EMBEDDED

Caitlin Press Inc.
3375 Ponderosa Way
Qualicum Beach, BC V9K 2J8
www.caitlinpress.com

Text and cover design by Vici Johnstone
Cover photo courtesy Gary Lunn
Photos pages 90-93 courtesy *Calgary Herald*

Printed in Canada

Caitlin Press Inc. acknowledges financial support from the Government of Canada and the Canada Council for the Arts, and the Province of British Columbia

through the British Columbia Arts Council and the Book Publisher's Tax Credit.
Library and Archives Canada Cataloguing in Publication
Embedded : the irreconcilable nature of war, loss and consequence / Catherine Lang.
Lang, Catherine, 1953- author.
Canadiana 20240352629 | ISBN 9781773861517 (softcover)
LCSH: Lang, Catherine, 1953- | LCSH: Lang, Michelle (Journalist)—Death and burial. |
   LCSH: Journalists—Canada—Biography. | LCSH: Embedded war correspondents—Canada—Biography. | LCSH: Embedded war correspondents—Afghanistan—Kandahār—Biography. | LCSH: Military ceremonies,   honors, and salutes—Canada. | LCSH: Bereavement—Psychological aspects. | LCGFT: Autobiographies.
LCC PN4913.L374 L36 2024 | DDC 070.92—dc23

EMBEDDED

The Irreconcilable Nature of War,
Loss and Consequence

by Catherine Lang

Caitlin Press

The author gratefully acknowledges that she lives on the traditional territory of the Lekwungen Peoples, also known as the Songhees, Esquimalt and W̱SÁNEĆ nations.

For Marissa Michelle

In whose likeness, Michelle's spirit lives on

CONTENTS

TIMELINE   8
FOREWORD   13

PART I   17

INTRODUCTION   18
NO TURNING BACK   20
STARS ABOVE MASUM GHAR   23
HEART OF TALIBAN TERRITORY   34
SHOCK LACED WITH ADRENALIN   40
REPATRIATION   45
VIEWING CEREMONY, KANDAHAR AIRFIELD   52
DEAR MICHELLE, JANUARY 19, 2015   58

PART II   71

UNDER THE GRAVENSTEIN   72
MAGENTA PASHMINA   80
SNOW ANGELS   87
CLOISONNÉ URNS   95
MEETING MELLISSA   101
DEAR MICHELLE, SEPTEMBER 8, 2015   108
DEAR MICHELLE, MARCH 26, 2016   111
CROWSNEST   116
YALETOWN   130
THE LOON'S CALL   138
NORTHEAST TO SOUTHWEST   152
UNCLE AXEL'S FARM   161
DEAR MICHELLE, APRIL 7, 2018   169

PART III   177

LANGUID LIGHT   178
A HIGH SCHOOL REMEMBRANCE   187
COMING TOGETHER, TEN YEARS ON   192
FROM KANDAHAR TO CALGARY TO MONTERREY   211

EPILOGUE   217

ACKNOWLEDGEMENTS   220
SUGGESTED READING   223
ENDNOTES   225
ABOUT THE AUTHOR   228

TIMELINE

This timeline incorporates a selection of major events in the Lang family and in the author's quest to document Michelle's life, interspersed with historical turning points, including those that led the West into the War on Terror. In part, this timeline is to provide insight into how these events are at play as we go about our daily lives.

September 1972	Art and Sandy travel overland to India through Turkey, Iran, Afghanistan and Pakistan
1972 to 1973	Catherine settles on Quadra Island
July 17, 1973	One month after Art and Sandy come home, Daoud Khan deposes Mohammad Zahir Shah, Afghanistan's king for forty years, in military coup
	Khan becomes the first president of the Republic of Afghanistan until April 1978
Autumn 1973	Catherine returns to Vancouver
Jan 31, 1975	Michelle Justine Lang is born in Vancouver
April 30, 1975	Fall of Saigon, Vietnam
1975 to 1976	Some 5,600 Vietnamese refugees are admitted to Canada
December 1977	Catherine moves to Sooke, southern Vancouver Island
April 1978	People's Democratic Party of Afghanistan overthrows Khan's regime in bloody coup d'etat and assassinate him and his family
June 1978	Mujahideen form to oppose Soviet-backed government
October 8, 1978	Cameron Arthur Lang is born in Vancouver
December 1979	Soviet Union invades Afghanistan
1979	US begins covert operation to arm mujahideen in Afghanistan

January 27, 1980	Ellen Sarah Newman is born in Victoria
March 24, 1980	Archbishop Óscar Romero is assassinated in San Salvador
June 1984	India's Golden Temple military raid
June 23, 1985	Air India bombing
Summer 1986	Vancouver hosts Expo 86
	Catherine's first reporting job, *Gulf Islands Driftwood*
September 1988	Al-Qaeda (international extremists) forms with goal of bringing jihad to the world
1988 to 1989	Catherine attends journalism program at Langara College, Vancouver
1989 to 1990	Catherine works as reporter for *Ladysmith-Chemainus Chronicle*
February 15, 1989	Soviet troops withdraw from Afghanistan
November 9, 1989	Fall of the Berlin Wall
1989 to 1996	Afghan Civil War, mujahideen factions wage war against each other
June 4, 1989	Tiananmen Square massacre, Beijing
1991	Soviet Union dissolves, end of Cold War
1992 to 1995	Bosnian War
1993	Michelle graduates from high school
April to July 1994	Rwandan genocide
July 3, 1994	Samuel Graeme Martin is born in Victoria
September 1994	Taliban emerge as Pashtun nationalist faction during Afghan Civil War
1994 to 1996	Taliban capture Kandahar, Herat, Jalalabad and Kabul
1996	Taliban establish the First Islamic Emirate of Afghanistan
1996	Catherine publishes first book, *O-Bon in Chimunesu: A Community Remembered*

1998 to 2000	Michelle's first reporting job, *Prince George Free Press*
Autumn 1998	Michelle's convocation, SFU
April to October 2000	Michelle works as reporter for *The Times-Herald*, Moose Jaw
2000 to 2002	Michelle works as reporter for *Regina Leader-Post*
September 11, 2001	Al-Qaeda attacks on the US
September 2001	Taliban refuse to extradite Osama bin Laden and other al-Qaeda leaders
	US declares War on Terror
October 4, 2001	NATO invokes Article 5 of *Washington Treaty*
October 7, 2001	US launches Operation Enduring Freedom
October 2001	Taliban flee to Pakistan
December 2001	First Canadian troops deploy to Afghanistan
2002 to 2009	Michelle works as reporter for *Calgary Herald*
April 17, 2002	Canada's first casualties in Afghanistan, four soldiers killed in a so-called "friendly fire incident"
September 2006	Operation Medusa, Kandahar province, counterinsurgency battle led by Canadian troops
February 3, 2008	Michelle's paternal grandmother dies
December 4, 2008	Prime Minister Stephen Harper prorogues Parliament to avoid non-confidence vote
December 11, 2009	Michelle arrives at Kandahar Airfield
December 23, 2009	Lt. Andrew Nuttall becomes the 134th Canadian casualty, Panjwaii
December 30, 2009	Taliban operatives detonate IED near Kandahar city, killing Michelle and four soldiers
	Prime Minister Stephen Harper prorogues Parliament, scandal re: torture of Afghan detainees

December 31, 2009	Art and Sandy Lang depart Monterrey, Mexico
January 1, 2010	Ramp ceremony, Kandahar Airfield, for Dec. 30 fatalities
January 2, 2010	Catherine and family members travel to Toronto
January 3, 2010	Repatriation ceremony, Trenton
January 4, 2010	Lt. Andrew Nuttall's memorial, Victoria
January 9, 2010	Memorials for Sgt. George Miok and Cpl. Zachery McCormack, Edmonton
	British journalist, Rupert Hamer, killed in Helmand province
January 11, 2010	Michelle's memorial, Vancouver
	Sgt. Kirk Taylor's memorial, Yarmouth, NS
January 12, 2010	Pte. Garrett Chidley's memorial, South Surrey, BC
	7.0 magnitude earthquake strikes Haiti
January 15, 2010	Canwest announces Michelle Lang Journalism Fellowship
January 18, 2010	Michelle's memorial, Calgary
January 2010	Tribute to Michelle from Right to Learn Afghanistan/Canadian Women for Women in Afghanistan
February 12 to 27, 2010	Vancouver hosts the 2010 Winter Olympics
April 10, 2010	Cameron Lang marries Sandra Benavides, Monterrey, Mexico
July 2010	Catherine, Bruce and Sam drive to Calgary, visit *Calgary Herald* newsroom
July 2011	Canadian troops withdraw from Kandahar
November 2011	Catherine flies to Calgary to visit Calgary Soldiers' Memorial
August 23, 2013	Inurning of Michelle's and her grandmother's ashes, Vancouver
February to March 2014	Russia annexes Crimea

March 2014	Canada's training mission ends in Afghanistan
April 2014	Art and Catherine meet Mellissa Fung, Vancouver
April 14, 2014	Boko Haram kidnaps 276 schoolgirls from Chibok, Nigeria
August 2016	Catherine travels to Calgary and Bellevue, Crowsnest Pass, Alberta
June 2017	Catherine to Yaletown
August 2017	Catherine, Colette Derworiz and Robin Summerfield travel to Lang Bay, Saskatchewan
September 30, 2017	Afghanistan Memorial unveiling, Victoria
February 2019	Trump administration begins "peace talks" with Taliban
July 2019	Bushra, Adil and Jahan Saeed-Khan meet Catherine in Victoria
August 2019	Art, Sandy, Margaret and Catherine attend Kandahar Cenotaph rededication, Ottawa
December 2019	Catherine and Jodie Densmore attend 10th anniversary gathering in Edmonton
January 8, 2020	Iran shoots down Ukrainian Airlines Flight 752
August 15, 2021	US troop withdrawal from Afghanistan and Taliban takeover
February 24, 2022	Russia invades Ukraine
October 7, 2023	Hamas attacks Israel, triggering Israel-Hamas war in Gaza
March 12, 2024	Tenth anniversary of Canada's withdrawal from Afghanistan

FOREWORD

Just a month after my one-year tenure with a Canadian media outlet end-ed, I was sitting in a cozy coffee shop in Toronto. The aroma of freshly roasted beans filled the air. I was nestled in a corner, scrolling on my lap-top, searching for job opportunities. Outside, the world was blanketed in snow, icy flakes shimmering through the wide windows. It was a cold day, but the warmth of the cafe offered a comforting contrast to the wintry scene.

Desperate and confused, I had fled the Taliban a year earlier. I found myself with no clear path for my future in journalism. Being a newbie, I worried my career might die after nearly a decade of reporting on the Afghanistan war for *The Wall Street Journal* in Kabul. As I clicked through LinkedIn, anxiety gnawing at me, a phrase caught my eye: The Michelle Lang Fellowship.

I googled it. The first link mentioned Afghanistan, my home coun-try where I had left everything behind: family, friends and an entire gen-eration. My heart ached as memories flooded back.

As I read further, my heart sank deeper still. Michelle had been killed by a Taliban roadside bomb in the southern province of Kanda-har while reporting for a Calgary-based newspaper. The tragedy struck a chord deep within me. Here was a fellow journalist who had shared my passion for reporting the truth, and she paid the ultimate price in the same land that I had lived my life. Her story was a stark reminder of the perilous path we journalists tread and the sacrifices we make for our craft.

I applied for the fellowship that day. I was lucky to get it, and I take to heart its mission to honour her legacy. The opportunity allows suc-cessful applicants to undertake an investigative project while also engag-ing in daily journalism at the *National Post* and the *Calgary Herald*. I write in the same pages where Michelle's words were published, following in the same tradition of pursuing the facts regardless of the cost.

The heavy toll of the work weighs on my mind. Every time I hear Michelle's name, it strikes me even more profoundly. It triggers memories of the many Afghan and foreign journalists killed, injured, and kidnapped in Afghanistan while reporting the brutal truths of a war that impact-ed the lives of hundreds of thousands of families both inside and outside the country. I am reminded of the 130 journalists and media workers, including sixteen foreigners, who were killed. Many were slain by the Taliban, the extremist group that now rules the country. Several of my brave colleagues remain in Afghanistan, still struggling on the uneven path toward freedom of speech, human values, and truth-telling.

Afghanistan, the birthplace of the renowned poet Rumi, who invited the world to peace and enlightenment, has been the epicenter of many tragedies. The stark contrast between the wisdom of Rumi and the ongoing oppression and gender apartheid by the Taliban underscores the profound loss and struggle that have defined my homeland. The thought of Michelle's sacrifice, alongside countless others, has deepened my resolve to respect their legacy and continue the fight for truth and justice through journalism.

When Lorne Motley, who was Michelle's editor and is now Vice President of Editorial for Postmedia in the West, called to say I had been selected for the fellowship program, I had mixed feelings. It was profoundly sad to be named a fellow in memory of a journalist who had been killed, especially when I had narrowly escaped the same fate multiple times in Afghanistan. Michelle's death in the country where I was born and raised made this opportunity feel both personal and painful. Adding to the poignancy, Canada, which I now call home, was where Michelle was from.

At the same time, it brought a heavy responsibility to my shoulders: to deliver a project to Canadian readers about the billions of dollars spent on developmental projects in Afghanistan. Schools built for Afghan girls and boys, clinics for villagers and women, roads and canals to help farmers sustain their livelihoods—these were the stories Michelle sought to tell in order to bring the real picture of a disastrous war and the human stories within it to light, highlighting the love and thirst for education among Afghan girls in Kandahar. Tragically, she died before she had the opportunity.

Now, some of the same schools are shut by the Taliban—the group responsible for her death—which has banned girls from attending secondary school and university. Women are being pushed from important parts of public life, with harsh restrictions imposed on them, and both men and women are being imprisoned for peacefully protesting and demanding access to education and freedom.

As I continued my fellowship, with Michelle's name always embedded in my mind and life, my old friend—better described as a friend of Afghanistan—Dr. Lauryn Oates told me that Michelle Lang's aunt,

Catherine Lang, wanted to talk to me. I got Catherine's phone number. I remember it was another snowy day when we spoke on the phone. She discussed her book about Afghanistan and shared stories about Michelle.

Through our conversation, I discovered that Catherine, like many other Canadians, is a true friend of Afghanistan. Despite the country taking her niece, it also drew her in, prompting her to learn more about Afghanistan, Canada's military involvement, and the country's complex history and multicultural society. Her dedication to understanding Afghanistan deeply moved me, reminding me of the shared bonds and sacrifices that link our two nations.

The book in your hands, *Embedded*, takes you deep into the beautiful life and mind of Michelle and her family, revealing the suffering and pain they feel every day after her death. It also showcases the profound dedication and passion Michelle had for journalism and her writing for Canadian readers. Catherine opens her world to you in her outstanding storytelling book, filled not with war, but with love and stories. Through her words, you experience the warmth, commitment and heartfelt connections that Michelle fostered. The book is a testament to Michelle's spirit and the legacy she left behind, capturing the essence of her life and the indelible mark she made on those who knew and loved her.

Ehsanullah Amiri,
recipient of the 2024 Michelle Lang Fellowship in Journalism[1]

PART I

But the force that draws a writer to one story rather than another does not tap politely at the front door. It shoots an invisible arrow into some murky region of the writer's unknown needs, and hits a target she didn't even know was there. That's when the trouble starts.

Helen Garner[2]

INTRODUCTION

I stroll east along Burdett Avenue on the fringes of downtown Victoria toward the looming structure that is Christ Church Cathedral. It's a cool February morning. The city is quiet as I gaze at the Gothic style inscription at the top of the church's central façade: *God So Loved the World*. I'm almost in the cathedral's shadow when I come to the end of the street to visit the Afghanistan Memorial.

My fingers sweep across my niece's name on the cold granite base of the memorial, and I ponder the value of her life's work and our shared belief in a free press, prompting a memory of my first visit to the *Calgary Herald* newsroom in July 2010. It was almost seven months after Michelle was killed on the job. Her desk remained more or less as she had left it, except that her colleagues had lovingly wrapped a magenta pashmina shawl around the back of her vacant chair.

On that first visit, the newsroom was massive, especially compared to those in community newspapers where I once worked as a reporter. It boasted a striking view of Calgary's downtown skyline. Wide swaths of desks, drafting tables and meeting rooms filled the space, where staff walked briskly between rows of desks from time to time. When I visited five years later, it was tucked behind that showcase space, where I had once stood watching a fork of lightning flash in the sky above Calgary's skyscrapers. By the thirteenth anniversary of Michelle's death, the newsroom no longer existed as a physical space, the building sold while staff worked from their respective homes, fallout from the COVID-19 pandemic, a declining industry and ever-changing work environments.

But this is not a story about the demise of print journalism. It began as a story about a young and vivacious woman who thrived within the humming, buzzing and oftentimes chaotic walls of those newsrooms—and loved pretty much every minute of it. Until, that is, the day Taliban operatives detonated a massive improvised explosive device beneath the light-armoured vehicle that was carrying Michelle, nine soldiers and another civilian back to Kandahar city, Afghanistan.

When the news of Michelle's death reached me at work on a quiet December day, my world shifted.

The very next day I began my dive into a morass of newspapers, dates, places, mementos—all fragments from her last days, her life. These facts that led to her end, the end of her breath, her heartbeat. I dove deep into the utter senselessness and uncertainty, the not knowing of time or value, the promise of secrets unrevealed or details unremembered, a complex mash of headlines and photos, mastheads and bylines. December 30, 2009, and on through the days, weeks, months, now ten years and counting.

CHAPTER I

NO TURNING BACK

The end of 2009 is approaching as I gaze at the Gorge waterway, glistening, glass-like in the fading light, from my office desk in Victoria, BC. The floor-to-ceiling windows arch along the entire side of the building, facing west above the Selkirk trestle bridge and Deadman's Island in the middle of the channel that flows to Victoria's Inner Harbour.

Most of my colleagues are on holiday, so it's quiet and free of the hectic buzz in the politically charged, dynamic work of provincial treaty negotiations with First Nations and the federal government. I'm updating consultation records, a relatively mindless task that suits me fine as the year winds down. When my phone rings, I'm startled out of my zone. It's my husband, Bruce, on the line.

"Hi, dear," I say.

"You'd better come *now*," he says. "I'm in the parking lot."

"But it's only four o'clock," I say. "I'll wrap up soon."

"Come now," he repeats.

Bruce often scolds me for staying later at work than I need to, but I dismiss his warning and finish my task before making a hasty round to water my plants. Spider plants. Christmas cacti. Large, gangly aloe vera plants propped up with chopsticks. They can't wait, I tell myself. No one will water them in my absence.

Tomorrow will be New Year's Eve, and as I shut down my computer and hustle down the hall, I sigh with relief at the prospect of a few days off. We have no special plans. Our son, Sam, is fifteen, so he'll be off with friends. I haven't called to ask my daughter Ellen about her New Year's plans. I won't be going to Vancouver to visit family, partly because my brother, Art, and his wife, Sandy, are in Mexico to meet their son's fiancée and her family. I think briefly about my niece's fiancé, Michael Louie. I bet he's sad Michelle won't be with him to ring in the New Year.

I exit the office and wait for the elevator, my brain still rolling through work-related tasks. The moment I walk out the main doors into the drab, grey parking lot is distilled. Bruce, leaning against the car, approaches me with a steady step.

He inhales and looks me in the eye. "Michelle was killed in Afghanistan today."

I freeze. My eyes cast around, resting in a pool of shadow in a corner of the parking lot. It's empty, dark. "No," I say, shaking my head.

I search Bruce's blue eyes. A plain and simple *no* rings through me, as if I'm telling someone *no, not ever.* Just an echo in my mind. *No. Afghanistan. Michelle. Killed.*

Some 800 kilometres away in the *Calgary Herald* newsroom, staff in the city's flagship newspaper were in the grips of a stunned silence following hours of anxious uncertainty. Reporters had been watching senior staff, some of whom were supposed to be on holidays, come and go from the chief editor's glassed-in office. They began to ask questions of themselves and each other. Had the paper been sold? Were they going to lose their jobs? Were they being sued? Then it started. A CBC clip announced that a reporter had been killed in Afghanistan and the *Edmonton Journal* called, awkwardly asking about the reporter they'd sent over. Reporters on the cop desk started sobbing after an RCMP officer phoned for the name of their journalist in Afghanistan without explaining why. By the time their boss, Lorne Motley, brought them together to break the news, they were already fighting to push their worst fears aside.

Lorne likely got the first phone call with the news of Michelle's death from his counterpart in Ottawa, who in turn learned the news via Canadian Press, through reporter Colin Perkel who was in the media tent at Kandahar Airfield. Reeling from shock and disbelief, he had to steel himself for his first, immediate task: to contact Michelle's parents and brother Cameron, in Mexico. But Art had left his cell phone in the hotel while out and about, and Lorne couldn't advise Michelle's anxious colleagues until he'd delivered the devastating news to family. Hours passed before he finally reached my brother. Soon after, he assembled staff together in a circle outside his office.

Reporter Sherri Zickefoose recalled the moment her boss, "ashen and devastated, choked the words out: 'Michelle Lang has been killed.' There were other details about the roadside IED, but I don't remember what else he said. Gasping and weeping, we fell into each other."

Saying it was the worst news he'd ever had to deliver, Lorne was equally shaken. He had offered the assignment to Michelle, his star reporter with the chestnut-brown ponytail and engaging smile. But now they needed to get to work. Michelle's death and the death of the four soldiers she was travelling with would garner front-page headlines across Canada for several days.

Soon, a Global TV crew showed up outside the *Herald*'s office, and three reporters—Colette Derworiz, Robert Remington and Gwendolyn Richards—bravely headed into the cold Calgary afternoon to face the cameras, bleary-eyed and heartbroken.

Back in the parking lot near the Gorge, I climbed into our Hyundai Tucson in a fog and strapped myself into the passenger seat. Bruce steered the vehicle into traffic, glancing sideways at me. But I was staring ahead, my mind tumbling. When did Michelle's parents tell me the *Herald* was sending her to Afghanistan? Three weeks ago? A month ago? My stomach churned. I hadn't called to congratulate and wish her well.

CHAPTER 2

STARS ABOVE MASUM GHAR

On Sunday, December 20, 2009, Michelle filed her first blog from Afghanistan. I imagine her sitting down in the media tent to share her personal experiences rather than write news reports. I expect she had her trademark jar of drinking water close at hand as she faced the screen and began compiling her thoughts, perhaps breathing deeply to manage her excitement about being there, doing what she loved. The journey that led her to Afghanistan involved a lifelong dream and years of hard work.

Her blog begins:

> Greetings from Afghanistan, where I will be reporting for the *Calgary Herald* for the next several weeks. I am currently at Kandahar Airfield, the sprawling military base near Kandahar city, perhaps best known for its dusty conditions and a very busy Tim Horton's. At the moment, Afghanistan's winter rains have turned that famous dust into a giant mud pit.

As a young child, Michelle paid little attention to the colourful pushpins crisscrossing a world map in her Vancouver home. The pins stuck out across Europe and overland through the Middle East to India and Nepal, documenting her parents' travels before she was born in 1975. Like most children, she delighted in exploring the streets and back alleys of her neighbourhood, but as she grew, her sense of the larger world grew too, especially when she heard her parents talk about adventures in countries like Afghanistan, where they had travelled in 1972.

My journeys weren't documented on that world map, but I had travelled with Art and Sandy in Europe after trekking around for a year on my own. My brother and his wife met me in England to travel across northern Europe and then south to Greece. In their late twenties then, Sandy often backcombed her long, dark hair into a French twist while Art wore Coke-bottle thick eyeglasses under a shaggy mane of shoulder-length brown hair. I'd left home after graduating from high school, desperate to escape my bickering parents and possessed by the invincibility of youth.

Naïve and foolish, I was eighteen and determined to see the world on my terms.

Art and Sandy also sought adventure, but a decade older than me, they were more measured in their approach. Following university and beginning their respective careers as a chartered accountant and a teacher, they had done their research, reading widely about ancient civilizations and plotting their routes in advance. Where I bought a bicycle in England with the idea of cycling through Europe, they had bought a used Volkswagen van. Where I managed to cycle through France with a map of Europe, staggering from youth hostel to youth hostel along the main southbound highway, they had guidebooks and maps of major cities on their itineraries like the sensible, if not seasoned, travellers they were.

It was a time of exploration for a generation of young western people. We were hippies who descended en masse, travelling these routes in the 1960s and '70s, seeking ways to challenge the status quo. Capitalism, greed, corruption and nasty politics ruled the world we lived in then, as now. At home in Vancouver, I joined the throngs on downtown streets, shouting slogans and singing songs against the war in Vietnam. While less anti-establishment than me, Art and Sandy were still caught up by a movement that sought to fashion a culture based on values of peace, equality and justice.

When they arrived in London, I was crashing with fellow hippies in a flat. After many months of vagabonding, my blue jeans were a patchwork of fabric squares that hung loosely from my hips, and my long, brunette hair was unruly in London's heavy, damp air. I caught Sandy admiring the long, flowing Carnaby Street dresses of women stepping lightly along busy sidewalks, but Art wouldn't be caught dead with a bandana wrapped around his head like many men in psychedelic shirts and bell-bottom pants wandering the streets. My brother and his wife held hands, stopping to study the Tower of London while I bounced past, eager to be done with sightseeing and flee the city for the open road.

Within days, we ferried across the English Channel, then travelled through Holland and Germany, before heading south and biting into a corner of the Italian Alps near Trieste. We camped under a starlit sky in the mountains one night. Today, I can almost smell the cutting frost in the night air and see the swirling cosmos high above, the wonder of the world enveloping me in fresh and startling ways.

I didn't have a driver's licence, and I don't remember Sandy driving either. Harried and exhausted, Art coaxed that dusty forest-green VW van south through what was then Yugoslavia. When we reached Albania, a communist country with a closed border, Art had no choice but to turn the van east and begin the long drive up and over a mountain. As we climbed one treacherous hairpin turn after another, fog swirled and night began to close in, so we set up camp. In the morning, streams of locals trundled by, staring as we rose, dishevelled, from our overnight camp beside a well-trodden foot path.

When we finally arrived in Athens, we toured the Acropolis and other sights in the blistering heat, camping on the outskirts of the city for a few days before amicably parting ways—they to continue their overland journey and me to wrap up mine. I found my way to the island of Ios where I lingered for six wonderful weeks, living outside, sleeping wherever, making friends with locals and other travellers, drinking ouzo and partying in the town square. I met an American man who was cute and thought I was too, so we soon became an item, trekking on foot to the other side of the island to stay with a Greek family. I remember the back-breaking labour of harvesting olives off the ground for long, hot hours, the mother of the family instructing me as we went, though we couldn't speak each other's language. A kind woman, she had a hard and simple life on this island where people crossed the dry, scrub-spotted, and hilly landscape on donkeys and mules, the sparkling Aegean Sea spread out before them. It was an idyllic time and place to complete my European adventure and rest from wanderings that had shaken my self-centred sense of place in the world.

Meanwhile, Art and Sandy travelled into more uncertain worlds—through Turkey, Iran and Afghanistan and on to India and Nepal. Their adventures just beginning, they covered the rough highways and byways of the Middle East, following one of many original Silk Road routes. When they came home to Vancouver a year later, my brother was terribly gaunt. He had suffered from dysentery in India, but the travelling bug had bit both of them for good. Still, they were also ready to settle down for a while and start a family. Less than two years later, Michelle was born.

By the time Michelle filed that first blog from Kandahar Airfield, she had already crossed paths with a cast of characters. Canwest reporter Matthew Fisher was the first to spot her when she stepped off a military aircraft from Dubai onto the tarmac on December 11. As his Christmas replacement, she was walking in the opposite direction on the other side of a chain-link fence, while he was waiting to leave the base for a holiday from war reporting.

Michelle Lang once badgered former Premier Ralph Klein into his quote about not reacting to "the reaction to the reaction to the reaction." In this photo, he appears to be trying to push her aside. Photo courtesy *Calgary Herald* archives

He recognized her because they had met in Calgary some months before, when she had peppered him with questions about reporting in Afghanistan. During a lengthy dinner at a steakhouse near Crowchild Trail, Michelle asked Matthew about everything from the logistics of filing stories from a massive army base to the state of the war, as well as how to weigh the risks when going after a story.

During a phone interview later, he recalled that she had expressed considerable apprehension about the dangers and wasn't overly interested in military combat operations. "She was more interested in the humanitarian side—women, children and how they were treated, and the hospital situation," Fisher told me.

She had cut her teeth in investigative reporting while on the health beat for the *Calgary Herald*. In 2008, on her first international assignment, she had reported from Johannesburg, diving into the ethics of the Alberta government recruiting South African doctors when the need was so much greater there. Even before winning a 2009 National Newspaper Award for her coverage of health issues in Alberta, the work had earned her the nickname Dr. Lang.

Padre André Gauthier, the senior chaplain of Canadian Armed Forces at KAF, was in the welcoming brigade who greeted Michelle after she disembarked. Like most everyone who met her, he took a liking to her right away. Soon, they were chatting about Canada's mission and life on the base.

Years later, I listen to his thick Francophone accent on the phone. He recalls how she was both excited and afraid, so he confided his own early fears to her. "I remember how nervous I was my first time, back in 2002, at the outset of this mission. It's normal and takes time. We just slowly learn to live with a certain degree of fear and accept that that's part of the overall experience," he said, adding, "The emotion comes, you know, and oftentimes it stays there for a while, and after that we have to let it go. The thing is, when we feed or nourish our fear, it becomes worse, and we feel a lot of anxiety."

I learn that Michelle wanted to do a story about André. Perhaps out of modesty, he referred her to another chaplain. On December 24, Canwest published her piece and photo of Padre Sandy Scott. He's smiling in the sun in his military fatigues, a tin box of Christmas goodies from Canada under his arm. But in her few short weeks on the base, she continued to visit André, not because she was religious, but because they enjoyed each other's company. I suspect she was homesick, and he was a man who offered consolation.

In this photo taken December 24, 2009, Canadian Forces Padre Sandy Scott holds a box of home-made Christmas goodies at forward operating base Masum Ghar. Photo by Michelle Lang/ Postmedia News Service

I don't know the details of what followed that first encounter with André, but Michelle soon settled into the media tent. *Globe and Mail* reporter Patrick White was there when she walked in, recalling how refreshingly humble she was compared to some macho men who often swaggered into the tent. But Patrick and most other reporters had been on assignment for a while and were ready to go home for Christmas. By her second week at KAF, only two other Canadian reporters remained: CBC's James Murray, and Canadian Press reporter Colin Perkel.

"I was there when she first arrived," Colin said during a phone call in 2016. "There's a photograph soon after her arrival, which I took of her, with a blue frag vest and a blue helmet, I think—not the greatest picture because it was taken with some cheap equipment in the media tent. It was more of a lark than anything else. But she was trying on this equipment, and a couple of guys were sitting around. We were giggling and teasing her a little bit.

Michelle Lang collects a season's greeting from a Canadian soldier at Kandahar Airfield, December 12, 2009. Photo by Colin Perkel/THE CANADIAN PRESS

"I moseyed over and punched her vest playfully, and I said, 'Oh, that's not going to stop a grenade or an artillery shell,' or something like that. She looked totally crestfallen. It was totally meant to be a joke, of course. I've always felt bad about that."

A veteran reporter, Colin's voice cracked as he told me about learning Michelle had been killed. "It couldn't have been worse if it had been my sister. I can't really explain it, but that's how I felt. A couple of days before she left, she came into the media tent. She wanted to tell me about a really bad nightmare she'd had. I was distracted with something else, and I was busy. I didn't really get a chance to sit down and listen to whatever it was she wanted to tell me," Colin said at the other end of the phone line. We both fell silent and hung up soon after. Letting his words sink in, I fell backwards onto my bed, staring blankly at the ceiling. What might she have revealed about her dream, given the chance?

Michelle sussed out stories about life on and near the base during her first days in the "giant mud pit" of Kandahar Airfield. In her first week, she wrote articles on topics ranging from bomb-sniffer dogs and their handlers to a successful operation in the Panjwaii area, supported by Canadian troops, but led by the Afghan National Army.

In an online dispatch dated December 22, Michelle wrote: "Last week I travelled to a Canadian forward operating base in Panjwaii, a district southwest of Kandahar city. I was struck by the beauty of the area, and I took this photo of the surrounding mountains." A gentle dark mound frames the foreground of the photo, with a jagged mountain peak rising

Michelle tries on her fragmentation vest and helmet at Kandahar Airfield, December 13, 2009. Photo by Colin Perkel/THE CANADIAN PRESS

through fog in the near distance in what she described as "a volatile and dangerous district" and the ongoing challenge the Taliban presented in the region.

She also found ways to offer her readers a glimpse of what life was like on the military bases, writing about civilian staff working as barbers and hairdressers, as well as how soldiers were celebrating the Christmas season, including a newly married couple who spent their first Christmas together in Afghanistan.

In all, her byline appeared in ten newspaper articles published by the *Calgary Herald* and other Canwest papers that December. Two of them involved her first encounter reporting on the inevitable outcome of war—a soldier's death and his ramp ceremony, when soldiers in uniform perform the solemn function of pallbearers, marching their comrade's flag-draped casket along the tarmac and up the ramp into the hold of a massive military cargo jet for repatriation to Canada.

She filed the first of two stories about Lt. Andrew Nuttall on December 24, 2009, the day after he was killed while leading a foot patrol near the village of Nakhonay in the Panjwaii district. A thirty-year-old soldier from Victoria, BC, Lt. Nuttall and an unnamed Afghan soldier were killed when an improvised explosive device was detonated on their path. Michelle quotes then Brigadier-General Daniel Ménard talking about Lt. Nuttall: "Andrew came to Afghanistan because he honestly believed that he could make a difference to the people of Afghanistan, and he demonstrated that every time he went on patrol."

That night, Michelle emailed a friend about fighting back tears while reporting on the tragedy. I imagine Ménard's words hit home, for he could have been describing why she was there too, believing that by raising awareness about Afghanistan in Canada, Canadians might care more about Afghans.

While reporting on life at KAF and the forward operating bases, she was also working contacts on the civilian side, staff like Renée Filiatrault, a powerhouse of a woman who managed the press on hot, controversial topics. Later, Renée recalled how she had scoffed at Michelle wanting to tell humanitarian stories when hardcore reporters were hounding her for details on Afghan detainees. Michelle had filed one story on the detainees, but she didn't always want to run with the pack.

One week to the day after Lt. Nuttall's repatriation, Renée shouldered the first of five caskets with a grim face. Over the years, I had studied the woman in civilian clothes in the front-page photo that splashed across Canadian newspapers on January 2, 2010. Now I know it was Renée—her commitment when dealing with the press from then on: to answer all questions straight on, in honour of Michelle.

Another civilian Michelle came to know was Adam Sweet, a public diplomacy officer with the Canadian International Development Agency. At 24, he coordinated opportunities for the press to accompany troops from his base at Camp Nathan Smith, the forward operating base in Kandahar city. It was in the military's interest to get stories to Canadians about the reconstruction work of the troops.

Adam knew how keen she was to report on stories beyond the bases. She also let him know about her fears—namely, that she wanted a relatively safe mission, if such a thing existed. She declined the first opportunity he offered. After weighing the risks of going out with troops to clear an area of land mines, she reluctantly turned it down. She had a fiancé waiting for her in Calgary, clinging to the promise she'd made to come home in one piece. Journalists like Patrick White had done crazy things to get stories, like hide under a blanket in the back of his fixer's car in order to pass through Kandahar Airfield's heavily guarded entrance. The pull to be where the action was couldn't have been more intense, but

Michelle sits next to Chief of Defence Staff Walt Natynczyk in a military vehicle on Christmas Day, 2009. Photo courtesy Gary Lunn

Michelle was neither reckless nor careless. She remembered her friend and colleague at the *Edmonton Journal* telling her about a close call she'd had while on assignment in Afghanistan. In fact, that friend had pleaded with Michelle not to go at all. Reporting on soldiers clearing land mines must have felt way too dangerous, so she stayed put.

It was an interesting time to be in Kandahar. Lt. Nuttall's was the first Canadian death in six weeks, so it had been relatively quiet on the combat front. Chief of Defence Staff General Walter Natynczyk arrived a few days before Christmas to bolster morale among the troops, giving Michelle an opportunity to report on his speech to troops. Soon she was hopping on a chopper to accompany him and other VIPs—including then Defence Minister Peter MacKay and Gary Lunn, then Minister responsible for the 2010 Olympics in Vancouver—to six forward operating bases and report how the troops celebrated Christmas and enjoy a special meal herself.

"There was a big turkey dinner, beer and even some entertainment, including comedian Mike MacDonald and Melanie Dekker, a singer-song-writer from Vancouver," she wrote in one of her online dispatches. They, too, had sacrificed spending the occasion with their families and loved ones.

On the morning of January 31, 2017, I phoned Gen. Natynczyk to talk about Michelle. Sunlight streamed through my window as I recalled shaking his hand at the repatriation ceremony in Trenton, Ontario, some seven years before. We had chatted briefly then, and I remembered his striking demeanour. But only three days after her death, it wasn't the time or place to ask questions.

It would have been Michelle's forty-second birthday when I found myself chit-chatting with him, my heart heavy and my voice shaky. I set out three topics I hoped to cover, including the military's relationship with the media, though what I really craved was a detailed account of exchanges they might have had.

"It was actually one of my best memories when I was the chief of defence," he said. "It was on Christmas Eve. We were at a large forward operating base outside of Kandahar Airfield proper called Masum Ghar. At this base, there were literally hundreds of soldiers. This is where we bedded down for the night.

"I still remember having a big town hall with all the troops. The Minister of Defence spoke. Parliamentary secretary Laurie Hawn and MP Gary Lunn spoke. I spoke. So you could imagine just a huge huddle of 200, 300 soldiers on this day, and then everyone broke, and we went in for supper together, including Michelle. Everyone went through the food lineup and so on, and after supper, the entertainers did their thing.

"Anyway, it was a really nice evening, and it went on for quite some time. When it was dark, we went up to the top of the mountain to visit the troops who were still on duty—senior non-commissioned officers who had assumed the duties of their subordinates so that the most junior soldiers could have the night off. Here were the sergeants and warrant officers on duty. I still remember Gary Lunn handing out the 2010 Winter Olympic mittens to everybody.

"It was a crystal clear, moonlit, starlit Christmas Eve. We were standing on top of a mountain. Actually, we were standing on top of a tank that was parked near the peak of the mountain overlooking the entire Kandahar region. There's a river valley below, and all was calm," he said, musing about the region's reputation as a crescent of instability.

"And one of the sergeants asked: 'Do you think anyone back home knows or cares that we're here?' This was pretty powerful. It goes to the point about the military-media relationship: no matter where we have sent Canadian sailors or soldiers or aircrew, defending the country from thousands of kilometres away, if it's not reported back to Canadians, nobody knows they're actually there, and no one can appreciate their service and sacrifice. Michelle's role and the role of all her colleagues is absolutely vital to the overall mission and to the defence of Canada—as it has been through every military campaign in which Canada has served.

"Now it's around ten or eleven o'clock at night and we're exhausted. On the side of a hill was a headquarters accommodation area for visitors, and so Michelle was accommodated in the same area as we were. I still remember, we went into this ramshackle little bathroom, ablutions area. If you can imagine a shack with a jury-rigged water tap and a beat-up wash basin. And what I recall was Michelle, Laurie Hawn and myself all together, trying to brush our teeth at the same time with a meagre drip-drip-drip of water coming out of this improvised tap-basin arrangement."

I wanted more details, more of Michelle, but it was time to wrap up the conversation, leaving me to imagine Michelle going to her barracks-style room and taking out her journal to jot down notes about this remarkable Christmas Eve before her head finally hit the pillow. Here she was, in the land that her parents had travelled through in 1972. Perhaps she smiled to herself, knowing they couldn't have imagined having a daughter who, thirty-seven years later, would be mingling with senior Canadian military officers and politicians under the moon and the stars, with a view of the Arghandab River Valley snaking its way across Kandahar province below.

CHAPTER 3

HEART OF TALIBAN TERRITORY

In all, Michelle travelled with Gen. Natynczyk and National Defence Minister Peter MacKay to the forward operating bases in a helicopter, not travelling by land, and therefore, not technically outside the wire. Provincial reconstruction teams were often deployed from these bases to consult with Afghan elders about their village's needs. Separate from the combat role of Canadian Forces, soldiers coordinated efforts between aid agencies and local Afghans to build schools, dig wells and other infrastructure. Scattered throughout Kandahar province, these bases were nonetheless in the heart of Taliban territory where Canadian troops were on one of the most dangerous assignments undertaken by NATO troops.

On the morning of December 30, Michelle rose from her bed in a SeaCan at Camp Nathan Smith. I expect she knew the history of how the camp came to be named after Private Nathan Smith, who was among the first casualties of our Afghanistan mission. It happened on April 17, 2002, when an American F-16 fighter jet mistakenly dropped a 500-pound bomb on a live-fire training exercise, killing four Canadian soldiers and seriously wounding eight. A subsequent investigation by the American administration ultimately laid blame on the US fighter pilots. For Canadians at home, it was a heart-wrenching tragedy that further called into question our role in Afghanistan.

I wonder if Michelle could have been mulling that over as she dressed to go outside the wire on the last Wednesday of 2009. Almost halfway through her assignment, she was finally going to get what she had come for: firsthand accounts of the Afghan people in their environment and Canadian soldiers building relations with them. Perhaps she was hopeful it would lead her on further missions, ones where she might learn what Afghans thought about our presence in their country.

Still, like most people, Michelle probably didn't sleep well the night before leaving the relatively secure base. As a teenager in Vancouver, she had taken to jogging to help manage panic attacks. But here in a walled compound in Kandahar city, she needed a different strategy to calm her nerves. As she prepared to hop into the back of a light-armoured vehicle with Canadian troops that morning, perhaps she was still trying to push away the nightmare she'd had days before.

Back at Kandahar Airfield, Canadian Press reporter Colin Perkel kept himself busy that morning. He was miffed, not at Michelle, but at the military. He had put his name forward to go out on a mission, but the powers that be had chosen Michelle instead. He had a job to do, too, and life at KAF was boring and often unproductive.

A few hours before heading out, Michelle phoned her fiancé, Michael, in Calgary, where he was winding down for the evening. I imagine she kept a positive, if somewhat aching, tone with him during the call, commenting on how quickly time was flying. With little more than three weeks left in her six-week stint, they certainly couldn't wait to hold one another again.

Though unhappy about her decision to go, Michael had finally given up trying to change her mind. Reluctantly, he came to understand it was something she simply had to do. Before leaving, he told her how he wanted to read about good things the troops were doing, and today she was hoping to write a piece about that very thing—or at least see for herself if the troops were indeed making progress with Afghan civilians and communities.

I imagine Michelle pausing briefly after saying goodbye to Michael that morning. Maybe he had done his best to sound brave, but fear and longing may have lingered in his voice. I expect doubt lingered in her heart, too, but she pushed on, preparing for her departure from Camp Nathan Smith.

I picture public diplomacy officer Adam Sweet making the last of the preparations throughout the morning. In charge of two reporters going out on convoys that day, he had spent time getting to know Michelle and decided to put the other reporter on a convoy with regular force soldiers.

"I actually made the decision to put Michelle on the reservist convoy because I knew that she was still fairly new to the military piece, and this was an opportunity to talk to guys who were outside the military structure—a little bit easier entry, if you will, into the relationship," Adam tells me during a telephone interview in 2016. "Also, they were from Alberta, young guys. They were going to go check out this village to see what was going on in Dand District—a positive story, with reservists.

"She was really excited," he said. "I remember she was interested in health care and education and how things were progressing in schools.

She wanted to see that work on the ground, but there was definitely some trepidation. She wasn't foolhardy, saying 'Yeah, let's do it. Let's go!' She wanted to check into it. She was so caring and wanted to learn."

Sometime after lunch, Adam escorted Michelle and a young foreign affairs diplomat, Bushra Saeed, to the pre-deployment briefing. In one of the last photos taken of them, they are standing at the back of the briefing room behind the soldiers, chatting as if they were college friends getting ready to head out for a night on the town, though their clothes clearly indicate that wasn't the case.

As I study the photo, I wonder what was going through Michelle's mind. Sunglasses are propped on the top of her head, her brown hair in a ponytail at the nape of her neck. She's not quite smiling; a distant look in her eyes makes me think she's preoccupied. Maybe she's thinking of her parents or her colleagues, a little lonely for all that's familiar and secure but also pleased with the prospect of telling them about the day's events when they next talk. The strap of a canvas bag is crossed over her grey flak vest, while Bushra stands to her left, attending to a backpack, a strand of dark hair falling down her cheek. She, too, is smiling.

Around two o'clock that afternoon, they were getting into "Charlie"—one of two light-armoured vehicles heading out—when Michelle

In one of the last photos taken of Michelle, she chats with Bushra Saeed, a civilian employee of the federal government, during a pre-deployment briefing at Camp Nathan Smith, Kandahar city, on December 30, 2009. Photo courtesy Adam Sweet

realized she had forgotten her sweater and had to return to the SeaCan.

"It was a little bit chaotic," Adam says. "The soldiers were like, 'Where is she? What's going on here?' She was clearly a newbie."

Michelle would have cursed herself as she ran back to her room. "Way to go, Michelle! First chance to ride in a convoy outside the wire, and you forget your friggin' sweater."

Adam trusted the soldiers that Michelle and Bushra were travelling with when they left the base in the early afternoon. They were good guys, and intelligence on the ground indicated this would be a relatively safe mission. Still, he knew she was nervous, and had told her earlier there was no shame in not going if she changed her mind.

Clearly, she didn't. The prospect of getting this story had too strong a pull.

A few times during our phone call, Adam stops to collect himself while I shake my head with a sense of dismay. Here he was, a young man of twenty-four, deciding with whom and when to send two civilians, both smart and engaging young women, outside the relative safety of the walled compound.

"As she was walking into the LAV, she turned to me and said: 'Don't worry, Adam. Everything will be fine. I'll talk to you when I get back.' And then she climbed into the LAV and never came back."

On the first anniversary of her death, I look at a half-page photo in the *Globe and Mail* of a light-armoured vehicle with a remote-controlled weapons station travelling toward the photographer. It is the latest edition of this military vehicle, offering better protection against mines and IEDs than the previous LAV III. Armed with a heavy 25-millimetre machine gun and a 7.6-millimetre machine gun in its main turret, it looks to me like an enormous, menacing bluebottle fly. You know, the kind where someone zooms in with a macroscopic lens and captures this beast-like image with hairy legs and bulging bug eyes. In this case, the bug eyes are headlights, and the hulk of the vehicle is equipped with soldiers and firearms and man-made antennae, everything seemingly captured through an ominous blue-grey filter.

The photo isn't one of Colin Perkel's, but the feature article is his.[3] Over a four-page spread, he details the convoy's movements that day, piecing it together from the survivors' accounts of events and a heavily redacted military incident report. It's as close as I'll ever come to knowing what unfolded over the course of the afternoon.

According to Colin's December 30, 2010, feature, the two-LAV convoy made its first stop at a nomadic Kuchi settlement about thirty minutes after leaving Kandahar city. Michelle and Bushra were in the second of the vehicles, the one called Charlie. I imagine the name gave Michelle pause. It was also the name of an Afghan man who had rescued her parents in 1972 when their VW van barely limped into his mechanic's shop in Kandahar city. After seeing pictures of him and hearing how he had helped her mother and father get back on the road, Michelle talked about trying to find him, if and when she had the opportunity. Art and Sandy quashed the idea. It would have been too dangerous for her, as well as for their former friend if he were even alive. After giving it some thought, Michelle had reluctantly agreed. But I wonder if, as she sat crunched in the hold of Charlie, Michelle imagined talking to the man who had helped her parents about all that he'd witnessed in his lifetime. He had taken Art and Sandy to a nomadic Kuchi settlement to watch bejewelled women dance in florid dresses during a rare time of peace in Afghanistan almost four decades earlier. What insights might he have imparted about his homeland during times of peace as well as war?

Meanwhile, Charlie's driver, twenty-one-year-old Garrett Chidley, was focused on Alpha, the LAV in front, leading the two-vehicle convoy from Camp Nathan Smith along Route Molson Ice to their first stop, a Kuchi settlement, where they scrambled into the light of day. I study Michelle's profile in a cropped photo of the scene. A slate-grey helmet on her head, Michelle was slightly bent over her notepad, behind three soldiers who were talking to a turbaned Afghan man. Bushra was to Michelle's right, and children on the periphery watched the clutch of soldiers and two women. One small girl in a pink dress and head scarf stood at the far left, and like the boys, her arms were crossed over her torso, curious but also a touch defiant.

In wider shots of the scene, a long irrigation ditch called a "wadi" stretched into the distance on one side of the road, and fabric tents and large trucks covered in canvas straddled the other side. Tall conical structures, which I later learn are brick kilns, were perched at one end of a string of trucks, tents and flapping tarps. The sun was shining on the sandy brown landscape, with no hint of green anywhere. A fabric scarf was wrapped around Michelle's neck several times, perhaps to ward off a chilly Afghan winter wind. Children and men outnumbered the soldiers, and women were nowhere to be seen.

Maybe Michelle had noticed the mood of the gathering as the men and children studied her and Bushra, two unarmed women among the soldiers, before a sentry remaining with the LAVs called one of the commanders on his radio and said curtly "Time to go. Crowd growing."

Huddled inside the LAV again, they carried on to the village of Hosi Aziz, where twenty-eight-year-old Sgt. Kirk Taylor, a civilian-military specialist, talked to the elders. As part of Bushra's job with Foreign Affairs, she stood close by, shadowing him in order to report on the civilian-military goals of Canada's mission. But a crowd began to gather there as well, so once again they got the order to climb back into Alpha and Charlie and head back to base. Michelle was thrilled because she had finally got what she had come for—a story about Afghans, a teeny glimpse into what their lives were like in an equally teeny part of the country. Bumping along on the muddy road, she had already started to organize her thoughts into the articles she planned to write the instant she got back to the base.

It was about 3:45 p.m. when the convoy came to a traffic jam near the outskirts of Kandahar city. Should they wait it out and risk being sitting targets? Or should they go back via the road they came in on? In the front LAV, twenty-nine-year-old section commander Sgt. Jimmy Collins had to make that dreadful decision quickly. He chose the latter. When I read this in the one-year anniversary feature, I swear. "Damned if he did; damned if he didn't."

Here is how Colin describes it. "After the stops to talk to locals, the LAVs lurch down the road at about 30 kilometres an hour, and Sgt. Collins surveys the landscape and soon recognizes the terrain. He knows the stories about convoys hitting IEDs on roads cleared just hours earlier. So he gets on the radio to Sgt. Miok, whose head he can see poking out from Charlie's hatch as it follows some 20 metres behind, and recommends stopping to perform another search."

The two soldiers had a brief and bawdy radio exchange seconds before shock waves engulfed Sgt. Collins' exposed head. The article continues: "The 20-tonne armour-plated assault vehicle lifts into the air like a toy. It appears to buckle in the middle as it begins to come apart. The turret, perfectly level, is spinning in the air toward Alpha. A soldier's lower body follows behind like a wet towel."

The only thing I know with certainty about the moment of Michelle's death is, again, from Colin's feature. "Enclosed in the steel cocoon of the light armoured vehicle, Ms. Saeed had been sitting across from and chatting amicably with Ms. Lang, the Calgary reporter. The day's outing would likely yield three stories, Ms. Lang had been saying. She did not finish her sentence."

CHAPTER 4

SHOCK LACED WITH ADRENALIN

I am sitting behind the wheel of our car waiting to board the 3:00 p.m. ferry to Vancouver from Swartz Bay, the BC Ferries port a half hour north of Victoria. After the incoming ship docks and begins unloading, I stare blankly as vehicles of every imaginable size and shape stream endlessly off the upper deck's ramp.

It is December 31, 2009, the day after I learned of my niece's death, and appropriately dark and stormy. Lead-grey clouds are saturated, unleashing walls of rain onto the pavement around us as we wait for the deckhand to wave us onboard. Suddenly, a stream of sunshine bursts through, the ferry railings and ship's paraphernalia gleaming white against the deep slate sea and sky.

I'm in shock watching this familiar scene unfold, as if I'm embedded in an oil painting, a speck of humanity pinned on a huge canvas. Somewhere outside of myself, I'm on my way to Vancouver with my fifteen-year-old son, Sam, and twenty-nine-year-old daughter, Ellen. My husband, Bruce, isn't with us, though I seem to be talking to him as I gaze stone-faced out the car window.

But no. Bruce isn't beside me because he has to stay with our dog, Tika. Art and Sandy won't be home yet. I've no idea whether they're still in Monterrey, Mexico, or whether they're on a flight back to Canada. I'm only aware that I need to be with those in my family who are on the Lower Mainland, where we'll gather round each other at my sister's home.

It's pitch black when Sam, Ellen and I arrive. Draping our dripping wet coats by the front door, we haul ourselves upstairs. Margie comes to hug us as we enter the living room, her hazel-grey eyes tired and teary. Her pregnant daughter-in-law, Vera, and son, Daniel, are sitting on the couch, trying to put on a brave face. Her husband, Al, is happy to see us, hoping we can inject some cheer into this New Year's Eve. But there's no way to cut through the shock and sorrow. On top of which, Daniel is worried about how his younger brother, Stephen, is coping with the loss of their older cousin. His shy, lanky brother stops by during the evening but doesn't stay.

I shuffle into the kitchen to phone my ninety-four-year-old father. My mother passed the year before, so he's by himself in his veteran's apartment on West Broadway.

"Hi, Dad. How are you doing?"

"Where are you?" he asks.

"At Margie and Al's. Ellen, Sam and I just got here. It's too bad you can't be here, too."

Silence. It's hard to know what to say. He's frail, distraught and bound to be lonely, but he lives on the other side of the city. I don't have the stamina to pick him up and then take him home later in the pouring rain, in the dark. Michelle was his first grandchild. He loved many things about her, not least her intellect and ardent curiosity.

At home in Vancouver, three-year-old Michelle cradles her baby brother, Cameron. Photo courtesy Lang family

"We have to carry on," he says, finally. His voice is shaky. "It can't be helped."

"Yes, I suppose. I still can't believe it, though." We chat haltingly for a few minutes. "I'll see you tomorrow, Dad. We'll be by in the morning. Love you," I say, hanging up.

I stand for a moment in my sister's kitchen, staring at the fridge door, a smattering of family pictures and household notes stuck to its surface. There's nothing I can do or say to comfort him. I feel numb.

We create a photo album for Art and Sandy throughout the evening. Margie and I reminisce about her early childhood as Daniel and Ellen recall fun times with their older cousin. Poring over images of Michelle from infancy on, we laugh at those where she's hamming it up and chat about her shyness with strangers. There are photos from grade school to graduation, in sports uniforms clutching a baseball bat with all her might, and summer holiday pictures, splashing with friends in Okanagan Lake, her younger brother, Cameron, often by her side. I giggle at one taken in her baby-blue-wallpapered bedroom. Sporting a flouncy hat, a silky blue blouse and a candy cigarette dangling from her mouth, Michelle bares one shoulder as she leans forward, her left hand on Cam's shoulder. It's hard to tell if her brother is wearing a woman's wig or a hat, but he's got a frilly dress over his jeans and white sneakers, his fingers stuck between lips plastered in red. No doubt it was Michelle who got him to dress up in that garb—just one of many occasions when she would get him to do her bidding. As the night wears on, we choose a Christmas photo of Michelle for the album cover—one of her as a young woman, wearing fake reindeer antlers, as always, smiling into the camera.

In the blur of unfolding events, I phone a reporter at the *Calgary Sun*. I reached out to them in error, thinking it was the *Herald*, and sent them a grade-school photo of Michelle to run with the story. In it, a fringe of brown bangs falls neatly across her forehead as she peers upward. Braces haven't yet straightened her overbite, her blue eyes clear. I can't explain why, but I'm desperate for others to see how sweet she was.

As soon as I hang up, the phone rings. It's Renata D'Aliesio, one of Michelle's friends and colleagues at the *Herald*. I tell her more or less what I'd just told the *Sun*, that Michelle was a fun-loving niece who held a special place in our hearts. Renata interviews my father, too. She quotes him in her article, published January 1, 2010: "I'll miss her presence," he said. "We have to live on with her memories."

One of the pictures in the photo album we made that New Year's Eve was of Michelle blowing out five candles on a birthday cake. Naturally, she was wearing pink, her favourite colour, in a pinafore-style dress. Soft ribbons were wrapped around two silky brown pigtails that hung from the top of her head. Her mother stood behind, smiling as Michelle gathered her breath to blow out the candles. About seven of her friends, all wearing party hats and grinning, sat around the heavy oak dining table, which was decorated in pink doilies, frilly pink crepe paper crisscrossing the ceiling above.

It was January 31, 1980, but I didn't go to her birthday party that year. Four days before, when I was twenty-six, I'd given birth to my first child—a six-pound baby girl. On the morning of Michelle's birthday, I sat with infant in my arms while I waited to be discharged from the Royal Jubilee Hospital in Victoria.

That day I gave my beautiful baby Ellen to Edith and Victor Newman, relinquishing all legal rights to her as my child, through a private adoption. Her Haida father and I had separated months before, before I even knew I was pregnant. I lacked the confidence to be a single parent and was far from financially stable, while the Newmans offered her a loving home that was steeped in Victor's Coast Salish and Kwakwaka'wakw heritage.

When we arrived at Edith's parents' house, we were standing near the stairwell that led to the door outside. Ellen was sleeping soundly, bundled in a receiving blanket and cradled in my arms. A wave of momentary relief flushed through me as I shifted her sweet, warm body into Victor's waiting arms, not Edith's. I couldn't bear the thought of giving her to her new mother. But perhaps I remember it that way because that's how I want to remember it. I listened to them descend the stairs, holding my breath until the door closed.

A different phase of life awaited me, yet Ellen and her adoptive family continued to be very much a part of it. Though torn by my decision to give her up, I visited the Newmans on a regular basis, forming a close bond during Ellen's infancy and childhood. Edith and Victor wanted her to know her biological parents and our families. As her birth mother, I came and went, showering her with as much affection as I dared, as did her birth father, Jerome, until his untimely death a few weeks short of Ellen's thirteenth birthday.

Having her with Sam and me the day after Michelle was killed was a comfort. She holds herself well in difficult circumstances and supported her half-brother in those early days. Some nineteen years younger than Michelle, Sam didn't have a strong connection to his cousin. But when Ellen was young, she often came with me to Vancouver to visit my side of her birth family, always delighted to play with her fun-loving cousins, especially Michelle.

On that New Year's Eve in my sister's living room, I came across a black-and-white photo that triggered memories of those days. It was a closeup I'd taken of Ellen and Michelle in an outdoor swimming pool, beads of water glistening on their grinning faces, side by side and gleeful.

Now it's New Year's Day, and Margie and I head to our brother's. He and Sandy had arrived home in the wee hours after a long flight from Monterrey and a dark drive in the rain from Seattle where they'd left their car. From the foyer of their townhome, I glimpse Sandy treading down the hallway, her body bent, heavy as rock. A few moments later, she shuffles past us to climb the stairs and lie down in her curtained bedroom, a vacancy in her eyes. The flight had taken its toll: her blood pressure is up, and she needs medication to cope with the unrelenting grief.

Margie and I talk to Art by the front door. He looks drawn and exhausted, and I expect he hasn't slept much. He'd already declined the military's invitation to the repatriation ceremony in Trenton, Ontario, while we had accepted the night before when the *Calgary Herald* offered to pay our expenses. But for them, it was too much, too soon to even consider another flight, let alone the inevitable mingling with others. Art stands grim-faced in the hall as we put a copy of our flight itinerary into his hands.

"Thanks for going there on our behalf," Art says. "Sandy isn't in any shape to travel."

"We understand, Art," Margie says, their eyes meeting briefly. It's hard to see him like this, but there's little to say. He opens the door, and I give him a hug. His body is stiff, as if it might fall apart if he lets go.

Moments after we leave, I turn to Margie. She maneuvers her yellow Aerio left off 33rd Avenue onto Granville Street, her hazel eyes watching for speeders coming over the rise toward us.

"Did you notice the photo album we made on the dining room table?" I ask.

Margie nods, glancing at me briefly. "Putting it together helped us," she replies, "but I don't think they'll be able look at it for a while."

I nod back. "I wish there was something we could do or say, but the truth is…" I falter, my eyes following the road south as Margie heads toward the Fraser River and home, each of us struggling to stare down this beast: the finality of untimely death.

CHAPTER 5

REPATRIATION

On January 2, three days after Michelle's death, Margie is at the wheel again. I point out an ethereal pink flush in the sky as we head to the airport, as if a spirit energy is marking its presence. It gives our sad hearts a momentary lift, this notion of Michelle lighting the sky in which we'll soon be airborne. My sister smiles brightly for the first time in days, her steady, familiar manner a comfort.

After takeoff, I take out my journal and note the airplane icon making its way across Canada on the back of the seat where Margie sits. Our sad motley group is scattered throughout the aircraft behind me: Sam, Ellen, and my nephew, Daniel, and his wife, Vera, each of us unsure what the next two days will bring.

It's already dark when we arrive at our downtown hotel in Toronto. In the Westin Prince lobby, I meet Michelle's fiancé for the second time. We first met on a beautiful, warm day just seven months prior. It was Dan and Vera's wedding, when rhododendrons were in full bloom on the university grounds of Cecil Green Park House. The deep blue of Vancouver's harbour and the North Shore mountains framed our view beyond the landscaped perimeter. Everyone in the family was delighted to meet Michelle's future husband, their affection for each other pulling them close. After the heartache of relationships that had fallen apart, she had finally found her soulmate.

My husband snapped pictures of the young lovebirds. They sat across from us at a perfectly adorned table—save for the clutter that guests were creating on the smooth white tablecloths, with empty hors d'oeuvres plates and half-full wine glasses attesting to the imbibing well underway. In one photo, Michelle holds up her arm—she wants to make sure her wrist-to-elbow cast is in the viewfinder—and flashes one of her winning smiles. Michael was with her when she broke her arm playing Ultimate Frisbee before boarding a plane to come to her cousin's wedding. But that painful night was behind them, and in the glow of a balmy dusk in May, they were radiant in love.

It was the last time I saw Michelle alive.

Michelle and her fiancé, Michael Louie, at a wedding reception in Vancouver, May 2009. Photo courtesy Bruce Martin

Now, Michael is a broken man as he approaches me in the gleaming dark backdrop of the bar behind the Westin Prince foyer. Holding a velvet case in the palm of his outstretched hand, he stares at the diamond ring between us. "What will I do with it now, Auntie Catherine?" he asks, his shoulders heaving, his face crumbling.

I'm at a complete loss. What can I possibly say? I wish my husband were here. He'd think of something comforting, even if only a strong hand on Michael's shoulder.

Michelle's friends from the *Herald*—Colette Derworiz, Renata D'Aliesio, Kelly Cryderman, and Gwendolyn Richards—come forward from the upscale bar to greet us. It's the first time we've met, and despite the circumstances, I'm buoyed by their camaraderie and warmth. They surround Michael, along with his friend, Phoebe Fung, who's never far from his side for the duration of this trip. All of four feet, eight inches tall, Phoebe sports short, thick black hair and a broad smile. It's not immediately apparent, but as I get to know her, I discover a resilience that belies her buzzing, friendly manner. Though petite, she's clearly in command.

We head out together for dinner at a nearby restaurant. It's been a kaleidoscope day, travelling from the wet West Coast to the chilly shores of Lake Ontario in the dead of winter, meeting Michael and Michelle's inner circle from Calgary, their long, sad faces like ours, still clinging to vibrant images of Michelle as if we expect her to round a corner and join us. A collective disbelief hangs in the air, and we voice our sense that this can't be happening, that we're going through motions on a movie set, standing outside of ourselves in this coming together of our family and her loved ones. My brain is still spinning when my head hits the pillow in the room I'm sharing with my sister. I turn toward Margie, lying in the bed beside me, just like when we were growing up together and shared a room, and listen to her breath, falling fitfully in and out of sleep.

The next day we are chauffeured from Toronto to the sprawling military base at Trenton, the largest in Canada. As we roll along the highway, sun shines through cloud cover, more silver and shrouded, like a moon in the mist. Our chaperone, a woman with a lovely manner and the bearing of a diplomat, escorts us into a private room inside one of the base's cavernous buildings. We're separate from the military families grieving their losses in the large hall, and I wonder if they've already had time with the dignitaries in this room, surrounded by the support of their military family. In time, I will meet many of them, but today, they are strangers whose names I do not know, people I dare not approach for fear of breaking protocol. I think of Art and Sandy, Cameron too, who remains with his fiancée in Mexico. I wish they were here, but in a way, I'm relieved they're not. What could possibly comfort them here?

A tall, finely groomed man approaches Margie and me, extending his hand. His forest-green serge suit is covered in military medals, the Order of Military Merit and the Meritorious Service Cross to name a few.

"I am so very sorry for your loss," Chief of Defence Staff Walter Natynczyk says, making direct eye contact. "Just the other day, I was brushing my teeth beside Michelle in a ramshackle shed," he offers, smiling and turning to Peter MacKay, the Minister of National Defence.

"My deepest condolences, as well," Mr. MacKay says, also extending his hand.

But I'm focused on Walter Natynczyk, disarmed by his confident charm, his easy but sincere smile. I suppose he has had many opportunities to speak with families of our fallen.

"She was a trooper and left her mark with everyone she talked to," Mr. Natynczyk says. "Her story about the couple together at Christmas Eve paid tribute to the soldiers, and it was so fitting. She went and made the rounds to meet as many as she could, to listen and to tell their stories."

"Yes, that would be Michelle," I say. "She always found ways to connect with those she met."

"Well, again, our deepest condolences," he says, shaking our hands warmly before turning to accompany Mr. MacKay to greet others in the room.

Margie and I retreat to a corner of the sectional couch when we see Governor General Michaëlle Jean approaching. She sits beside us, taking our hands in hers, offering what comfort she can. I sink into the depth of her eyes and hang on her every word.

"You know that Michelle died doing what she loved, don't you?" she asks. Leaning in closer and recalling her own experience as a foreign correspondent, she continues: "Michelle would have been so full of excitement when she arrived at Kandahar Airfield. I can remember the moment I landed in conflict zones in Africa, covering civil wars and famine for the CBC. It's this adrenalin of being on the ground where people's lives hang in the balance. It's the sense of immediacy, the urgency of getting to the stories. Not to mention getting under the stories, assembling, and analyzing facts, interviewing whoever will talk to you and provide context. And getting it right. Of course, you're under the deadline pressure of a national news network back in Canada."

Sitting there, I remember that adrenalin, as well as the longing to experience it abroad. The closest I came to it was covering two snowmobilers lost on a mountain overnight in winter. Working as a reporter for a community newspaper in 1989, I also felt the impact of lives hanging in the balance. The scope of the drama hardly worthy of a national newscast, but the urgency was real to those of us watching snow falling outside the newsroom window, waiting for search-and-rescue updates, tracking down folks who knew the missing men, scrambling to get as many facts as possible before deadline. I know that the same adrenalin was coursing through Michelle's veins. But it doesn't make me feel better because I can't move past the harsh reality that no matter how much she loved it, her job *wasn't* worth the cost—her brilliant self violently ripped from our world.

As Ms. Jean speaks, I am thinking: *Is her death in vain?* I want to know, as if, like a fact, she can tell me definitively: *No, she did not die in vain.*

We are outside now, where the wind howls. Wisps of snow skate across the tarmac like a ghostly dancer's shadow.

The mammoth hulk of the Hercules aircraft is parked to our right, so massive it's a wonder it can lift off the ground with cargo. It towers over the line of mourners and military guard. In front of us and to our left, a gaggle of press stands roped off in a corner of the tarmac. Lenses the lengths of a forearm perch on tripods, waiting like the rest of us.

This is the first of many military memorials I will attend over the coming years. In time, I will be able to anticipate the rigour, the discipline, the military regalia, and ceremony. But today, it's nothing like anything I've experienced in my fifty-plus years.

The aircraft's exit ramp unfolds slowly, revealing a hole like the maw of an oversized grey whale. A silver-haired chaplain stands by, his long robe fluttering like a bleached sheet on a Prairie clothesline in winter—whip, whip, whip. I hear the crackling of frost on cotton from the winters of my youth in Saskatchewan.

The repatriation ceremony begins. I stomp my feet as quietly as I can to keep blood flowing in my cramping toes. Even though we're somewhat sheltered under an awning, it has been decades since I've stood outside in sub-zero temperatures. I turn my head and spot Michelle's friend, the dancer from Montreal in a crowded row behind, brushing tears from her rosy cheeks. She had introduced herself earlier. "Michelle had a photo of you leaping through air in a flowing dress," I said. "She raved about how magical it was to see you dance."

A lone bugler on the tarmac begins "The Last Post." I've never heard the mournful melody with such clarity before, and the notes cut into me. Pallbearers, six per casket, descend the ramp. One by one, they march before us with their heavy loads. We watch as if caught in the reels of a slow-motion movie. And between each of the five flag-draped caskets, the bugler's lament fills the air again. The slow passage from Hercules aircraft to the black limousines parked in a row a short distance away on the tarmac.

We lay red roses on caskets, now firmly inside the open backs of gleaming hearses. Windblown and sad, Margie and I each clutch a rose to place on her flag-draped coffin as our escort guides us to the first limousine. Michael walks alone a short distance behind us. His lips brush the rose petals, sobbing as he lays it on her coffin before turning to walk solemnly back to his friends.

I look over at families of the fallen soldiers, a mass of conjoined long, black coats, huddling in semi-circles at the back of each open hearse. Then a thud: the mother of one of the soldiers falls chest first onto her son's casket, the echo of her wail a mile long.

Pallbearers lift Michelle's casket into hearse at Trenton military base, January 3, 2010. Photo courtesy Postmedia

Michaëlle Jean, not only Governor General but Canadian Forces Commander-in-Chief, flanked by senior ranking officers and the minister of national defence, begins her remarks. "Let's hope that life triumphs over terror in 2010."

She pauses. Four days have come and gone since an improvised explosive device killed my niece and four Canadian soldiers, all but one of them reservists, on the outskirts of Kandahar city. Five others were wounded on that hard, muddy road in the heart of Taliban territory.

Family, friends and fiancé under awning during repatriation ceremony, Trenton, January 3, 2010. R to L: Catherine Lang, military escort, Michael Louie, Phoebe Fung, Margaret Menzies, military escort, Gov.-Gen. Michaëlle Jean, Minister of National Defence Peter MacKay, Chief of Defence Staff, Walt Natynczyk. Photo courtesy Postmedia

One of those five, also a civilian, is fighting for her life in a German hospital while we listen to Ms. Jean offer prayers for her survival and bear witness.

I stand erect between Margie and Sam, looking out at the vast windswept tarmac where Michaëlle Jean speaks of comfort and hope and sacrifice and commitment, her beauty fierce and ablaze on this bleak, grey afternoon. It is nine days before a 7.0 magnitude earthquake shatters Haiti, the country she fled as a refugee. She, too, will soon be whirling in a vortex of grief like those of us assembled on the tarmac of this freezing January afternoon.

After the repatriation ceremony, we speed mile after mile along the Highway of Heroes in a convoy of limos. I'm cocooned inside luxury on wheels for hours, crunched up against a back corner, staring out the window. Hundreds upon hundreds of men, women, and children are lining both sides of the highway and crammed onto overpasses above, arms and sometimes entire bodies waving. Police officers, firefighters, and paramedics stand on top of emergency vehicles, silhouetted against a deepening twilight sky. *This must be nationhood*, I think. I've never felt anything like it before, a sudden awakening to the notion of service embedded in our common humanity, like a very large extended family. Unbelievably to me, the rows of people we stream past for 170 kilometres are still lining Toronto's downtown streets, paying tribute as we arrive at our destination, the caskets delivered to the coroner's office. Whisked away by our escorts, we are done for the day.

CHAPTER 6

VIEWING CEREMONY, KANDAHAR AIRFIELD

When I cast my thoughts back to those early days of January 2010, I recall how oblivious I was to certain details, unable to connect the dots back then. Years later, it hit me that as we flew from the Pacific Ocean to Toronto, a Hercules cargo plane had already lifted off the Kandahar Airfield tarmac some 10,000 kilometres away. So while we flew east, Michelle's remains were in the air, flying west, almost home.

Nine days after Michelle reported on the ramp ceremony for Lt. Andrew Nuttall at KAF—the 134th casualty since Canada's mission had begun in 2001—a female civilian and five soldiers in uniform marched my niece's casket onto the aircraft ramp on the same Kandahar airfield. I learned about her ramp ceremony in Kandahar from news reports, the backdrop to the moment-to-moment drama we were living in Canada. It was when I talked to Padre André Gauthier nine years later that I got a more visceral picture of how the drama unfolded in Kandahar, in the midst of war on the ground.

I'm not a religious person, but meeting this chaplain became important for reasons I can't explain. We had spoken a few times by phone,

Pallbearers carry the caskets of journalist Michelle Lang and four Canadian soldiers, Sgt. Kirk Taylor, Sgt. George Miok, Cpl. Zachery McCormack and Pte. Garrett Chidley, at Kandahar Airfield, January 1, 2010. Photo by Colin Perkel/THE CANADIAN PRESS

telling me how he had been the only one among the military who knew Michelle well enough to identify her at the Kandahar morgue. It pained him then. I think it will always pain him. Listening to his sweet-natured voice and hearing about his ministrations to the dead, the dying, the injured, I had pictured him down by their sides on the dusty roads and fields, reciting prayers and blessings. Talking to him also made it clear why Michelle wanted to interview him shortly after her arrival. The chaplains weren't soldiers, but they faced danger nonetheless. The caring, compassionate aspect of their work inspired me too. Simply being there. In war zones. Working through his personal fears, praying that God would take care of him, and if not, that God would take care of him in an afterlife.

So when I unexpectedly heard his voice on the phone one January morning in 2019, I leapt to attention. He was in Victoria and asked if I'd like to meet. Pumped with adrenalin, I dropped what I was doing and drove to the Esquimalt naval base that sunny afternoon. I took a few wrong turns and, cursing myself, arrived late. While he was waiting, he held a rosary in his hand and prayed for Michelle in case she wasn't at peace. It made me wonder if that's why my thoughts went to my mother and her sisters and my grandmother, my Nanny Gray, in the hours after I first learned Michelle was killed. A part of me wanted then and wants now to believe that their energy instantly rushed to envelope her, to guide and comfort her on her journey into the spirit world. I guess that makes me an agnostic, someone who doesn't know what they believe.

André and I talked for two hours, the soft winter sun falling on his chestnut brown eyes and his clean-shaven face, framed by a salt-and-pepper brush cut. In the luxury and stillness of an empty wardroom on the base, we pulled two plush chairs in front of a wide picture window with an expansive view of Juan de Fuca Strait. Race Rocks Lighthouse was barely visible, as if behind a filtered screen, bathed in a winter glow on the horizon. Throughout the afternoon, I paused every now and then to point out the marine and bird life congregating around rocky islets near the shore. As the hours passed, we watched the light descend to the west, the islets growing dark, silhouetted against the rocking, silver sea. Walking outside later, I came to a sudden stop. An iridescent full moon, truly the size of a huge saucer, hovered above the horizon just as I was beginning to process all I had learned that afternoon.

I wonder if Michelle knew that André didn't learn English until he joined the military. He was in his early thirties at the time, and still today his accent is thick and luxurious, calling me "Cat-er-een" with the enthusiasm of a youngster. When he talks about the viewing time he organized after she was killed, his voice is soft and tender. Listening to him speak, I am deeply moved and comforted by the efforts he and others went to, to ensure a sacred space surrounded all five caskets, side by side in a row.

A sentinel guard stood by while Canadian and coalition military came and went, offering their respects for three hours prior to the ramp ceremony. It was next to the Canadian cenotaph in a security zone for the Afghanistan Joint Task Force where a seating area had been set up behind the row of caskets. When André struggled to find the words to describe the afternoon, I asked if he would write about it for me, in French. Later, a bilingual friend translated it for me:

> Right at the start of the viewing, I invited all the chaplains who were there to pray together for each of the deceased military members and for Michelle Lang. We placed our hands on each of the caskets, one after the other, praying for divine mercy and that these people be welcomed into the realm of God. We also prayed for all the family and friends of the deceased, that they may have the strength to overcome such a difficult trial. We prayed for the rest of all their souls. When we finished, we went to the back to welcome those who were coming to offer their respects.
>
> The viewing area was dominated by a great silence, a silence occasionally broken by restrained sobs. The military personnel arrived in groups of five or six at once. One at a time, they advanced to the casket of the person they had come to grieve. They prayed in silence, then collected themselves. Some spontaneously placed their hands on a casket with the greatest respect. Just before leaving, they saluted their departed colleagues with grace and dignity. After sitting down, some stayed for twenty or thirty minutes, or occasionally for an hour or two. And then, before leaving, they went through the same ritual as on arrival, collecting themselves in front of the casket for a few moments, looking at the photo of the deceased, touching the casket and offering another salute, often with tears in their eyes. Occasionally, a personnel member burst into tears, unable to hold in their grief. Spontaneously, their friends

or a chaplain offered comfort and empathy with a hug or a hand on their shoulder.

We passed boxes of tissues around and emptied many. I was touched by the compassion of the military and civilian personnel throughout the viewing. We sensed an atmosphere of unity and cohesion despite the sadness and feelings of loss and suffering. I felt that what was happening was in the domain of the sacred, where life still speaks to us more strongly than death. Only a very thin veil separated us from the dead.

I noticed that a smaller number of people offered their respects to Michelle and came to stand in front of her casket because she was not as well known to the military personnel. However, she was better known by the people at HQ, the civilians working there and her fellow journalists. They stood by her casket and looked at her photo and her magnificent smile.

Finally, the three hours of the viewing came to an end. The chaplains went forward together. We gathered ourselves in front of each of the caskets and said a prayer for the souls of the departed and their families in Canada, as well as their colleagues, their friends and all those who would suffer from their loss. We asked the Lord to give them the strength and grace necessary to get through this difficult trial, and we prayed that the mutual support and comfort that they give each other would bring a balm to their hearts and their souls.

Naturally, I wish I had been there to witness the sanctity he spoke of, all in the midst of so much sorrow. The one place I can't go is where Michelle went, where furrowed rows of grapevines and poppy fields might have encircled her for miles. I can't pause along the stretch of road where she died, any more than I can listen for echoes of that past ringing in my ears.

Nine years on, I continue to ponder the speculations of others. For example, was the armoured vehicle Charlie targeted on purpose? Some vigorously denied it, but others suggested that her assassins got paid extra because she was a woman and a high-profile target. André had heard that the Taliban thought someone even more "important," like a brigadier-general, was on that convoy. Other analysis points to the Taliban's

In this image taken on December 30, 2009, a helicopter flies over the road on which an improvised explosive device was detonated remotely under the light-armoured vehicle carrying reporter Michelle Lang, federal policy analyst Bushra Saeed and Canadian troops. Photo: Allauddin Khan/ Associated Press

efforts to make a big statement on the land during the Christmas season, in an area where coalition forces and Afghan authorities were pouring resources into reconstruction projects. The blast was seen for miles, warning villagers and the Afghan army of the dangers of messing with them on their home turf. Still others point to the underlying betrayal of Canadian troops by those with whom they thought they were building a trust and who did not warn them about the tunnel of bombs they were sure to encounter.

But no matter how much time and effort I make, I am always and forever viewing that muddy road and the surrounding countryside as an outsider. I circle around, skittering this way and that, overturning the same stones repeatedly, until my thoughts compress into a tangle of knots I can't penetrate. Looking for what I do not know. Quietly and without warning, it comes to me. I'm seeking Michelle's version of events. In writing and in voice.

January 19, 2015

Dear Michelle,
Looking back on it now, the days and weeks following your death seem like a long, wild dream, a storm of emotions. Day after day, week after week, reporters, columnists, editors and publishers wrote about you and the soldiers who died alongside you. It was often front-page news, this chronology of events that began on December 30, 2009. Suddenly, we were pawns in a geopolitical war game beyond our grasp, slashing into the once-solid girth of our family. A gut-wrenching yank from the protected bubble of our white-privileged society, where the realities of war, while deeply saddening, failed to penetrate the zone in which we passed our day-to-day lives.

On the last day of 2009, I grabbed the first set of newspapers, my heart sinking as your smiling face popped out on the front page above the fold and the *Calgary Herald* headline:

'Brave' Herald reporter, 4 soldiers die in blast: Roadside bomb kills Canadians in Kandahar

My hands flipped below the fold to see the *Herald* headline under your beautiful face

Deadly day for Canada: Taliban blast targets rebuilding team

The coverage spilled on to the inside pages, tearful editorials and articles by your colleagues.

LANG: 'Excelled in journalism'

Dedicated journalist went after the real story

Photos of you giggling at something, in your flak vest and helmet, or you smiling sweetly beside Chief of Defence Staff Walter Natynczyk in the back of a military vehicle on Christmas Day, or you shoving a tape recorder into the agitated face of then Premier Ralph Klein. The editorial cartoon space was a black square, with your name in the centre.

Headlines in newspapers across the country declared it one of the deadliest days for Canada in Afghanistan, with a large photo of you glancing over your shoulder, smiling at a soldier, your brown hair in a ponytail and sunglasses propped on top of your head. Over and over, news articles noted you were the first Canadian journalist killed in Afghanistan since Canada joined the NATO mission that began in 2001, following the 9/11 terrorist attacks on the Twin Towers and the Pentagon. As it turns out, you were the only Canadian journalist killed before our combat mission ended two years later, in 2011. Nor were any Canadian journalists killed during the remaining three years of Canada's mission, helping to train the Afghan National Army in combat and adherence to international laws and protection of human rights, something near and dear to you and me.

> **Roadside bomb kills four soldiers and a Canadian journalist, injures five others in one of the deadliest attacks on troops since the mission began**

> **Brazen strike in relatively peaceful area signals dramatic upsurge in violence around Kandahar city, threatening to undermine soldiers' advances in the district**

> **An award-winning journalist and bride-to-be who loved the work and knew the risks**

And on it went. First online and then in print the following day, newspaper reports framed the month of January 2010 for me. It was just the beginning. I threw every newspaper I came across during those days and weeks into a cardboard box, a mishmash of articles about your demise and the importance of a free press to report on our mission, the military status of the combat and reconstruction efforts—the mounting deaths, including the one you covered yourself, that of Lt. Andrew Nuttall who was killed one week to the day before you.

In the months and years to follow, I stashed more articles, in print and online, in file folders that came to resemble my random emotional journey. Without a clear sense of how to focus or consolidate, folders with your name for the title emerged: Michelle—clips from Dec. 30, 2009 and on; Michelle's death—columns, articles; Michelle—memorials, tributes, etc. All of them grew thicker by the day, month, year. And as the jumble of files expanded, so too did my knowledge of you, spiralling down pathways of my troubled heart.

Slain Canadians begin journey home, dateline: Kandahar Airfield

January 2, 2010. The ramp ceremony in Kandahar on New Year's Day. Front-page photos, images of pallbearers shouldering your flag-draped casket on the tarmac, four more caskets falling in behind yours as they marched toward the cameras. The massive cargo plane somewhere outside the camera frames.

While Aunt Margie, your cousins and I flew to Toronto the day after that cargo plane lifted into the skies above Afghanistan, I didn't have the wherewithal to contemplate the efforts involved in bringing your body home. I was of no mind to retain details. Except for the photos. Somehow, they stayed with me. Stay with me still.

Sombre return for five Canadians

Supporters line sombre Highway of Heroes

Stiff salutes and a vigilant public

January 4, 2010. Newspapers reported on the repatriation ceremony at Trenton. They wrote about the hundreds who lined the Highway of Heroes for miles and miles in the falling light of a grim winter day. Your parents at home in Vancouver, in the darkest days of their grief and shock, did not make the news. I doubt they were looking at newspapers; I doubt they saw the photo of Aunt Margie and Michael Louie in their sorrow, flanked by military and civilian escorts.

A No. 1 that should not be: Four soldiers, one journalist and endless grief

Did I read the January 4 *National Post* front-page commentary by Don Martin back then? I've no idea. It moves me to tears, as do many accounts, these years on.

"Ironically, the last time I talked to Ms. Lang, she was attending a tribute in Calgary to Nichola Goddard, the first female soldier casualty of the mission. Now she's set a tragic precedent of her own that we only hope will never be repeated. Michelle Lang is now home, but she was on a flight you never want to catch for a homecoming every family with a Kandahar connection dreads."

The significance of your death as a journalist was not lost on us. In the same *National Post* column on January 4, Mr. Martin also wrote: "It's an enormous credit to the senior brass of the Canadian Forces that they gave Ms. Lang the first civilian ramp-to-repatriation salute in Canadian military history. ... when she died alongside soldiers in an armoured vehicle hit by a massive Taliban-planted bomb last week, senior officials decided she was an on-the-job victim of combat as much as the troops and treated her as an equal."

She was our witness

January 4, 2010. I read the *Ottawa Citizen* editorial in the *Vancouver Sun*, wondering if Randy Newell, your Afghanistan assignment editor at the *Citizen*, had a hand in writing it. It had a personal touch, referring to you as "a sensitive reporter." I think you'd have been pleased with how they described why journalists take on dangerous assignments and why it's important work, how you and other journalists risk your lives in order to "make sure the story gets out"—not a soldier, but "very much an agent of democracy."

Remembering

January 9, 2010. A large photo of you surrounded in black. It was the full-page commemoration that Canwest published in all its newspapers across Canada—your picture and name above the fold, the photos of the soldiers you died with lined up in a row beneath the tribute to you: *A great friend, colleague and award-winning journalist.*

What female reporters bring to a combat zone

January 12, 2010. The *Province* published an opinion piece by Kathy Gannon, the Associated Press correspondent who has been covering Pakistan and Afghanistan for decades now.

"Michelle wasn't a soldier who had been trained for battle,

who chose to go to a war zone to fight an enemy. Michelle strapped on the flak jacket and a helmet and stepped into a military vehicle to go out on a road she knew to be dangerous because she was a brave reporter, like so many of our colleagues both men and women, who want to try to understand what these conflicts are all about. To understand the people involved in war—the soldiers, the ordinary people and, yes, even the enemy."

The target of an attack herself in Kabul in 2014, she survived, though she needed emergency surgery. A German photojournalist accompanying Ms. Gannon did not. It meant a lot that someone of Ms. Gannon's stature paid you tribute, but I've no idea if things that matter to the living no longer do to you, out there in the beyond.

Hundreds turn out to mourn fallen journalist

Slain journalist remembered for gusto, courage, fairness, and wicked humour

January 12, 2010. They reported on your service at the Italian Cultural Centre in Vancouver. Photos of your flag-draped casket on a steel trolley, surrounded by friends and relatives, pallbearers in black suits: your brother Cam, your cousins Daniel and Stephen, my cousin Keith and others I don't recognize. A front-page photo of your mother and father seated in the front row, heads bent together as they listened to Aunt Margie at the podium.

Just as with the day of Andrew Nuttall's service on January 3, it was pouring rain that Monday. Before the service began, I stood in a medley of people arriving, a swirl of folks who came from across Canada to pay their tributes, including an entourage of RCMP officers in red serge. Your Saskatchewan comrade Mike O'Brien and his soulmate, Robin Summerfield, pregnant with the boy they would name Will Lang O'Brien, were among those I met, along with family from the farm where you visited during your Saskatchewan newspaper stints.

Art and Sandy, heads bowed low, walked behind your flag-draped coffin into the cultural centre's main hall. Where was your love, Michael? I don't remember. He's quoted in the *Province*, saying: "Her heart was bigger than life itself."

Your brother choked up when he said your name, but he still managed to make everyone laugh out loud describing the noodle soup fight

Margaret Menzies pays tribute to her niece, Michelle Lang, at the memorial service in Vancouver on January 11, 2010. In front row, parents Art and Sandy Lang mourn their loss. Photo courtesy Postmedia

and the punch you delivered that sent both of you flying through a large picture window when you were school kids. More friends and colleagues plucked up the courage to tell more stories, while happy photos flashed across the screen behind—you in grade school, high school, university and all the newspapers where you worked. Your frail ninety-four-year-old grandfather shook, his speech incomprehensible, propped up by your cousin Sam, fifteen, braces on his teeth, awkward beside our failing patriarch. I spoke at the podium too. I called you a lioness with a golden flower, a line from Lawrence Durrell's *Justine*, both your middle name and the title of the second novel in his renowned quartet.

Then it was your father at the podium, his 1972 slides from Afghanistan up on the screen, as he addressed the crowd of mourners. "Michelle went to Afghanistan to tell us what had happened to that tragic country," your Dad said. He expressed a slim hope, one that Afghanistan might be at peace again, a more stable nation, so that your "death and all the other deaths will not be in vain."

Afterwards, we retreated to your parents' place, numb and exhausted. I poured myself more than one scotch.

Fellowship created to honour slain Canwest journalist Michelle Lang

January 15, 2010. Canwest Publishing announced the Michelle Lang Fellowship, "intended to inspire young writers to strive for the same excellence pursued by the award-winning *Calgary Herald* journalist." You were a hard act to follow for the inaugural recipient, Laura Stone, now the *Globe and Mail's* Queen's Park reporter.

Memorial service honours life and work of Calgary Herald reporter Michelle Lang

January 18, 2010. The *Herald* reported on your Calgary memorial service at First Alliance Church, the fourth and final public memorial service after those in Kandahar, Trenton and Vancouver. I didn't go, but when I saw the photo of your newsroom mates hugging on stage, I knew it was another day of stories, of laughter and tears. I was exhausted, spent, wanting to cocoon at home with Bruce and Sam.

On January 22, no one reported on what would have been your homecoming from Kandahar, the moment your Michael had been longing for ever since you disappeared from view through the airport departure gates. And on January 31, they didn't report on what would have been your thirty-fifth birthday, though everyone in the family hadn't stopped thinking of you since it all began.

WAR IN AFGHANISTAN: THE LONDON PLAN, THE AFGHAN ENDGAME BEGINS: NATO countries make broad compromise to end the war with unanimous deal that includes making peace with the Taliban

January 29, 2010. The *Globe and Mail* published a series of articles under a photo cropped to focus on a line of men's hands resting on their knees. All sported black pants except for the green-purple-black striped piece of cloth—perhaps handwoven, perhaps ceremonial—covering the lap of Afghan president Hamid Karzai. The camera flash glints on the polished black shoes of the Aga Khan, Karzai, British PM Gordon Brown and UN Secretary-General Ban Ki-moon. And so the bargaining began: one month less a day after the bomb blast propelled you into the roof of the LAV, killing you instantly, so they said.

The word *incomprehensible* takes on new meaning, new depth. Not just your death, but the negotiations with your assassins. You had slipped further into the mystic when, a little more than a year later, Canadian troops withdrew from combat, leaving behind a contingent to keep training the Afghan army and police for another three years. Alas, the laudable goal of preparing Afghan security forces to keep the peace when NATO troops departed was short-sighted. How I wish you'd still been with us to report on the complicated machinations of the mission's shortcomings, ones that cost everyone so dearly.

Military unveils plaque for Calgary Herald reporter slain in Afghanistan

Forces unveil front-line memorial for journalist slain in Afghanistan

March 13, 2010. They reported on the military unveiling of your plaque between two media tents in the Canadian compound of Kandahar Airfield. The plaque, made by army engineers, was mounted on a wooden plinth so very far away from us. The Canadian Press reporter Steve Rennie noted that "it stands as a reminder to journalists covering the war of the perils that come with reporting from the front lines," while Padre Yvonne Mills paid tribute with these words: "May Michelle's spirit not be forgotten by those who work in this space."

The military unveil a plaque near the media tent where Michelle worked at Kandahar Airfield, March 13, 2010. Photo courtesy Postmedia

Art and Sandy Lang with Gov.-Gen. Michaëlle Jean at Rideau Hall on May 27, 2010, when the Michener-Baxter Special Award was awarded posthumously to Michelle. Photo courtesy Postmedia

Slain journalist Lang wins press freedom award

May 3, 2010. They reported that you were the twelfth recipient of the Canadian World Press Freedom Award, the first time it was awarded posthumously. They honoured you with a moment of silence at the awards ceremony in Ottawa. The next day a small group of journalists and soldiers witnessed a master corporal place a bouquet of flowers at your plaque outside the Kandahar media tents. British journalists attended as well to honour their colleague, Rupert Hamer, a father of young kids, killed in Helmand province ten days after you.

Also in May 2010, your name was one of ten etched on the 2009 glass pillar of the Freedom Forum Journalists Memorial in Washington, D.C.

Michelle Lang honoured at Michener awards

May 27, 2010. They reported on Art and Sandy accepting the Michener-Baxter Special Award for Exceptional Service to Canadian Journalism on your behalf. The photo at the black-tie ceremony in Rideau Hall gives me pause: a tearful Sandy in a sparkling black dress, a stoic Art in tuxedo, a sombre Governor General Michaëlle Jean, her white cardigan curved against her plain black dress. Art is tipping a small box containing an engraved pendant, as he holds it out for the camera.

But you weren't there, and little else mattered.

BEFORE AND AFTER: The Bushra Saeed story

September 11, 2010, the ninth anniversary of 9/11. The *Ottawa Citizen* published a front-page photo of you and Bushra Saeed, the two of you standing in a briefing room before you and the troops hit the road on the day you died. You're leaning against what looks like a blackboard as Bushra tells you a story. You've got your flak vest on, hair in a ponytail. Your expression is reflective, and I wonder what you're thinking. Your instinct for story never far below the surface.

But the feature is about Bushra, the woman and civilian sitting across from you when the IED detonated. Miraculously, she survived, though barely. We've met a few times and keep in touch. Her story is remarkable, as is she. When I read the article, I didn't wish she had died and you had survived. I wished both of you had survived. I still do.

Reporter slain in Afghanistan honoured: Plaque recognizes journalist Michelle Lang and 14 soldiers who have died during Canada's mission

October 23, 2010. They reported on the unveiling of an Afghanistan plaque at the Saskatchewan War Memorial in Regina. The front-page photo shows your mother wiping a tear from her face, your father following behind. Capt. Nichola Goddard's name is the first on the plaque, and yours is the last, right below Lt. Andrew Nuttall.

As a reporter for the *Moose Jaw Times Herald* and *Regina Leader-Post*, you had ties to Saskatchewan. That's why they added your name to the plaque, one plaque of many on the Saskatchewan legislative grounds. The memorial is like a maze, with separate structures that list the names of Canada's war dead going back as far as the Boer War, in which your paternal great-grandfather served. I wonder now if he went willingly with a sense of purpose, or perhaps reluctantly, with dread.

Families pay tribute to soldiers in Afghanistan

November 12, 2010. Newspapers reported on the Remembrance Day service in Kandahar, families of some of the fallen in attendance. Canwest reporter Matthew Fisher quoted Rear-Admiral Andrew Smith: "There were some highs and lows and some heart-rendering sobs, but the families who came here wanted to smell the air and taste the dust." Oh, to have been there to do just that...

Remembrance Day services have never been the same since. The sadness I felt in previous years remains, but now it's personal. Some days, the headlines and photos flash before me. Other days, I glance at current headlines, on the lookout for any that contain "Afghanistan" or "journalist killed" or "Taliban" or "bombings."

I don't read the news the same way anymore, either.

The full story of one of Canada's deadliest days

December 30, 2010. The *Globe and Mail* published a four-page spread on the first anniversary of your demise, Michelle. I can't count the number of times I've referred to it over the years, but I know that your media tent buddy and veteran Canadian Press reporter Colin Perkel pulled out all the stops and used everything in his toolbox to assemble the facts and shape them into a story that ought to have won an award.

Reluctantly, silently, Sergeant Jimmy Collins lifts his sleeve.

There, tattooed on the inside of his wrist along with images of a palm tree and a maple leaf, are the initials of five fellow Canadians—victims of one wrenching instant of violence on a muddy road in Afghanistan one year ago today.

Kandahar

Always remember GC-GM-ZM-KT-ML

Garrett Chidley. George Miok. Zachery McCormack. Kirk Taylor. Michelle Lang.

I read Colin's feature with trepidation, an inconclusive underscoring of suspicions that the blast was a targeted explosion, aimed at the LAV in which you and Bushra travelled. It might have been random, but you were both high-value targets—civilian, professional women. It brings home to me the nature of this war: distant and perverse; the very fact that we are at war obscured from our national conscience, because most of us just can't fathom its existence in a place so foreign and far away. Misery brought on by poverty and greed, power and corruption, fanaticism gone berserk, humankind's seemingly insatiable appetite to control and dominate. And it has been ever thus.

Such was my mindset to sum up the year gone by. Our first-year wrestling with the gaping hole you left behind.

Years later, I read the reports, attentive to bylines of those who got on the job right away, even though they, too, were in shock, pushing back the walls of grief. Bylines by those I would meet, like Colin Perkel and Renata D'Aliesio, Colette Derworiz, Kelly Cryderman. I still look for their bylines. The coverage about you and Afghanistan didn't end with 2010, nor did my interest in following it.

But I'm struck by what they produced under the circumstances. I imagine being among them, writing under a tighter-than-tight deadline, feeling the gamut of emotions we were all feeling, gathering the facts, talking to military spokespeople, soldiers and padres, triple-checking ranks and titles, describing the weather, the setting, the prevailing grave and sombre mood. And those who talked to family and your Michael, scribbling quotes like mad about someone they not only knew but loved, holding back their urge to sob alongside. If you ever needed evidence of the depth of professionalism and dedication of those who write our news, you'll not find a better example. They were your peeps, and they did you proud.

Love, Aunt Catherine

PART II

From prehistory, we have been both communal and narrative creatures, longing for the means to share with each other the great privilege and burden of what it means to know our mortality.

Brandy Schillace[4]

CHAPTER 7

UNDER THE GRAVENSTEIN

I walk onto East Hastings Street in Burnaby to catch a bus home on a sunny day in 1982. As I pass by a storefront window, I turn to look at my reflection wavering back at me. I can't see my face clearly, but I'm definitely talking to the persona I see before me. *Of course, you want to be a journalist.* I'm bursting with optimism at the prospect. Why hadn't I thought of it till now? I knew I wanted to write, but journalism hadn't occurred to me, and then suddenly, there it was before me, clear as a starlit sky on a mountaintop.

At twenty-nine, I had finally hit upon my calling in life. I had just been to a clairvoyant recommended by my Aunt Marg and Aunt Jean. I want to call them my Scottish aunties, though they were born in Canada. Their parents, my mother's parents, were Scottish immigrants, so they were only one generation removed from Scotland. The clairvoyant was also Scottish, an older woman with grey hair, her face weathered. As I recall, the room was dimly lit as she studied me: my wavy brunette head of hair, my unblemished face, my brown eyes. "You'll have three children," she said, with a pause, as if perplexed and a little uncertain about that prediction. "You'll marry a man who works in the same profession as you. You want to be a journalist."

She escorted me outside when it was time to leave and gave me a look that bore into my core. I wasn't sure what to do with that otherworldly stare, but I took her last projection to heart. Once back home in Victoria, I decided to quit my full-time, permanent job as an elementary school secretary and registered in the creative writing program at the University of Victoria. By the summer of 1986, I had an internship as a co-op student for the *Gulf Islands Driftwood*; my "beat" was the outer Gulf Islands—Pender, Galiano, Mayne and Saturna.

In May 1986, I settled into a small cottage high on a rock bluff overlooking Haro Strait. Idyllic, for sure, though I was seldom there and often wrestled with my insecurity around losing my man, Bruce Martin. He was working as a sound engineer at Expo 86 in Vancouver, rode a Honda motorcycle in his denim vest, his masculinity like a magnet whenever I laid my eyes on him. Mindful of waves of visitors and celebrities coming and going to Vancouver's World Fair, I imagined him catching the eye of some chick prettier and hotter than me, stoking a deep-seated fear of loss. I'd had many lovers come and go in my life. I couldn't stomach the notion of losing him, too.

But I didn't have time to dwell on it while working. I was busy from the get-go with weekly travel to Salt Spring Island where the newspaper's office was housed in a small squat building in the heart of Ganges. I joined another co-op student reporter, the editor, a photographer, and a small handful of staff who managed the business end of things. On Mondays and Tuesdays, we manually laid out the pages—now a bygone trademark of newspaper production. I spent hours in the darkroom, too, developing rolls and rolls of black-and-white film. I loved seeing how my pictures turned out, scanning the contact sheets for the best ones to publish.

We were a good crew, and the editor gave me free rein to cover whatever I fancied. I wrote feature articles about artists and writers, beekeepers and pioneering families who settled the land with double-bitted axes and cross-cut saws. I reported on findings unearthed by SFU students at the Pender Canal archaeological dig, a story that mainstream press in Victoria and Vancouver also covered. A significant dig, it was undertaken without the consent of nearby Sencoten nations who had probable links to the summer villages under excavation. Few, including me, seemed to question that at the time.

I was tickled pink to interview author William Deverell on his forested Pender property, recounting how he'd hung out at the corner of Hastings and Columbia Streets in Vancouver to research the city's street life for his 1979 novel *Needles*. A good-looking, confident man, he was likely amused by my attention, this young reporter barely able to contain her enthusiasm and admiration, but he was kind enough to not let on.

I have a fond memory of my interview with local legend Eve Smith, a sweet-tempered woman who had been ahead of her time throughout life, penning countless letters to the editor on disarmament, animal rights, the environment and health issues. By the time I met her, she was elderly and frail, bedridden but mentally spry, propped up by pillows. She wore a lacy white cardigan and smiled sweetly when I lifted my Pentax 150 to snap her photo, all the while talking about the issues she still wrote about in her mind, having lost the physical stamina to put pen to paper.

I'd hop on a ferry to Galiano or Mayne and talk to locals about what was going on, always on the hunt for story, always finding one or two.

Often, it was pure joy—the inter-island travel on beautiful sunny days, meeting characters who either chose or were born into the island life. I met a couple who became my friends and, one day on a hike, we discovered a rare red-tailed snake of interest to the local parks people. Even that became a story.

The Saturna lamb roast on the Campbell family property was perhaps the biggest event of the summer. A fundraiser for Saturna's community hall, it was supported by folks who'd come from neighbouring islands and beyond. That year I made my way there with the local RCMP officers in their aluminum skiff—in a deluge of rain. As the young, blonde, and blue-eyed officer pointed the skiff's bow southeast into Haro Strait, he revved up the motor and declared we weren't far from the "lamb poach." As rain fell relentlessly, about 400 people donned foulies and gathered in circles on tarps laid out on the ground. Kids played at the coconut toss booth and folks sold their crafts and homemade goodies. Musicians sang and played guitars, wooden spoons, and bones under a tent in the beer and wine garden. I watched the patriarch, Jim Campbell, overseeing his helpers slow-roast the lambs Argentinian style, on spits, hissing over the fires and was moved to write about how the community rallied in the downpour that never let up.

When the summer was over, the publisher offered to extend my co-op term for another four months. But I was keen to finish my degree, not to mention get home to Bruce, so I declined. I would miss writing my stories and seeing my byline in the newspaper every week. I'd miss the pride I felt introducing myself as the local reporter, the licence to ask questions of people from various walks of life. But it was only the beginning of my career, or so I thought then. There would be other opportunities, I was sure. My goal: to work as a reporter for the *Vancouver Sun*. I think the other co-op student stayed, married, and had a family. I didn't want to put limits on where I might go. In hindsight, I can't help but wonder about the life I might have had, had I stayed too.

When I returned to Victoria in September that year, I moved back in with Bruce. While his son from a previous marriage joined us, I continued my creative writing classes at UVic, and Bruce started up an appliance repair business, leaving behind his years in broadcasting. A year later and much closer to finally graduating, I spotted an ad about the Penny Wise[5] scholarship for the Langara journalism program in Vancouver. I didn't have to think for long about whether or not to apply. Though I didn't yet have the required bachelor's degree, I was in my early 30s and thought I might have a chance as a so-called "mature" student. It didn't occur to me then that I might not return to finish my degree, but I'd exhausted all the non-fiction courses at UVic and was hungry to try my hand more seriously at journalism.

I won the scholarship. Soon enough, I was packing up to move to Vancouver.

The Langara College campus sits on 49th Avenue near Cambie Street, relatively close to Art and Sandy's house in Kerrisdale. I found a place to live nearby in a house with four other women. The living room looked right across the street at the elementary school where Michelle had played with her friends. By then, at thirteen, she had moved on to the high school up the street, Magee Secondary, but I remembered taking her to the playground during my visits when she was little. Now I was in the 'hood again, about five minutes walking distance from the roughshod back alleys where Michelle played as a child.

Late afternoon on a warm spring day in 1989, I sauntered over to my brother's home. Michelle and a classmate were poring over a school assignment, trying to write and design the front page of a newspaper. It was a rare opportunity to help my niece with schoolwork. Eager to share my passion, as well as elements of the trade I'd been learning over the previous months, I sat on the lawn beside Michelle and her friend, and we began.

My memory of that afternoon: full sun in the backyard, splayed out on the grass. Michelle's nut-brown hair, cut in a chin-length bob, shines. The braces on her teeth are a necessary discomfort to correct a prominent overbite. She is almost all legs and thin as an alder sapling. Her friend Lindsay is a true redhead, with a face full of freckles. Magazines and books lie scattered around us on the grass. The shade from the Gravenstein apple tree by the back deck didn't beckon us. Although absorbed in our task, we are young and hungry for sun and its warmth.

I explain what a lead is, as well as the five principles of reporting: who, what, when, where and sometimes why. Down another layer yet: how proximity, drama, timeliness, and controversy all factor into determining what's newsworthy and what's not. Michelle catches on quickly and is soon taking the pen and writing the lead, bouncing ideas past me for this or that approach. Lindsay is content to let her friend do the work on this occasion, and I'm delighted with how the lesson triggers Michelle's enthusiasm.

I never asked if that afternoon sparked something that led her to journalism, but I know that her unending curiosity and love of language and learning were key to her success as a reporter. Turns out, she also inherited our family's dogged determination, and no doubt it helped that her parents read newspapers and listened to CBC, often debating politics and current events. But first, she had to overcome an almost debilitating shyness.

After graduating from Langara, I moved back to Vancouver Island for my first (and as it turns out, my only) full-time permanent job as a reporter, while Michelle, now in her mid-teens, joined the high school drama class. It was her mother's idea, a way to help her daughter come out of her shy self. Leafing through a photo album now, I spot her with peers huddled together on stage, a pre-performance black-and-white shot, orchestrated to look spontaneous. She seems in her element, an intent look in her eyes, a beautiful cascade of hair draped over her shoulders. Regrettably, I never had the chance to attend any of the plays, nor did she share with me the ups and downs of her brief stage life, for I hardly ever saw Michelle during those years.

I recall stepping off the bus and looking up a super steep hill at the town of Ladysmith on a bright, clear day. A warmth came over me, a sense that I'd arrived where I wanted and needed to be. It's funny in hindsight. The city girl arriving in Ladysmith thinking she had "made" it somehow. Working for the *Ladysmith-Chemainus Chronicle* wasn't my end goal, but a stepping stone to something bigger that I was sure awaited me.

Just like my time at the *Gulf Islands Driftwood*, I loved the job. Of course, I had to endure boring municipal council meetings and monitor local RCMP reports, along with the regional hospital board, which at one point decided to withdraw abortion services. But the most meaningful assignments were those that took me into the heart of the community and its characters—accompanying the Aboriginal police liaison officer on a night shift or profiling students at North Oyster Elementary School, most of whom were from the local Chemainus (Stz'uminus) band, artists, organic farmers, the volunteer fire department on Kuper Island, and renowned selective forester Merv Wilkinson on his 77-acre woodlot. I could often be found speeding along the old highway between Ladysmith and Chemainus in my pale green Toyota station wagon, windows down in summertime to catch the salt air and glimpses of Satellite Channel beyond residential neighbourhoods.

Alas, within a year I was fired. I hadn't learned to zip my lips, especially when feeling wronged. My boss and those above her were primarily focused on the bottom line when what mattered to me was excelling in journalism. I couldn't separate my need to do as good a job as I possibly could with the practical side of putting in the time to move up and on. The final straw for management was when I spent long hours getting stories just right and then had the gall to charge overtime. That's when life and my reporting career went sideways. I was offered a job with a Duncan newspaper, but it was a rag—so many car ads and little worthwhile content. I had hoped to do so much better and decided to try my hand at freelancing in Victoria. But first, the *Chronicle* had given me a story I wanted to turn into a book. And I did.

One of the last stories I wrote for the newspaper featured a former resident, Bill Isoki, and his wife Hana, both Japanese Canadians who, like thousands along BC's coast, were shipped to internment camps in the province's interior after Japan bombed Pearl Harbor in December 1941. Bill and Hana went to Lemon Creek, one of a handful of camps in the Slocan Valley. When World War II ended three years later, Canada shut the camps, offering internees two choices: move east of the Rockies or move "back" to war-ravaged Japan. By the time restrictions forbidding them from returning to the West Coast were lifted in 1949, most residents, including Bill and Hana Isoki, had eventually begun anew in Toronto. That's where the Chemainus murals society reached them in 1990, with an invitation to come and help organize a reunion for the summer of 1991.

After interviewing the Isokis during their visit, I watched Bill and Hana stroll together through the towering cedars of Waterwheel Park to Old Town, their first time in almost 50 years. The redemptive elements of the story tugged at my heart as they sauntered off. I was struck by the absence of any hint that a once-thriving community had existed in Old Town. The idea to welcome back those kicked out so unceremoniously during wartime included plans to commemorate the contributions of Japanese Canadians with two murals.

Determined that this story was worth more than a few articles in a community newspaper, I set about contacting former residents. My goal was to create a picture of the former community and the characters who inhabited it. Those I interviewed were eager to share their stories, to shed some of the grief and shame that accompanied them on their journey, to demonstrate how they picked up the pieces and did whatever they could to make sure their children were educated, good citizens. It was gratifying to have their trust and gratitude, and through them, I learned how gracious people can be in the face of injustice.

Seven years later, *O-Bon in Chimunesu: A Community Remembered* won the Hubert Evans Non-Fiction Prize at the BC and Yukon Book Prizes. But freelancing was a bust for the most part. I didn't have enough hustle in me to make a go of it financially, though I did write and get published. Some articles came about because of the subject matter of my book. By the time it was published in 1996, Bruce and I had a two-year-old son. As with the arrival of any child, life takes on new meaning and new challenges. I'd been working as an editor of provincial legislative debates during legislative sessions, which allowed me the freedom to write my book during off months. But it wasn't sustainable. When Sam was five months old, Bruce had bypass surgery for the second time in his life. He had already shut his appliance repair business down because he was barely breaking even, so a good deal of the financial responsibility fell to me. It doesn't take much to trigger memories of stress during Sam's early years, though of course moments of joy came along with a sense of completion. This time I wasn't experiencing motherhood from afar, as I had with Ellen. While my journalism career became a casualty of sorts, the skills I'd acquired eventually opened a door at the provincial ministry for Indigenous affairs.

While I was writing news releases and issues notes for government, Michelle had her first reporting job at the *Prince George Citizen*. When our paths crossed occasionally at her parents' home in Vancouver, she'd tell me about her assignments and I'd ask if she covered anything related to the treaty negotiations with the Lheidli T'enneh First Nation in Prince George. But for Michelle, it was just one of many stories, and while interested, she wasn't consumed by the subject matter that so captivated me at the time.

I'd always been interested in social justice matters, especially anything involving Canada's treatment of Indigenous people. My job offered opportunities to learn about our legal and constitutional frameworks as they relate to the original inhabitants of this land, as well as associated public policy issues. I had the privilege of attending negotiation sessions in remote communities, where I met many people immersed in a culture that challenged my place and privilege in life. The work was challenging, dynamic and sometimes rewarding—more politically driven by parties on all sides than I could have imagined. When it came to building relationships with those across the table from us—Indigenous representatives as well as our federal counterparts—I thrived. But I often felt on the wrong side of the table, not at all confident in the task of actual negotiation.

Over fourteen-plus years I worked in the ministry, I bounced from the treaty negotiations branch to communications and back again. It's where I was working the late December day when Bruce phoned, urging me to drop whatever I was doing and leave the office. My father, barely able to speak, had phoned him with the news of Michelle's death, and Bruce drove straight to my workplace to tell me in person.

It was another turning point. I still needed an income, but I began to consider the possibility of semi-retirement in order to pick up my pen, pick up my passion again. And there was little I felt more passionate about than the senseless, devastating loss of Michelle, my niece who had gone where I had not in journalism, Michelle who was on an upward trajectory, Michelle who brought light and laughter into our lives. Suddenly, I wanted to know about Canada's mission in Afghanistan as well. I hadn't paid much attention until the Taliban assassinated her. I knew a little and was as concerned about the plight of Afghan people as I was about the countless instances of humanitarian misery the globe over. Now I zeroed in on Afghanistan as never before. Canada's mission and the war became personal in a flash.

The irony of Michelle's death coming while on the job she loved, the job I also loved but didn't pursue, hit home hard. And much like Michelle, my instinct for story rose to the surface even in the midst of shock and grief. I would honour her, pay tribute to her legacy, make sure she wasn't forgotten. I was on a mission again, with writing at its core.

CHAPTER 8

MAGENTA PASHMINA

Michael Louie is behind the wheel of his sleek, black VW sedan, cruising southwest of Calgary to the Millarville Market in mid-July 2010. I watch the rolling hills of ranch country through my back seat window, my sixteen-year-old son, Sam, beside me, and my husband, Bruce, in the passenger seat up front. It's Big Sky country where cattle and horses graze in vast, open pastures. Cloudy when the four of us set out from Calgary, we stroll through the outdoor market along one length of a flat expanse of dry field. Bruce and I are celebrating our seventeenth wedding anniversary, and I'm delighted when the sun punches through, suddenly penetrating our bones with sweet, dry heat. Dressed in blue jeans and a smart T-shirt over his slim frame, Michael is relaxed and grinning as he points out his favourite vendors. He chats to the woman selling a range of preserves and sauces, claiming she makes the best butter chicken sauce ever. Like me, he enjoys his food spicy hot, though he's also a big fan of good burgers and just about anything deep-fried, including bacon of all things.

Michael is different from the man we saw a few short months before, in April. That was when Michelle's brother Cameron married his sweetheart, Sandra Benavides, in her hometown of Monterrey, Mexico. The wedding was our first opportunity to come together as a family for a happy occasion, less than four months after Michelle was killed. Immediate family, including my ninety-four-year-old father, flew out of Vancouver on a rainy day for the biggest Mexican-style party of our lives. For Art and Sandy, it was a time to rejoice and at least temporarily set aside the still-raw memory of their only daughter in order to celebrate their son's marriage to a vibrant, sophisticated young woman—an anesthesiologist in great demand at the Monterrey hospital. But for Michael, the celebration was more bitter than sweet. He stood on the periphery, as if looking from afar on so much celebration and joy. Bruce caught up to him during a bad moment, told him that he was family and escorted him gently into our fold. But it must have been tempting to walk away: his wedding date with Michelle yanked from his grasp for all time.

But here in July, Michael is on home turf, relaxed and eager to show us around. Whatever grief he's carrying is sequestered in a private space.

We left home earlier in the week, Sam and his acoustic guitar surrounded by a pile of stuff crammed into the back seat while we sped through the Fraser Valley, along the Coquihalla Highway into the Okanagan, and finally into Revelstoke on the BC side of the Rockies for the night. Sam is mostly good-natured about this road trip across the province with his parents, strumming folk songs on his guitar in between long stretches of punching buttons on his scuffed-up, metallic-blue Gameboy. He looks out the window as we head into Rogers Pass, the spiky mountain peaks on either side of the highway catching his eye for the very first time. I can't help but wonder how he remembers that first encounter with the world-renowned mountain range which separates BC from Alberta and the rest of Canada. Did it plant an early seed for the cross-country bike trip he would do through Rogers Pass all the way to Prince Edward Island five or six years later? Perhaps.

Our second day on the road, we drive east through the foothills and over the plains to Calgary. We're staying with Michael's close friends, Phoebe and Rob Fung, in a modern suburb, southwest of the city's core. Tiny, bouncy Phoebe greets us at the door with her broad smile and welcomes us inside their spacious home. It's the fourth time I've met her in seven months; every other time she was at Michael's side. At the repatriation ceremony in Trenton, at the Vancouver memorial in January and at Cameron's wedding in April. I wonder if their friendship goes back to childhood, long before she made her professional debut as proprietor of Vin Room, a brand-new upscale wine bar, on a bustling Calgary street. Her husband, Rob, is working from home for British Petroleum Oil. A soft-spoken, gentle man, he's preoccupied with the aftermath of a catastrophic oil spill in the Gulf of Mexico. We pop our heads into his study to say hello and he apologizes for not coming to greet us. The timing of our stay could clearly have been better for him, but he finds time later to join us for a movie in their downstairs den, decked out with a huge, panoramic television screen and high-end sound system.

Over the next few days, Michael will set aside whatever tasks he's managing in emergency planning with the Red Cross and show us around "Cowtown." It's Calgary Stampede time, so locals and tourists in cowboy hats and boots will be raising a bit of hell. Even though stampedes are not really our thing, we think Sam ought to be able to see what all the fuss is about for himself. Still, it's not the reason for our trip to the city.

The full-page memorial ad published in Canwest newspapers across Canada on January 9, 2010. Photo courtesy Postmedia

This summer road trip is my idea, prompted primarily because the reporter in me yearns to visit the *Calgary Herald* newsroom where Michelle spent so many waking hours. Having never been to Calgary, I suppose I also needed to experience the city she had come to make home—for in my mind, she was always at home in Vancouver.

The next day, with the help of our GPS, we find our way along a maze of highways and overpasses to the Calgary Herald, a modern, red-brick building the size of a football field, in the southeast part of town. Bruce and I hold hands as we approach the main entrance, Sam sauntering along close beside us. All three of us come to a full stop, staring at the full-page *In Memoriam* that we first saw featured in the newspaper after Michelle was killed. I guess it's been posted to the entrance ever since. REMEMBERING MICHELLE LANG, *January 31, 1975–December 30, 2009: a great friend, colleague and award-winning journalist,* Michelle's face surrounded in black, the four soldiers in smaller photos across the bottom. I suppress a gasp as I push past the glass door where reporter Colette Derworiz greets us in the open concept foyer before leading us up a spiralling staircase adorned with large, framed photos of the Calgary Stampede taken by *Herald* photographers over the years.

The entire second floor is a mass of desks, computers, filing cabinets, drafting tables, much like the newsroom scene in *All the President's Men*. As Colette escorts Bruce, Sam and I into the room, we are greeted by editor-in-chief Lorne Motley, and reporters Renata D'Aliesio, Kelly Cryderman and Gwendolyn Richards. I hold my breath in an attempt to halt my rising emotions as they lead us to Michelle's desk, now tidy from its former chaos. Thankfully, it's not without some clutter, her awards and photos propped to the right of the computer monitor and tools of the trade stacked up on its left—steno pads and piles of newspapers. Her chair is enveloped in a rich magenta pashmina, tied around the chair's back, where she sat pounding out her stories. A pashmina to commemorate, perhaps to lighten absence with radiant colour.

I stand over her desk thinking of my time in community newspaper newsrooms, which were nothing so grand as this, when a thunderstorm erupts. We hasten to the wall of windows overlooking Calgary's skyline. Rain, hail, pelting and lashing against the windows, the sky varying depths of stormy slate grey, a split-second fork of lightning creases the sky in a distant vertical jag, a striking, silver filament of light. A boom of thunder crashes, then only the sound of the slashing rain and wind. My heart is near my throat. I want to keep it together, want to express so much—grief, gratitude, our collective, palpable sorrow. Kelly Cryderman—a tall, good-looking blonde and one of Michelle's close colleagues—says what we're all thinking. "It must be Michelle, vying for our attention." We smile at the thought of Michelle poking us alive, the graceful sweep of the pashmina, tied in that gentle knot, vivid in my mind.

Back at her desk, we listen to editor Chris Farcoe tell us the "shoe" story, one of many illustrating Michelle's zany enthusiasm for diving into action. In the spring of 2005, she approached the town of High River to report on the river's flooding banks.

"The gum boots she brought never made it out of the trunk," Chris recalls, smiling. "Alarmed at the pace of the flood, she decided there wasn't time to grab her boots and went into the flooding waters wearing heels that probably set her back a few hundred bucks. It was me she came to afterwards, hoping the *Herald* would reimburse her. I reminded her about the gum boots she'd left in the trunk, and she shot me a mournful glance before shuffling back to her desk."

We all laugh as I imagine Michelle running into rising water, her nude-coloured designer heels sinking into the riverbed, a pen braced between her teeth like a lover's rose while she gripped her note pad as if it were a lifeline. I would probably have done the same and think of weather-related stories I once covered. None of them involved flooding rivers, but I'd tried to shelter my steno pad during torrential rains often enough.

Colette interrupts my reverie and escorts Bruce, Sam and me to a space by the newsroom entrance. She tells us about the plans staff have for transforming the area into one of quiet contemplation, dedicated to Michelle. She's heading up a committee that includes graphic designers and reporters to choose colour schemes and which of Michelle's front-page stories will line the wall above an L-shaped couch. Colette introduces us to the graphic designer who pulls out coloured renditions of the space, including a standing light sculpture inscribed with Michelle's name.

"It's already taking shape in our collective imagination as a place to reflect and relax, to welcome the creative and think about meaning in life and Michelle," Colette says, her crystal blue eyes penetrating mine.

"Oh, it's going to be so lovely," I say to Colette, gazing at the image of the light sculpture. "I definitely have to come back when it's complete."

"You'll be welcome any time, Catherine. Let me show you the tree and bench outside that we're also working on to commemorate Michelle," Colette says, leading us back to the spiral staircase down to the foyer and out the main door.

During a brief ceremony at the Calgary Herald in November 2011, Art Lang shakes hands with Chief of Defence Staff Walt Natynczyk by the military plaque made at Kandahar Airfield. Photo courtesy Postmedia

She leads us along a path a short distance away to a spindly seedling they have planted near a bench with a plaque. The seedling is a Russian Mountain Ash, which they chose because of its strength. At its base, Colette planted some pretty pink and purple petunias.

"I check on the flowers every morning before heading into work, but the bunnies are a problem," she says, winking. "They've been nibbling away at the flowers, and it's hard to keep them at bay. I guess I'll have to put a little fence around them."

It's time to go, so we bid our farewells and head out. I'm still holding onto the image of the magenta pashmina wrapped so lovingly around Michelle's chair when I go for a walk later in the afternoon. The sky to the east is a now familiar stormy grey slate. But to the west, the sun is blasting through to a valley floor, casting its reflection on houses perched on a ridge, their facades illuminated against the black sky. Then finding my way to a path, I feel a cold wind threatening to bring the rain down again. Suddenly, I'm at a standstill in front of voluptuous peonies the same rich colour of the pashmina. I whisper: *I'll bring a peony bush like this for the Herald garden, flowers befitting Michelle Justine, my Laurence Durrell niece.*

On our last night in Calgary, Michael takes us to 4th Street, SW, and we enter Phoebe's wine bar in a happy-go-lucky mood. After greeting us at the door of Vin Room, Phoebe quickly bustles off to attend to customers, the consummate businesswoman. Just as *Herald* reporters Colette and Kelly arrive, Michael suggests we dine on the rooftop patio. I nod, always eager to sit in sunshine, which I can see at the top of a flight of stairs. But the next instant clouds burst open and a thrashing hail storm descends. Everyone laughs. "Welcome to Calgary," Colette says with a giggle.

We grab an indoor table in this gleaming establishment, and soon we're sipping very fine wine and nibbling sticky soy sesame steak and mushroom bites when the sun bursts through the windows again. "Welcome to Calgary," Colette hollers again. I'm quickly learning that the city Michelle came to call home can turn from summer to winter and back again in short order. It's nothing like Vancouver, save perhaps for the adrenalin so characteristic of Canada's big cities strung across the country above the forty-ninth parallel. Now settled in, we begin to reminisce about Michelle.

Almost a week later, we left Calgary via Pincher Creek to the southwest. Bitter cold wind blew us toward a line of towering windmills in the distance and then west through Crowsnest Pass into the East and West Kootenays. When we arrive at our B & B in Nelson, BC, it's still daylight and peaceful and quiet high above Kootenay Lake. On this side of the Rockies, it's summer again. A breeze is rustling the birch stands behind and above me, rooted into a steep hillside. Grapevine leaves over an arbour are backlit by the sun and a hot, gentle breeze caresses my face.

Our B & B overlooks this town where I once lived, having followed one of my early loves here in the mid-1970s. But I don't linger on those long-ago memories now. We're hungry and ready to kick back, so we unpack our leftovers of Chateaubriand, rice and corn. It's almost as delicious as it was last night, our final dinner at Phoebe and Rob's.

We'll be home tomorrow, and I contemplate whether I accomplished what I set out for. Was it just to stand in the newsroom where Michelle had found her stride, covering stories worthy of a National Newspaper Award? Of course, it was more, even though I hadn't realized that I also needed to experience this wealthy, vibrant city, to feel the city's pulse as she once had, surrounded by her love and dynamic friends.

Turning to Bruce and Sam, I raise my glass of wine. "To Michelle," I offer, smiling in the heat on this hillside, high above a sparkling blue Kootenay Lake.

CHAPTER 9

SNOW ANGELS

On Friday, November 9, 2012, I sit and wait at the Victoria airport for my flight to Calgary. Michael is set to pick me up on arrival, so I text updates to him as the hours tick by. Midway through the evening, Air Canada announces it's cancelling the flight due to blizzard conditions at the Calgary airport. I slouch further into the grey upholstered chair, luggage piled at my feet and try to focus on my breathing, a half-hearted effort to keep anxiety at bay. Too tired to read, I watch the usual airport gig unfold around me: families juggling babies and kids as announcements come and go; solo guys in chairs, thighs pumping to release pent-up energy; older couples leaning on each other; pretty much all of us on our devices, scrolling through screens. If WestJet cancels too, I won't be joining Michelle's friends at the Calgary Soldiers' Memorial on Remembrance Day. It's the reason for my trip, so if I can't get there today, I may not go at all. And I want so badly to be with Colette and two other colleagues, Leah Hennel and Gwendolyn Richards, to hear how life goes on at the *Calgary Herald*, to remember Michelle together on Remembrance Day.

It's about 1:30 a.m. when the aircraft finally takes off, and Michael and I have agreed that I'll make my own way to Phoebe and Rob's. I doze as best I can during the flight, knowing I'm not going to get much sleep whatever happens now. A mercifully short flight, I'm soon looking through the window at utter blackness as we begin our descent over Calgary's main runway. Snow swirls wildly in every direction, but we land safely and shuffle off the plane onto the freezing tarmac like penguins huddled together for warmth. In a stupor, I find my way to the WestJet checkout where we've been instructed to go. WestJet will find complimentary hotel rooms for those who've missed connecting flights. They're in the same long, stringy line in the dimly lit airport as me, waiting my turn to get a taxi chit into town at no charge. We inch toward the sleep-deprived folks staffing the counter. Even at this hour, I'm driven to get the taxi chit, my Scots blood boiling because I have to wait in the same line as those who need more complicated arrangements. A sensible person would have said to hell with it and hailed a cab on their own.

It's about 4:30 a.m. when I finally arrive at Phoebe and Rob's. Snow is lighter but steady, steady, steady. I pile my suitcase and backpack on top of the snow and fumble over and over again with the key lock. I have the number code on my phone, but it isn't working. Damn! In desperation, I ring the doorbell.

Rob opens the door gingerly in the dark. He's gracious about this very early morning interruption and helps me inside with my gear. Tip-toeing back to bed, he whispers: "We left the door unlocked for you."

The next morning the sky is a solid grey. I'm tired but excited too. Colette will be by to pick me up soon, so I shower, dress and head into the modern, spacious kitchen for breakfast. I'm alone in this lovely home, my only company a Pomeranian called "Dom"—short for Dom Pérignon. I bend to pet his fluffy bronze fur when the doorbell rings. Then I'm out the door into the winter wonderland of this Calgary suburb, climbing into Colette's sedan, bundled up in all the winter gear I could muster at home—long johns, a wool turtleneck, mittens, scarf and white down knee-length coat with a fake fur-trimmed hood that I bought for the occasion. Turns out I'm not as cold as I thought I'd be. Perhaps a teeny bit of my early childhood Prairie blood insulates me, though more likely it's because it's not as cold as it could be.

Colette points out various landmarks as we drive downtown. Despite the summer road trip here two years ago, I still don't know this city, so it's hard to retain what she's telling me. I've no way yet to anchor east from west, north from south, and Calgary seems to spread every which way, with overpasses and looping highways around and within its sprawl. When we reach the downtown area, the Bow River comes into view as we turn onto Memorial Drive.

"Over there is the Field of Crosses," Colette says, pointing to an embankment dotted with thousands of white wooden crosses and red poppies. "The ceremony is at dawn, so it's over now. Every year between November 1 and November 11, people place 3,500 white crosses here. Some refer to it as a temporary art installation. Gwendolyn and I went two years ago, the first Remembrance Day following Michelle's death."

My heart sinks when she says today's ceremony is over, and suddenly I wish I could have been there with them in 2010. I cast my thoughts back to the Remembrance Day service I attended on the legislative grounds in Victoria that first year, one of hundreds gathered around the cenotaph, my heart a bit raw as I stared at rows of elderly veterans whose memories of warfare, though distant, were still profound. I searched the crowd for younger veterans, hoping for a connection that wasn't there.

At the same time in Calgary, in front of TV camera crews, Colette and Gwendolyn spoke about the personal cost of war, losing their colleague Michelle and how it was in her honour that they came to witness the dawn ceremony. I watched their breath billowing into the freezing air on the TV screen, a crystal-clear morning if ever there was one. At least that's how I remember it, the cameras zooming in on their red cheeks, their voices strong as they spoke of their friend and colleague, almost a year from when they last caught a glimpse of her—rushing to her desk with a Mason jar of water, relentlessly phoning sources to confirm one last factoid or intent at her computer monitor, surrounded by clutter as she finessed her main story of the day.

Today we carry on past the Field of Crosses, farther along Memorial Drive. Once a central feature in an Indigenous trail network, the road is built along the dirt route where Calgarians came to remember their war dead five years after the First World War. In 1922, Calgary's mayor planted the first poplars on an embankment above a treeless Bow River, and by 1928, crews had planted 3,278 trees to commemorate the fallen. I can't imagine how it must have been before then. Where did the families of those who didn't come home commemorate their dead in the early post-war years? And once the trees were planted, did they choose a specific one to represent the person they had lost so they could speak their names out loud?

Canada's current practice of repatriating the bodies of its war dead didn't begin until 1970, a fact that takes me aback. When I attended the repatriation ceremony of Michelle's remains in Trenton, it felt like a century's old military tradition to me, steeped in the timeless symbolism that accompanies solemn ceremony. But it's actually more contemporary: a century ago, such efforts would have been pointless, not just because of transportation logistics but also because tens of thousands of soldiers were killed across swaths of bloody battlefields. The Great War, indeed.

It's about minus five degrees Celsius when Colette and I walk from her car along the snow-covered path to the Calgary Soldiers' Memorial where we meet Leah and Gwendolyn on the wooden platform. We hug and they lead me straight to the towering white marble slab inscribed with Michelle's name. At the bottom of the last column of six pillars, set equidistance apart along the broad platform, I read: *M. Lang, journalist.* I trace my fingers over her name and look for the names of those who died with her. They are all here, too: Garrett Chidley, Zachery McCormack, George Miok, Kirk Taylor. At 34, Michelle was the oldest among them.

Pte. Garrett Chidley, 21, of Langley, BC, and Cambridge, Ontario.

Pte. Zachery McCormack, 21, of Edmonton, Alberta.

Sgt. Kirk Taylor, 28, of Yarmouth, NS.

Sgt. George Miok, 28, of Edmonton, Alberta.

I wander around each smooth marble column, inspecting names from Calgary's army reserve regiments who fought and died in World War I, World War II, and Afghanistan. Of the 3,000-plus names on the six columns, those from Afghanistan are from across Canada, unlike those from the First and Second World Wars who were from the Calgary area. Afghanistan's fallen came home in flag-draped caskets in recent memory. Some, only months before the memorial was unveiled in April 2011, the ninety-fourth anniversary of the First World War battle of Vimy Ridge. When I read the inscription on an outside facing column, I pause. It's a simple, powerful line from John McRae's poem *In Flanders Fields*:

WE LIVED
FELT DAWN
SAW SUNSET GLOW

Leah, Gwendolyn, and Colette are standing by the bench behind the marble pillars, respecting my privacy as I shed quiet tears for my niece and the multitude of casualties commemorated here.

When we are done talking, done with sadness, we plod through knee-deep snow to the embankment below. It's been ages since I made a snow angel, but I don't hesitate for a second, falling backward without fear alongside her friends into the white, fluffy drift, arms and legs splayed out, swishing them back and forth, back and forth. Below the memorial, we giggle and squirm, calling out to Michelle while we shape snow angels in her memory. I imagine her happy, smiling as our laughter echoes over the mighty Bow River.

I tell Michael about the snow angels when I'm back at Rob and Phoebe's for dinner. I tiptoe around what to say to him, censoring myself a lot. I don't want to cause him grief, and I understand he doesn't want to dwell on Michelle's death. All I really know is that he's doing the best he can to move on with life. Yet a part of me aches. If only he had come with us. He could have made a snow angel beside ours, drawing energy from the blanket of crusty snow beneath us. So many if only's....

CHAPTER 10

CLOISONNÉ URNS

To inurn: a verb meaning to place or bury (something, especially ashes after cremation) in an urn.

Against the hazy blue backdrop of the North Shore mountains in Coast Salish territory, we sprinkle Mom's and Michelle's ashes at Mountain View Cemetery. We gather as families do on such occasions—a semi-circle of sombre, sad hearts and faces around the brand-new headstone. The bond between us palpable, we shift our weight under the hot Vancouver sky while my brother Art reads a poem that his wife came upon while sorting through Michelle's belongings—a poem Michelle had handwritten onto a piece of blue stationery during her high school years. *Remember*, by Christina Georgina Rossetti. A poem to a loved one, a lyrical plea to cast aside lament following death.

> *Remember me when I am gone away,*
> *Gone far away into the silent land;*
> *When you can no more hold me by the hand,*
> *Nor I half turn to go yet turning stay.*
> *Remember me when no more day by day*
> *You tell me of our future that you plann'd:*
> *Only remember me; you understand*
> *It will be late to counsel then or pray.*
> *Yet if you should forget me for a while*
> *And afterwards remember, do not grieve:*
> *For if the darkness and corruption leave*
> *A vestige of the thoughts that once I had,*
> *Better by far you should forget and smile*
> *Than that you should remember and be sad.*

It is August 23, 2013, and Sandy wonders aloud if Michelle had a premonition of untimely death. The thought must have hit her like a hammer when she discovered the poem. I picture her sitting on the edge of

Michelle's bed, the blue stationery slipping from her hand onto the floor. But why Michelle chose to write it in longhand will always be a mystery. Maybe it *was* a premonition or maybe a school assignment? Maybe there was something about its turning of phrase that spoke to her? Perhaps she simply regarded it as a thing of beauty and wanted to preserve it for herself. We'll never know.

Art falters now and then as he reads the poem, his voice cracking. Still close to the surface after three-and-a-half years for everyone gathered: her fiancé, Michael; brother, Cameron; her Aunt Margie, Uncle Al; grandfather, Art Sr.; and Bruce and me. Those who grew up with her as well: cousins Dan and Stephen, Ellen, too. Sam, the youngest cousin, and then the children who never met her, the sons and daughters of the generation who came after: her niece, Marissa, and cousin Dan's children, Olivia, William. Dan's wife, Vera, had been pregnant with Olivia when Michelle was killed.

Cameron stands to the side, shaking his head at the irreconcilable, still fraught with disbelief. His wife, Sandra, dressed in a snazzy black-and-white dress, looks lost in thought at his side. She's also beside Michael, considered a brother-in-law even though he and Michelle never married. In his designer jeans, classy shades and dark blazer, Mike is focused, calm, though we can't see into his eyes. I hope it's a comfort for him to be in the company of his vivacious sister-in-law. He's stronger than when I saw him in Toronto mere days after Michelle's death. Stronger, but I think his loss will always be tangible to those who know him well.

Art chokes out the last stanza of the poem and kneels in his dark dress pants, with one leg stretched backwards and one arm deep in the hole. He braces his shoulder against the ground as he stabilizes the empty rust-brown cloisonné urn in its place. It shimmers in the sun. Its shape so womanly, so elegant.

No one speaks.

One by one, every family member approaches two square depressions at the foot of the black marble headstone. Silently, each of us in turn scoops ashes from an emerald-green, wooden box. Clutching the sand-coloured ashes in our palms, we let the grains fall into and around the urns, first Michelle's, then Mom's.

When my mother, Catherine Smith Gray, was born in February 1912, Canada was a relatively young colonial country. In her later years, I often reflected on the fact that she was my living link to a way of life and world events long passed. She was the second oldest of five children born to her Scottish immigrant parents, Alexander and Catherine Gray, in what was then a rural community far on the outskirts of Winnipeg's city core. My mother didn't talk about what led her parents to Canada, but she occasionally talked about a shelter they lived in while her father built their tiny bungalow. Evidently, they had to take cover one day while a cyclone whipped across the land, mercifully missing their wee plot of land—a memory that remained vivid for her over many decades.

Her older brother, Jack, died of a massive heart attack when my mother was still a relatively young woman. As a child, I didn't appreciate how deeply it must have hurt her to lose him, the brother who perhaps was her protector, buffering some of life's harshness. Her father was next, dying shortly after I was born in 1953 when my mother was forty-one. I was eight or nine when her mother, my Nanny Gray, died. I have a vague memory of Mom walking into my bedroom after my grandmother's funeral, red-eyed and tired. I sensed her sadness, but for the most part, she kept her grief private. I have memories of playing canasta and drinking pot after pot of Red Rose tea with my Nanny Gray. She's in many of our early black-and-white Brownie-box photos, holding me in her arms as a baby, holding my sister's hands, little circles of her white hair held in place with bobby pins—nothing bouffant for my Scottish grandmother. Now I regret how little I knew about her, other than that she delighted in cheating me at canasta, had a beautiful singing voice and was very pretty as a young woman.

People called my mother Kay, short for Catherine. She grew up with few of the expectations I had as a young woman. As the oldest daughter, she left school in grade eight and worked as a sales clerk for the Hudson's Bay Company near the corner of Portage and Main where the winter wind cut sharply into her face as she stepped off the street car, day after day, year after year. Until, that is, she married my father and began her life as a wife and mother. It was 1942, and soon after their wedding and so-called honeymoon, my father went into training, deploying a few short months later to Europe with the Royal Canadian Engineers. When the Second World War ended and he returned, my brother was a toddler. My sister followed in 1948 and I in 1953, by which time we were a typical nuclear family, living first in Edmonton, Alberta, and then in Prince Albert, Saskatchewan. Those may have been my mother's happiest adult years. Her husband had a good job with the Canadian National Railway. In Prince Albert, they owned their modest house, and Mom was busy living the domestic life expected of her. But life got rocky when my ambitious father quit his job because he saw no chance for advancement. We moved to Winnipeg, then Vancouver, where Mom took on boarders and looked after other people's children to help make ends meet. Though cliché, family really was everything to her. Whenever she had a chance to get away, which wasn't often, she'd travel to be with her sisters in Winnipeg, and when my brother, sister and I grew up and became independent, she lived for and doted on the generation that followed, beginning with her first grandchild, Michelle.

The summer after my mother died in 2008, three days shy of her ninety-sixth birthday, my sister took some of her ashes and scattered them at Winnipeg Beach near Mom's sisters, our Aunt Marg and Aunt Jean. The three of them had once had the times of their lives riding the Moonlight Special from Winnipeg to the dance pavilion where they danced the foxtrot and waltz with many suitors before boarding the train home at midnight. Winnipeg Beach was also where Mom took Margie and me for summer vacations with her sisters and their kids. By scattering some of Mom's ashes there, Margie wanted to cast Mom back to those more carefree times.

Dad kept her remaining ashes in the container the funeral home gave him, not wanting to let go just yet or maybe not knowing how, when or where to put them. They had had a fractious marriage and he had plenty of regrets. I know he loved her, though I'm not sure she loved as much in return, for as she showered her children and grandchildren with affection, she blamed him for the headstrong, reckless ways in which he derailed the security she craved.

And so it was that we interred Mom's ashes beside Michelle's, five and three years, respectively, after their deaths. Art and Sandy ordered the headstone and began making the other necessary arrangements for the memorial service well in advance—the final one for Michelle a private family matter.

Sam and I escort my father, each of us on either side of him, as he stumbles forward on the uneven ground: gaunt, his frail ninety-eight-year-old body decrepit but determined as ever. He can't lean over to reach the box on the ground, so my nephew's wife approaches, her bare feet padding the grass while Sam and I keep Dad stable. She lifts the emerald-painted box up to him with both hands, and I watch as my father reaches in with long, thin fingers, almost translucent, the strength of their grip almost entirely gone. Grasping no more than a teaspoon, he is grim-faced as he lets them fall from the tips of his fingers into the ground: ashes of his first grandchild and then those of his wife of sixty-six years. The space between his shoulder blades concave and narrow, like an eagle's hunched wings at the moment of landing.

Sam is next, Dad's youngest grandchild at nineteen, not quite a man but no longer a boy. He is stone-faced, too, perhaps more stricken by the grief of his relatives than by the loss of Michelle. He had not known her well, born as he was in another city when Michelle was nineteen herself, on the cusp of venturing into the big wide world beyond Vancouver.

Now it's my turn. I roll as much ash as I can hold into my palm, wrap my fingers around it to make a fist. It's neither coarse nor fine, but I can feel texture and substance—tiny bits of bone burned into grit. My mind goes blank when it cascades from my grip. I make my fist into a funnel to slow the letting go, positioning it directly over the urn so that it spills over and onto the sides and then float my hand in a circle to fill in a wee bit of empty space around the vessel. And the same again, over Mom's beautiful light jade-coloured cloisonné urn, feeling an urge to ask her forgiveness for my hurtful ways in growing-up years.

Margie's son, my nephew Stephen, is the last to approach the hole in the ground. Over six feet tall and strong, he's shy and rarely express-es himself. But on this occasion, when none of us could find words, he somehow does.

"How I loved you, Michelle," he begins. "I'll never forget you. I think of you every day and carry your memory inside. None of us will ever, ever forget you no matter how much time passes."

And kneeling above his grandmother's urn, he says: "Nanny, you were the sweetest person any of us will ever know."

It feels like a birthing. The simple truth laid bare by the one person in the family everyone—save his mother, my sister—seems to know the least. The depth of his feeling exposed to the sun, saying farewell for us all. He places a smaller second bouquet—pink and magenta gerberas—next to the huge spray of lilies, roses, baby's breath.

Over the course of the morning, the branches of our family mingled at the grave in groupings that moved about. Conversation would come later—an intuitive stillness that even the youngest seemed to embrace. Michelle's brother Cameron holding his baby, Marissa Michelle. Golden light in her hair. A puzzlement in her wide blue eyes, a slight frown creas-ing her brow. Her skin smooth like peony petals over cherub cheeks, staring intently, safe in her daddy's arms. Time standing still in the heat. We did not weep openly. Not there and then. Yes, tears streamed down our cheeks. We held hands, my husband and I. Sam beside his sister Ellen. My family—strong and soft—a clutch, together in grief. Slowly, we begin to move away, leaving the urns open to the sky. Cemetery staff will come to cover them with dirt and grass sod after we've gone. Beauty, once gleaming, will soon be buried from view.

I long to linger, glancing backwards as Bruce and I move toward our car. The black marble headstone, the wild splash of flowers reflected in the inscription *Forever Loved*. I cast my eyes around at headstones worn by time, pocked by weather, their lustre long gone, while the one for Michelle and Mom glistens in the heat, dark and vibrant. The residue of sandy ash on my palm. A primeval element between us the living, and them, the dead.

Back at Sandy and Art's afterwards, I found myself in the den alone for a moment, my eyes falling on dappled light caressing fuchsia tendrils in a hanging basket outside. And I thought of my mother again and how she died almost two years before her first grandchild was killed. I remembered the odd sense of relief that rushed over me because Mom was already gone. She had suffered enough loss, as anyone who lives to such an age inevitably does, but I don't know if she could have survived Michelle's death or the way in which it happened. With the inurnment of her and Michelle's ashes, I felt her wrapping a shawl around us, ever so slowly mending our family together.

Chapter II

MEETING MELLISSA

It's an unseasonably warm day in late April 2014, warm enough to wait outside the Bean Around the World coffee bar in Kitsilano. My brother is sitting across from me at the wobbly patio table in this trendy Vancouver neighbourhood. My nostrils twitch at the tumbled smells of the city—a mix of gasoline fumes and salt air. Cars stream by. I listen to the low rumble of engines and gaze at the blur flashing past, an incessant whirr of tires spinning on dry pavement. Speeding motorists, cyclists careening across lanes, everyone in a hurry. If I had my camera, I could try that technique I learned in journalism school long ago, panning while taking a shot of fast-moving objects—a technique I didn't practise often enough to get good at. I was more interested in photographing people, capturing a characteristic expression in time.

Art and I sit near a bursting canopy of oak trees along the side street. Dust motes swirl in tree-dappled sunlight as I glance down the street. Mellissa Fung is nowhere to be seen. Because I organized this meeting, I'm nervous, not quite sure if it's a good idea after all. I glance at our wavy reflections in the window. Art is wearing a striped polo-shirt, more casual than I expect of my accountant brother, with his thick-lens eyeglasses and short grey hair. But then, he is retired, with nothing in particular to prove. Life over the last few years has been more about getting through the days, helping Sandy get through them, too.

The smell of roasted coffee wafts over me, and I inhale deeply. She will be here, I'm sure. It won't be long now. I watch a grey squirrel twitch its bushy tail at the base of a tree before scampering down the street.

"Mellissa is giving a presentation at the planetarium after we meet," I say to Art. "You're welcome to join us if you want."

"Thanks, Catherine. I'll probably pass," he responds, checking his watch.

I nod. Mellissa's presentation will take place just a few blocks from the coffee shop. She'll speak at an event organized by Canadian Women for Women in Afghanistan,[6] and Art's capacity for the topic will only stretch so far. Unlike me, he isn't drawn to get involved in causes. I don't think it's because he doesn't care, and it certainly isn't because he isn't knowledgeable. Perhaps it's pragmatism, acutely aware of how insignificant we are in the machinations of international politics.

We sit in silence and wait. Thoughts are bouncing around my brain, and I'm working hard to stay in the moment. What *am* I doing here? It's as if I'm compelled to reach for anything and anyone who has a connection to the place where Michelle took her last breath, as well as the profession in which she toiled, the same that took her life some four-and-a-half years ago now. Mellissa has a deep connection on both counts—journalism and Afghanistan.

I look away from my brother and suddenly she appears, crossing the street to approach us, her crisp, white, tailored shirt almost ablaze in the bright light. Her black hair is neatly coiffed at the nape of her neck. As she gets closer, I gaze at her face—skin like porcelain, a brown mole near her lips. High cheekbones and eyes the colour of onyx.

"I'm terribly sorry I'm late," she says, extending her hand to Art, then me.

"No worries," I reply. "Thank you for coming. I know how busy you must be."

The three of us dive deep into conversation about Afghanistan right away. It's been over five years since Mellissa was kidnapped and held hostage for a month in a deep hole in the ground and about three years since her memoir, *Under an Afghan Sky*, was published. Mellissa Fung, former CBC reporter, living in Washington, DC, with her partner Paul Workman, a CTV reporter, remains committed to her profession—and to Afghanistan—nonetheless.

"I fell into a depression when I learned about Michelle," Mellissa says, turning to Art. "I can't explain it. It's so unfair, her fate so much worse than mine."

"Not necessarily worse, just different," I offer, Art nodding in agreement.

My brother turns to Mellissa. "Sandy wanted to meet you, but it's still too raw for her. We travelled overland through Afghanistan in the 1970s. I guess we were lucky. It was a time of relative peace. The monarch at the time didn't try to exert control over the traditional tribal groupings. One coup d'etat in 1973 and another in 1978 set the stage for the Soviet invasion. And of course, the United States wasn't going to sit idly by when that happened," he adds, shaking his head.

I listen intently as he speaks, realizing how little I know of the history, making a point to get him to talk about it more later. Mellissa gets it, though. She's well briefed.

"Yes, you were fortunate to visit Afghanistan during that period. It's hard to imagine today that women in Kabul wore miniskirts and an entire generation went to university and became professionals."

"We have very fond memories of our journey, and yes, Kabul was very modern," Art says. "We had vehicle troubles just outside Kandahar city and the owner of a mechanics shop took us under his wing. We went to his home, and Sandy went inside to meet his wife. Sandy said it was difficult to communicate because of the language barrier, but it was clearly a conservative environment. I don't think it would have occurred to his wife to come outside to meet me. It just wasn't done."

"I'm sure that's true, Art. I hope that will change with the younger generation. Many of them have aspirations that women in those homes might not have dreamed of forty years ago," Mellissa says.

Changing the subject, he asks: "I gather you're not with CBC anymore, Mellissa? Sandy and I miss your feature reports."

"I couldn't stay with CBC after my kidnapping," she says. "They assigned me to stories like behind the scenes of *Battle of the Blades*, and I just couldn't do it. Here I was, still traumatized and needing to report on meaningful topics. It just wasn't going to work.

"CTV helped me out a great deal when I was held hostage. Paul was working so hard behind the scenes to get me released, and CTV just stepped up to the plate in ways I wouldn't have expected."

She tells us that she's freelancing now and plans to return to Afghanistan to finish telling the story she had set out to tell when she was abducted, stories about ordinary Afghans, many of them internally displaced and living in refugee camps.

"You're brave," I say. "Those are the kinds of stories Michelle wanted to report on as well. She was okay with letting other reporters go after the more political stories. The scandal associated with Canada's handling of Afghan detainees was a very hot topic at the time, but she wanted to focus on topics she knew something about from the beats she covered back home—health care and agriculture. She was skeptical about Canada's program to give farmers grains to grow as a substitute for opium and asked civilian staff at KAF if it was working on the ground. Were women and children getting an education? Did citizens have access to adequate health care?" I pause. "These were some of the stories she never got to write."

Mellissa sighs audibly and her brow furrows. "The Afghan detainee story was important, but so are those topics," she says, her voice trailing off.

Art listens intently, wanting to know if she has insight about what's going on, on the ground. "Why don't the imams speak out more forcefully against the violence?" he asks, his eyes searching hers.

"As with everything, it's complicated," she responds. "Many of them are afraid of reprisals, and rightly so. They have families, too. It's almost impossible for outsiders like us to grasp the cultural and religious underpinnings of Afghan society, as you probably already know."

Art nods, his shoulders slumping. "Yes, I do. But I thought you might have witnessed something—clerics speaking about the situation perhaps."

I look at my brother, a bit perplexed. I know he already knows these things Mellissa is saying, so why ask the question? Is it because he feels so helpless? Might things have been different for Michelle if more imams had decreed an end to the violence?

"I sometimes wonder too, Art. The true teachings of Islam are peaceful, not violent," Mellissa says.

I sit listening intently, longing to talk about my own journalism leanings, but I hold back. Mellissa is in a different league, and though I hate to admit it, I can't go back now. Still, I muster the nerve to say: "I'm writing a book about Michelle. Art and Sandy have given me their blessing."

But her attention seems elsewhere, and it's time to go. Art stands and extends his arm forward.

"Thank you, Mellissa. It's been a pleasure to meet you."

She takes his hand and gently cups her other hand over top. "I'll always remember Michelle," she says.

Their eyes meet briefly before my brother turns to go. "See you later, Catherine." I watch him walk away, his gait not unlike my father's— head set against the elements as he rounds a corner and is gone. Mellissa and I walk along the tree-lined streets to the planetarium, talking about her family and mine, ordinary things that folks say when getting to know one another. My time with her is up when we reach the fountain in the public square outside our destination. A blonde woman has spotted her, rushes over, and swirls her away in a flash. They need to prepare for the presentation under the planetarium's dome.

Mellissa waves goodbye. I stand and listen to the roar of water gushing through an art installation of a giant metal crab, ablaze in the late afternoon light. She is everything I aspired to be as a reporter, going where others might not dare in order to uncover stories that matter, stories that might make a small difference in some lives by drawing attention to their plight, stories that will help document the facts for future historians so that one day we might learn from history.

It's also what Michelle did, covering those stories wherever and whenever she could. That she died doing what she loved is little consolation. Somehow, I must accept it's the risk she accepted because of her devotion to the profession. A risk that I, too, might once have taken. At least I think I would have, though some days I also wonder if the work I found was what I was meant to do after all. I just couldn't see it at the time, hanging on to a passion for storytelling that never left me but which didn't serve practical needs to earn a living.

I'm back home in Victoria now, sitting with a glass of red wine in my hand, gazing at the Garry oak meadow outside our dining area. Tall camas flower stalks infuse the rock bluffs with a mauve and green wash that sunlight streams through. I contemplate the fact that Mellissa, Art and I hadn't discussed Canada's withdrawal of training forces six weeks earlier in March, when the majority of NATO troops also left Afghanistan.[7] I had heard the news on CBC en route to work that morning and struggled to stay focused at my job after reading an article in the *Globe and Mail*. A handful of kind colleagues came by my desk to offer their support. I'm not sure how they knew how deeply it would affect me. I'm not sure I knew either.

While we didn't talk about the withdrawal, Art's question on why more imams didn't speak out against the violence gave me pause. As he already knew, it was a question as complicated as the forces that drew the West into the conflict in the first place. I lean over to the bookcase behind me to pull out my notes from *The Unexpected War*, by Janice Gross Stein and Eugene Lang (no relation).[8] I've forgotten the details, though I remember the overall outline of how our involvement in Afghanistan began.

On October 4, 2001, the secretary-general of the North Atlantic Treaty Organization (NATO) invoked Article 5 of the *Washington Treaty*[9] in response to the al-Qaeda strikes in Washington, DC, and New York City on September 11. It was the first time in the fifty-year history of NATO that the article had been invoked. According to Gross Stein and Lang, it's the "provision that requires member states to come to the defence of members when attacked." Canada felt obliged to respond, and so we went to war, tentatively at first, with relatively short deployments in and around Kabul. Four years and three prime ministers later, not to mention an even more-revolving door of ministers of national defence, a bold and innovative new chief of defence, Rick Hillier, instructed his staff to draw up a proposal to take Canada into the heart of the hornet's nest that was Kandahar province, the homeland of the Taliban.

Canada was drawn in through a web of international dealings and persuasions, with our American neighbours to the south influencing every political decision in some major way or another, our counterparts in the European Union also in the mix. *The Unexpected War* details the story of how we came to be in Afghanistan in ways that demonstrate how very little the public knows about what goes on behind closed doors, including what military and political influences are brought to bear in the context of war. When I first read it, I found myself asking the same question repeatedly: Why do I even bother to speak out about the consequences of those decisions when I'm so far removed from the levers of power? And even if I were closer, what could I possibly do to alter the course of events? It's a hard reality to reconcile, though heaven knows it's not the first time I've felt this way. It's just that in this instance, the consequences are more personal than they've ever been. They are still rippling through the fabric of my family and many, many others—on both sides of the Atlantic.

Promises were made, or so I wanted to think, that we were there to assist on the humanitarian front, and goodness knows, Canadian Forces did accomplish some positive measures through consultations with tribal elders and reconstruction projects. Schools were built. Roads repaired. With increased security came more resources from the international community and more opportunity for Afghan organizations to operate in the open. Pockets of women and girls tasted freedom and exercised their right to go to school, daring to dream they could live as equals to men.

Soldiers put their lives on the line to gain the trust of the Afghan people and help where they could. But it was messy, too. Civilian casualties, mainly from US airstrikes, killed an estimated 50,000 Afghans. Of course, soldiers also died[10] in executing what seems to have been an impossible task, at least in the shorter term. The forces of war are as malevolent as ever, and in this case at least, the magnitude of goodwill by many honest, principled men and women fighting the war on the ground was no match against a corrupt Afghan government that did little to support its army or protect its people or the whims and political fortunes of powerful US presidents trying to appease an American public tired of the costs of war.

Closing my notebook, I sigh. My wine glass is empty, and I'm getting peckish. It's dusk, and the light in the meadow outside my window holds me in place. The breeze rippling through the tips of spear grass tumbles down a little dip in the ground. I find myself thinking about Mellissa again and feel the impact her presence had on me. While Michelle was the only Canadian journalist killed during our mission in Afghanistan, Mellissa was also a casualty of that war—the difference, of course, that she carries her work on with perhaps even more passion than before. Captivity changed her, strengthening instead of dissipating her resolve.

On occasion over the coming years, Mellissa and I keep in touch through email, and I learn that she's added filmmaking to her repertoire. During the COVID-19 pandemic, I watch one of her films online. She's bringing the plight of Afghan women into our homes. It includes footage of interviews with Afghan women. When the camera spins to her face, I see her furrowed brow and anxious eyes as she does her life's work. Perhaps for a while it was a way to deal with the personal trauma she endured during captivity, not knowing if she would ever see daylight and walk again in the world. Most of us in the west, thankfully, can only imagine what that must be like, but Mellissa not only knows but also walks among those who don't take their freedom for granted. It's clearly very painful work, but she simply refuses to look the other way.

A number of the film's images keep flashing through my brain; the young, bearded Taliban leader who says women lack general knowledge and are "mindless;" the university woman who talks about the denial of basic human rights, and ends her sentence in outrage, exclaiming: "I don't know what [the international community] is waiting for!" Finally, the scene with a slight woman cowering beneath a blue burqa on a dusty patch of ground while a man whips her for some alleged infraction, her body reeling, swaying violently. With each crack of the whip, she moans. It is not an easy film to watch. I can't imagine what it took to make it, to put everything you have to offer into such darkness in order to tell the world that these things go on in the twenty-first century.

After watching the film, I sit stone-faced for a time and decide to walk the dog, see if I can shake off this deepening despondency. Shuffling into our dining area, my eyes fall on the framed photograph of Michelle on the wall. It's one of those photos where she looks like a fashion model, taken while reporting for the *Calgary Herald*. I know that image by heart now and conjure her spirit as if it's shining a light in the universe. It's a fantastical notion, I know, but it brings a small measure of comfort as I head out the door into the twilight, thinking of her smile, as I once wrote, as broad as the horizon.

September 8, 2015

Dear Michelle,

I took Tika to the shopping plaza across the street for her walk this morning. She's too old to wander far now, but her nose works just fine, always keen to find a scrap of something disgusting to eat. Dogs! Garbage guts is what you guys used to call Natasha, the rescue dog I picked up in my travels long ago.

Do you remember what she looked like? I think you were just a toddler. She had short white fur with brown patches, big brown eyes, and a bum that wiggled up the length of her spine when she was happy. Her early years were on Quadra Island with me, where she roamed the woods and bluffs around our secluded bay, dog-paddling out to sticks I threw into the salt chuck. She wasn't fat back then, just full of life and free. Hard to believe now, but I used to hitchhike up and down island with her when I came to visit you guys in Vancouver. Until, that is, I left without her one day and she became your dog.

The thing I loved most about those days on Quadra was the absence of clocks or watches. We got up with the sun and let the days pass, warping my sense of time. I bet your family summer vacations in the Okanagan were similar, though more short-lived. I don't know if I could ever retrieve that sensation of floating through time, but I'm lucky to have experienced it at all. To be outside the world where wars and famines and injustice abound, where toxins are released into the atmosphere, oceans, rivers, and lakes, but also where people work to feed their families, and for those lucky enough, to find and follow a purpose, to contribute in meaningful ways to their communities.

On this morning's walk with Tika, I thought once more about the elusive nature of purpose. Though my journalism took a back seat, I brought two children into this world. You didn't have that opportunity, though you and Michael were as ready as anyone for parenthood. Life is fraught with disappointment. We don't always recognize the little accomplishments along the way that fulfil our *raison d'être*.

I recently came across the blog you posted from Masum Ghar where you took a picture of a sweet bundle of fluff, a light brown puppy named Crypto. He was standing on some stairs in the dust at the forward operating base where the military planned their efforts to help local Afghans build schools and hospitals and infrastructure for clean water. You wrote about the strays that found their way into these camps, how some soldiers adopted them, and others shunned them because they carried fleas and disease. I imagine you wanting ever so badly to cuddle him against your cheek, smell his sweet puppy breath as you once did with Thatcher and Humphrey, the basset hound pups that became part of your family after Natasha was gone. It wouldn't surprise me if you were plotting a way to bring Crypto home. To watch him run through green fields as you threw sticks or Frisbees for him to fetch. And your love, Michael. He would have felt your joy vicariously, watching you watching Crypto.

But it was not to be. Not a dog owner, not a wife, not a mother. Not long after the Taliban killed you, Granddad wondered why the military didn't use bomb-sniffer dogs that day. He had seen your article about a bomb-sniffing dog and thought that maybe dogs could have saved your life. Shaking his head, he asked me to write a letter to the Chief of Defence, Walt Natynczyk. As you know, his handwriting was illegible at the best of times, and he was ninety-four by then. I started to write the letter, but didn't get far. My heart sank as I thought about his need to know whether dogs could have meant the difference between life and death. It was too late, so what was the point in asking? But his question lingered with me, and eventually, I sent Natynczyk an email asking why the soldiers didn't use bomb-sniffing dogs that day. His response seemed a bit lame, explaining that canines were mainly under the purview of American forces. No doubt tactical and practical matters were at play, but obviously, Canadian Forces didn't have the resources nor much access to US dogs. Of course, we'll never know whether it would have made a difference anyway. Those bombs were buried so deeply under the road.

Remember when your mom and dad took you and your brother to Stanley Park for the Basset Hound Walk? I went along one year, when you were in elementary school and Thatcher was young. It was hilarious, all those nose-to-the-ground, heavy beasts running a race, long ears flapping. We laughed and laughed. After Thatcher was gone, Humphrey wiggled his way into your home and hearts. Of course, you'd begun your reporting career elsewhere by then, but no matter. You still fell in love with him.

Ricky the bomb dog on patrol with Canadian soldiers southwest of Kandahar city. Photo courtesy Postmedia

I marvelled at the lengths your dad went to over the years to keep that beast healthy and happy—stooped over to give him a bath in the backyard or kneeling on one knee on the grass, soaking his frequently infected paws in salty water. Walking him along the back alleys, the leash slack in his hands, your father was uncharacteristically patient, stopping every foot or so to let Humphrey sniff and snuffle. As time went on, he moved achingly slowly, though he could still sprint and send his ears flying if food was involved.

Sadly, he bit the dust in July. Your Michael adored him, too. I chuckle at the photo he posted on Facebook. Humphrey is caged between your long legs, his infected front paws soaking in a basin on your parents' back deck. You're smiling, almost smirking at the camera, a broadsheet newspaper in your hands. Humphrey, stuck as he was in your grip, eyed the camera mournfully, his long, silky ears in a slump. Michael ended his post saying that Humphrey was probably loving the big off-leash park in the sky with you.

Your brother, Cam, wrote a tribute as well, describing Humphrey's final opportunistic sprint out the door. *We will never know what he did with his hour of freedom rummaging around Shaughnessy Gardens. I like to think he paid one last visit to all of his four-legged friends that he'd met throughout the years. Rest in peace, Humphrey. There are no gates in doggy heaven.*

A dog family. That's what we are and always will be.

Love, Aunt Catherine

March 26, 2016

Dear Michelle,
Your father placed a section of the *Globe and Mail* on Granddad's chest soon after he passed around 8:00 a.m. at the end of February. Aunt Margie and I stood by, glancing at each other. I could see Aunt Margie was puzzled, as if asking: what the hell's that about? But I

Straddling the family dog, Michelle reads a newspaper while soaking Humphrey's infected paws at her parents' home in Vancouver. Photo courtesy Lang family

think I knew what the gesture meant—a final farewell, a *ça ne fait rien*, if you will, through one of the ways father and son had communicated over the decades. Talking about news. Arguing about politics, maybe even religion, though I doubt it. Economics, for sure. Probably the stock market. I never thought to ask if Granddad had any memories of the 1929 crash that precipitated the Depression. He would've been fourteen. So many things I never thought to ask, damn it all anyway.

It was hard to watch his precipitous decline in his last months. It took a very long time for him to finally give up. His body failed him long before his mind. But then in those last months at the long-term care home where he died, his will to carry on diminished almost daily. Before then, at Clarendon Court, the assisted-living facility where he lived in his late nineties, he had friends and could come and go more or less as he pleased. When I came to Vancouver to visit, I'd join him during the lunch hour and talk to his table mates. Sweet Harold. Surly Jack. Murray was the character who kept us all entertained with stories about working in the woods or trucking along Vancouver Island during the heyday of logging, some of it probably old-growth forests.

I was there when he said goodbye to those friends. Everyone knew they wouldn't see him again. I pushed him through the lobby in a wheelchair and, with his back to all his cohorts, he lifted that long, thin arm of his high in the air and waved his fingers in farewell as if tickling the air. I didn't turn to see their expressions. Neither did he. Soon after Granddad moved to his new home at the German-Canadian care home, I went to the dining area with him there, a warehouse-sized room complete with failing bodies, hunched forward in chairs, dribbling food while staff walked briskly about in their hospital shoes attending to various chores. Granddad was sitting on his walker when he reached out and tugged on a man's sleeve.

"Were you in the war?" he asked.

The man didn't even look at him, just kept going to his table. Granddad slumped further on his walker. His speech was so garbled by then even we had difficulty, straining to hear, asking him to repeat what he'd said, him straining the words back at us. He must have felt like the bottom had fallen out of his heart. It had, for his days as a conversationalist, his love of exploring meaning in literature and art with others had come to an end. Hard to imagine, I know. The grandfather who accompanied you to your university classes, insisting on sitting at the front and repeatedly hogging the prof's time with questions, embarrassing the hell out of you. I honestly don't know how you put up with it. But at the end, he might as well have been mute, unable to form words, express his ideas out loud. I doubt he ever really stopped thinking, though. I'd like to think he was having the conversation of a lifetime—with someone like Noam Chomsky or even Winston Churchill—during his final hours when morphine coursed through him. Wouldn't that have been a hoot? But on reflection, what I witnessed didn't look like much fun. I think he was still fighting, trying to come to terms with regret or still trying to persuade someone or something that he was right in his beliefs.

Conversation aside, food was one of Granddad's other great pleasures in life. Remember how he'd pile up his plate at Christmas dinner and go back for seconds, even thirds? But because he never stopped refusing to wear dentures, he developed aspirational pneumonia as time went on, meaning he couldn't chew or swallow solid food anymore. In his few weeks at the long-term facility, the food was an unpalatable sickly mush of varying shades of grey or brown or green. Before it got that bad, I bought him a snack-sized container of HÄAGEN-DAZS ice cream. He might have had two teaspoons before handing it back to me. Imagine him turning from that life's pleasure—heaps of rare beef, mashed potatoes and gravy, homemade berry pies, gone from the scoreboard, the tally of savoury, sweet moments a thing of the past.

It was really hard to watch, Michelle. I'd think about the kind of world he grew up in as Aunt Margie and I sat in his room during his last days. And how, as the oldest of five children, he outlived all his siblings except for the youngest, his sister Ellen. That's how determined he was, though of course you already know that. About nine months before, as he approached his hundredth birthday, he looked around his messy apartment and turned to me: "I'm old, but life is *still* interesting." I sure loved him for that.

I slept, or rather tried to, in a chair in his room two nights before he died. We were sure he was going to go that night, and I wanted to be there, like I was when Nanny died. Aunt Margie and I sat with him for hours the following night, cocooned in the soft light of the tiny room, a basket of treats on a tea tray that staff delivered to comfort us. We didn't talk much, just sat in the quiet, darkening space to keep him company while he slept fitfully, tossing and turning. Sometimes he'd let out a cry. I sketched a picture earlier in the day of all six-plus feet of him: in his narrow bed, a wretched shell of the man he once was, his skin translucent, pocked with purple blotches, bruises from the slightest grazing against the metal bedframe. It was time. He had to go, but as with everything he did in life, he fought against that dying light.

The nurses gave him morphine towards the end, but they resisted at first, telling us he wasn't suffering. I knew they were wrong. His breathing so laboured, just like when Nanny was dying. And he specifically told me that he didn't want to go through what she'd gone through. I felt so helpless, though the nurse on duty when his heart stopped beating was kind.

At his memorial service, I stepped up to the podium and spoke to those gathered:

> The day after Dad departed, I woke to sunshine. I took the compost out and discovered my daffodils blooming. Walking the dog later, I turned a corner when a sudden gust of wind swept across the surface of a pond—a darkening cat's paw. It came and went with such brief and sudden intensity, ferocity even, that it took my breath away. Of course, I imagined it was Dad's spirit bidding me or the world a final farewell.

I think his love of art and language and his quest for knowledge were his bedrock, the place he went for solace in his chaotic search for meaning. During one of my last visits to Clarendon Court, I found him lying in bed reading war poems by Wilfred Owen. The sun shone through his window and all was quiet. He didn't know I was there, and that's how I wanted it, just to stand for a few moments, without intruding, allowing the stillness to settle and for time itself to pause. I studied his profile and reflected on the long life he had lived. I knew he would not always be with us, but at the same time a part of me also did not believe he would ever go.

Enough sadness. At his memorial service, your cousin Daniel followed me at the podium and gave the funniest farewell tribute ever. You would have loved it. He did a great job of sharing what it was like to have him as a grandfather. I bet you would've written something equally hilarious. Here goes.

Having Art Lang as a grandfather was an adventure. You never knew what was coming your way, and I'm not just talking about his driving. A simple visit could turn into an epic quest to pick up some item he got a "really great deal" on from a friend (or some guy he happened to meet on the street). Looking back, I think we're all glad that Granddad's years of wheeling and dealing happened before the advent of Craigslist.

Family gatherings were prime time for his incessant attempts to broaden our horizons. A conversation would start with "How's school?" or "What are ya' reading?" Unfazed by my one-word response, he would press for more. This was no softball interview; this was one-on-one with Arthur Lang. If he didn't have a newspaper article or a book to give you, rest assured he'd call days later about some program on CBC or Knowledge Network that you really should watch.

When he wasn't resting like a champion, he'd try to plant some seeds of knowledge. You reap what you sow, and Granddad wasn't one to hold back with the sowing: a visit to the art gallery, leading us into the national pavilions at Expo 86 instead of the rides, or perhaps even getting better acquainted with the importance of a good manure for your garden.

I've never been able to hill my corn in the garden like Granddad insisted I should, and I certainly can't say when knowing how to grow a fruit tree from a cutting is going to come in handy, but I still tend the same garden he used to with the dubious help of his great-grandchildren. And I'm keeping an eye on his beloved rhubarb, even though I don't care for it nearly as much as he did.

Looking back, I realize his ways of imparting knowledge were actually thoughtful gestures. He learned what made you tick and then took it upon himself to share something useful or meaningful which might just help you on your own life's journey. If he gave you something or took you somewhere, it meant you were important to him. Just about anything he took an interest in, I'll wager you know more about it because of him. I've certainly learned and appreciate more about more subjects from Granddad than anyone else I know.

He really was a larger-than-life figure, the archetypal wizard who could take someone out of their small little world and show them there was so much more out there, if they would only follow him to go looking for it. The best way to honour his memory is to live your life fully, though maybe not quite the way he did. For Pete's sake, if you invite a stranger to dinner, call ahead, but keep your eyes and ears open and try new things. As Granddad was so fond of saying, you just might learn something.

Oh, how we all wished you were there to have a belly laugh with us, Michelle, to express our grudging love and affection for your dear old Granddad Lang.

Love, Aunt Catherine

CHAPTER 12

CROWSNEST

On a Saturday morning in August, I haul myself out of bed before 4:00 a.m. to catch a flight to Calgary. I'm exhausted. It's six months almost to the day since my father died and only a week since we interred some of his ashes in the plot where we interred Mom's and Michelle's ashes three years ago, in 2013.

The short flight to Calgary is a blur. Colette Derworiz is waiting, with a few preplanned stops to make before we head to our ultimate destination in the Crowsnest Pass. First, she drives to a city park, near Michelle's condo in Inglewood. The bench that staff dedicated to their colleague and friend is here now, relocated from the *Herald* grounds when the building went up for sale. Now we sit on the bench, facing the Ripple,[11] a stone walking circle with seven pathways that wind toward a central meditative space, representing the swirls created by a stone cast into water. The sound of the river beyond envelopes me, cleanses.

The Bow River winds through central and southern Alberta for almost 600 kilometres. The first people who walked this land remain here today, the Nakoda, Tsuu T'ina and the Blackfoot Confederacy, tribes I know next to nothing about. Because of my work in treaty negotiations for BC, my knowledge of Indigenous nations stops at the BC-Alberta border. Rightly or wrongly, the Blackfoot Confederacy triggers images of proud warrior men on horseback, mounted on the ridge of foothills, their flamboyant eagle-feather headdresses lined up across an unending blue sky. For centuries before settlers came, they built trade routes, harvested the abundant resources of this land and its waters and lived along this river, live along it still, while the river—like the green, dark forest of Gordon Lightfoot's "Railroad Trilogy"—was too silent to be real, millennia before humans walked this land.

Thinking about nature in this way helps me put life in perspective. I'm learning on this journey that death, too, is timeless. It's a good place for remembrance, and I'm comforted by the fact that Michelle is commemorated here in this park, close to the Bow River which flows on through time, and also where residents and visitors come to appreciate the sanctuary that moving water and earth bring to our souls.

Then Colette steers her car away from the park onto a highway before veering onto an off ramp and into the large parking lot at the *Herald*. We push the front doors open past the same full-page ad of Michelle that was posted here on my previous visits. Her face surrounded by a thick, black border every time staff enter the building, six and a half years on. It doesn't jolt me like it did the first time. I'm reassured by this, contemplating how the large banner headline *Remembering Michelle* hits those who still enter to report the news.

We step inside the newsroom, relocated to another part of the building. Gone is the wide swath of rows of desks. Gone is the view of Calgary's skyline. File cabinets and desks clutter the space more haphazardly, though the room is bright with light. A few folks come to greet us, but most carry on with their work. The space dedicated to Michelle is no longer at the spacious entrance of the former newsroom but tucked into a corner off the hallway, across from a display of sports jerseys and the like. I pause to take it all in: the welcoming couch, the light sculpture, her awards and Kandahar plaque, the display of framed front-page stories hanging on the wall. Headlines in thick black font above her byline: *Old before her time*; *We need our doctors, South Africans plead*; *Health cuts cripple small-town hospitals*; and the ones headlining her demise *'Brave' Herald reporter, 4 soldiers die in blast*; *'We will remember her'*; *'Our shining star.'*

The alcove is as lovely as when I first saw it, but without the sweep of open space around, it's irreconcilably altered. I wonder if any staff take a few moments for themselves here, to think in a quiet space, surrounded by memorabilia honouring their fallen comrade. Some stalwarts remain, like her former city editor, Chris Varcoe, but those who didn't know her surely don't feel the gaping hole of her absence, once so intense. I'm mute in the face of these changes, a bit crestfallen that such a dynamic place could be so diminished in six short years.

The once spindly Russian Mountain Ash her friends planted outside is about twelve feet high now, with a substantial trunk and fern-like foliage, full and lovely. Unlike the park bench, it's rooted too deeply to move. Shrubs at its base are flush, unkempt but healthy. I think Colette gave up on planting annuals and tulip bulbs. Too many bunnies. Too little time. Too few hands to help her tend this little patch of earth.

I snap a photo of her by the tree. She's in her late 30s, blonde hair tied back, sunglasses propped on top of her head, smiling and accomplished. Since Michelle's death, she has lost other close friends, most to cancer. I know she misses the years working alongside her fabulous women friends and colleagues. Nothing stays the same, neither of us able to turn the clock back to a happier time. Still, she laughs freely as we chat, lighthearted and spontaneous.

Soon we hit the open road and head for the Crowsnest Highway and big sky, ranching country. We're driving to the town of Bellevue, one of three hamlets nestled in the Rocky Mountain pass, where another former colleague has a cabin. It's the reason I've come to Alberta again, my tape recorder and notebook in tow. We'll have more time to reflect on life since Michelle's death and to talk about journalism, including war reporting in Afghanistan.

As Colette speeds through the Turner Valley, I jot down impressions en route: cattle, horses, Swainson's hawks perched on fenceposts. Rolling hills beyond long stretches of flat highway. Sheep River Public Library. We stop at the Navajo Mug for a bite to eat in Longview, an eatery that singer-songwriter Ian Tyson had a hand in running. Too bad he's not around when I buy Colette the "best egg salad sandwich," an abundance of ranching knick-knacks everywhere I look. As we walk back to the car, I hum lyrics to "Four Strong Winds," the thought of things that do not change stuck in my brain from an earlier time. Ian and Sylvia harmonies spinning around my brother's turntable, just one of Art's LPs when he and Sandy belonged to UBC's folk song fan club, not yet husband and wife, and me still in grade school.

The countryside is picturesque, and I listen to Colette tell me about ranchers, Tyson included, who are trying to protect the lands, and their ranching lifestyle, through a covenant to keep the realtors out. But it's not a straightforward process, as is almost always the case when big-moneyed interests are at stake.

"I'm one of few reporters left at the *Herald* from when Michelle died," Colette replies when I ask how things are going at work. "Renata went to the *Globe* and now Kelly is there, too. Gwendolyn got caught up in the first round of lay-offs. It's been tough. I worked hard to carve out my beat as the environment reporter, but they're adding on assignments that should be going to a general news reporter. Been there, done that. We're so short-staffed, and I'm not happy."

"Doesn't sound good, Col," I say, glancing at her tanned hands on the wheel. "What are you going to do?"

"I'm hoping they'll offer me a buy-out."

I study her profile and know from previous conversations how strongly she feels about journalism. She's at a juncture, assertive like I never could be about getting her career needs met.

Past the town of Longview, we stop at the wooden Bar-U Ranch sign, a national historic site. A giant cut-out of a rancher, with an equally giant cowboy hat, holds a neatly coiled lasso in one hand. Behind his towering silhouette, cut rows of hay and long grass sweep the land. Patches of cloud, some white, some grey, sculpt the big sky like abstract fibre art, a jagged pool of sky-blue offset in the distance, a marine mammal-like shape that seems to soar through space. Careful to avoid the barbed wire, Colette leans on a fence post, tucks her chin down and smiles sweetly, mischievously, into my camera again. She's relaxed in this environment, the Saskatchewan-Alberta girl that she is.

Soon after, the car rolls toward a stop sign, and I snap another photo—this flat-as-far-as-the-eye-can-see in every direction is a novelty to me now, decades after my father uprooted us from our prairie beginnings to the West Coast. The highway has the throughway here, and all these roads are paved, but studying the picture years later, I'm reminded of the intersection where the Humboldt bus crash happened, another story of death and destruction that Colette reported on, far too close to home. Her two nephews in Prince Albert, Saskatchewan, could have easily been on a bus just like it, rumbling from town to town to score hockey goals in ice arenas across the prairies. The emotional toll of covering these stories is tough. Journalists who cover crime, war, natural disasters and more are witness to trauma of various kinds, searching out facts, talking to the bereaved or victims along with those we hold accountable, somehow keeping it all together inside. When the reporters themselves go somewhere private to process what they've witnessed, how do they cope? How do they carry on? I wonder if, for some, it's by writing through it. That's what reporter Renata D'Aliesio said about getting straight to work to write about Michelle's death within an hour of learning the news. Doing her job was a way to help her stay focused while she processed the loss of a dear friend in Afghanistan, where she, too, had reported only three years earlier.

Violet-tinged mountains rise behind the foothills as we drive farther west. It's hot at mid-day, and the road bends and sways as we coast up and over rises, a languid tilt into curves. I find myself gazing at the horizon, expecting a glimpse of mercurial light reflecting off the Pacific Ocean in the distance. *Good grief*, I whisper, shaking my head, *we're hundreds of miles from the sea*. The highway keeps climbing, and suddenly we're on the pass entering the Rockies. Jagged, vertical peaks on either side, we cut our way through.

It's late Saturday afternoon when Colette and I pull up to Renata's early 1900s bungalow on a quiet residential street on the slopes of the mountain town of Bellevue. The first of Michelle's close colleagues to leave the *Herald* for another newsroom, Renata landed a job with the *Globe and Mail* in Toronto a few years ago. A petite, dark-haired woman with a subdued, ever-observant manner, she's on holidays and has brought her mother, Bozena, for a getaway in the mountains. Kelly Cryderman, now also a *Globe and Mail* reporter but still based in Calgary, knocks on the door to join us not long after Colette and I settle in. Kelly has the bearing of a model with her classic good looks, blonde hair and tall, lean frame. Both Kelly and Renata had been to Afghanistan for the *Calgary Herald*: Renata in 2006 and Kelly in 2007.

After dinner, I take out my tape recorder for a wide-ranging conversation about Michelle, Afghanistan, and journalism. These dynamic women are living the life I aspired to, spending many of their waking hours on their respective beats, offering me a glimpse into the tight-knit crew that Michelle belonged to, as well as the highs and lows that come with the territory over time. Michelle and her buddies were full of serendipity and fun and hard work, or as their senior male colleague, Bob Remington, described them: "energetic, funny, delightfully bitchy and cleverly foul-mouthed."

I relished being in the company of these women whose careers progressed in the years since Michelle went on her fateful assignment. Renata and Kelly talk about their time in Afghanistan, helping me picture what it may have been like for Michelle. I learned about the risks they took— many—and how it was a roll of the dice for them as well. Renata, the first of Michelle's colleagues to go, went into high gear the instant she arrived, figuring stuff out on the fly. It was fear of failure, not for her safety, that plagued her as she launched into the task at hand. She gave herself pep talks, returning to the basic tenets of journalism—the five Ws—even though the enemy, the terrain, the infantry, the military hierarchy, and operational decisions were like nothing she'd ever been thrown into before. At the time, Canadian troops were involved in Operation Medusa—a defensive campaign to defeat the Taliban from regaining control of

Kandahar city in the fall of 2006 and Canada's biggest military operation since the Korean War.

Renata knew she had to gain the soldiers' trust in order to get the stories, which involved demonstrating that she could look after herself. "I could sleep in the sand. I would eat what they would eat. There were no washrooms. I'd just squat where I could, and most importantly, not complain about any of it."

At the time, Canwest only had a "fixer," a local Afghan interpreter and guide, in Kabul, not Kandahar. So, unlike reporters with other major news platforms, she could only leave the base as an embedded reporter, with one exception. She went to Kabul to report on infant mortality, interviewing a midwife while walking with her from home to home. "Kabul was safer back then," she says.

We talk about the lack of training she was given prior to leaving Canada, how poorly equipped she was, wearing a flak vest intended for someone six feet tall. She rode on dirt roads in an open G-wagon or a LAV in the suffocating forty-degree heat, not a clue what was outside the armoured metal box carrying her and soldiers into enemy territory.

"Toward the end of my six-week stint, I wasn't ready to leave. I felt like I'd just started figuring things out, started seeing what the more important stories were, gaining the confidence to ask for certain things. Suddenly, I was gone, and it just didn't seem right."

For her part, Kelly tells us about the time she was stranded outside Kabul airport at night. After calling someone she knew, she hiked across an empty field in the pitch black to reach his vehicle. I'm dumbfounded to hear this, while everyone else wonders aloud if it was any riskier than when she was a cub reporter sent to interview a suspect of a violent crime on a quiet rural road in Alberta. One day at Kandahar Airfield, she got a call from her Calgary editor pressing her to file a story just as a rocket exploded nearby. Not in serious danger but alarmed nonetheless, she blurted "Holy fuck!" Across the phone lines, her editor wasn't fazed in the least. He was in a Canadian newsroom looking at his watch, responsible for feeding the beast, as it were.

Renata tells me about an incident sleeping on the roof of a farmer's house, beside a soldier who insisted she take a gun, the enemy close by and active. Even though she could hear gunfire, she felt that accepting the firearm would violate a journalistic code. "But I could see how scared he was," she says. "So I took it to give him some peace of mind."

So yes, journalism can be a dangerous and traumatic profession, often without acknowledgement by bosses who, like the rest of us, can only imagine the terror of bombs exploding nearby. Or what it's like to report on drug deals going down in the back alleys of Vancouver's Downtown Eastside. Or how it feels to head toward wildfires raging through towns like Fort McMurray when everyone else is frantically trying to flee.

It was like a girls' pajama party that first night, Bozena and I the matriarchs in the mix, all five of us drinking wine, laughing and talking—most of it serious. Bozena often interrupted with her fiery opinions. She's short like her daughter, but more solid, a real toughness beneath the charming, mischievous gleam in her eye. She grew up post-World War II in Warsaw. She hints that she didn't suffer like others did, and I'm left to speculate what she might have witnessed before immigrating to Canada as a young woman. Did post-war Poland set the foundation for her sometimes black-and-white views, I wonder, mindful that I've never experienced the ravages that war leaves in its wake or how such trauma manifests itself as people struggle to rebuild their shattered lives.

After coffee the next morning, Kelly, now the mother of a toddler, returns to Calgary. Colette will have to leave for work on Monday before the day is out, but she's keen to spend time with us in the mountains. An avid hiker, the Rockies are her place of solace, and she's in no rush to head back to the city.

It's overcast when Colette, Renata, Bozena, and I head out after breakfast to hike the trails at the Frank Slide Interpretive Centre[12] on Turtle Mountain. From Renata's backyard, we can see the slide that decimated the mountainside, giving us some perspective of the massive sweep of rock that buried the town of Frank in 1903, killing about ninety of the 600 people living there. Hiking along the trails, it's hard to get that perspective. Boulders the size of houses and a jumbled mass of rock spreads out and across from every vantage point as we wander up, down and around. When I learn that a one-metre-wide and six-metre-high wall could be built from Victoria, BC, to Halifax, NS, with this rock, I feel very small indeed.

We carry on to the town of Blairmore, a hop, skip and a jump away, and Renata and Colette pose in front of the weathered Green Hill Hotel Lobby Tavern, the venue for a girls' shindig—a Valentine's Day pub crawl—in 2011. Evidently, it was a wild night. Colette and Renata laugh at the memory, smiling perfectly in my viewfinder, their thoughts turning to how Michelle would have been in her element had she been with them that night.

Across the street we pay a visit to the Launstein Image Wildlife Art Gallery and meet the proprietor and his teenage daughter, Jenaya. She shows me around, explaining the stories behind the striking images on the walls. I'm not only inspired by her talent but also by her passion for their arduous wilderness treks in all seasons. It's hard to push down my enthusiasm, and I muse about writing a feature on this ambitious young woman's dedication to her art. It's the reporter in me again, but I lack the energy and ambition to chase down markets. Still, I learn something else about myself and this country, for the places I've been and the people I've met deepen my affection for this land I'm lucky enough to call home.

As the afternoon wears on, Colette says farewell and hits the road, while I stay behind in Bellevue. Colette will return the following weekend, but for now, I'll linger in this sleepy, tiny town.

On a hot day mid-week, Renata drives to Chinook Lake Provincial Park. It's soon clear why she keeps coming back to this part of the country. Stepping outside the car, we stand before emerald-turquoise waters set below a jagged mountain peak and breathe in the picture-postcard view, a pine forest trimming the lake's edge, save for a sandy beach at our feet. We wind our way around the trail in less than an hour, though I yearn to stroll for hours more.

Renata D'Aliesio (L) and Colette Derworiz reminisce about Michelle in front of the Green Hill Hotel, Blairmore, Alberta, in August 2016. Photo by Catherine Lang

On the far side of the lake, I spot a golden eagle cruising alongside the pines. Pointing it out to the others, we follow it with our eyes from one length of the lake to the other. Alert to the breadth of its wingspan, I imagine being drawn into its core as it glides effortlessly through air, wing tips arched skyward. We all agree it must be Michelle, coming to pay us a visit, letting us know how free she is, how she still cares for us. Her presence almost tangible.

Later, I read Eve Joseph's memoir *In the Slender Margin*, gaining perspective on this and other such moments: "*A sign is a combination of things—a confluence of our hopes, memories, beliefs—a moment in which the veil seems to drop and we are granted a glimpse of another reality.*"

We come full circle, back to the sandy beach where we began. The sky clouds over, taking the intense heat with it. But I decide to swim anyway. It's likely my only opportunity to bathe in this silky glacier-fed lake in the middle of these majestic mountains. Renata and Bozena sit on a bench and watch me wade in, splashing my upper body before making the plunge. It's not the take-your-breath away cold I remember from diving into Lake Louise when my brother drove my mother, sister and me across the country, from Winnipeg to Vancouver in 1963, but it's not a bath either. I sweep my arms wide in a breaststroke, dunk under and surface until I'm thoroughly cleansed, my brain less chatty, my senses tingly.

Renata and I retreat to a picnic bench, the dry forest floor under our feet. I pull out my tape recorder and press record as she climbs back into memory, reporting on Operation Medusa a decade earlier. Every now and then Bozena interrupts, putting in her two bits. I ask how she felt when she learned her daughter was going to Afghanistan. "Angry and afraid," she says bluntly. She questions why Canada would go into Afghanistan. "Let Afghans solve their own problems," she says, referring disdainfully to "western influence." A few moments later, she's also unequivocal when she answers her own question: "Canada had to go into Afghanistan because we didn't join the Americans in Iraq." I know there's a fair bit of truth to that.

Renata speaks softly, explaining how and when she told her parents about her decision. She didn't want them to worry, but knew she'd go regardless. As it was for Michelle, so it was for her—a calling to do her job and do it well, a relatively rare opportunity to cover history in the making.

After a while, the weather shifts again, threatening rain, so we retreat to Renata's backyard. We continue the conversation for another hour when a sudden thunderstorm erupts. I grab my phone to scan a video of the little backyard as if I were on a merry-go-round. Renata glances my way briefly, and I wonder if she's thinking the same thing as me. Is Michelle unleashing her energy again? Renata tucks her chin and hurries inside, but I crave the adrenalin of this wind lashing against my body, whipping fabric against skin. I feel it pushing me in all directions as it circles around the yard. Pausing a moment at the edge of her property, I look down. A steep slope plummets into a neighbour's yard and beyond to the railroad crossing and a farmhouse on the other side of the tracks. I stare at the modest green hill where sunlight dances across a pretty white house and think about my interview with Renata. The scene is a stark contrast to the one I'm imagining—Renata's tiny frame lying beside a soldier, a gun tucked beside her, on the roof of a farmer's house, surrounded by the flat sand-coloured roofs of his extended family, the dark outline of a maze carved out of the earth beneath them. Active gunfire and rockets in the near distance.

Turning back to the bungalow again, I glance at my watch. We'd been talking about Afghanistan for over two hours and it's time for dinner.

I don't remember the drive back to Calgary with Colette. Maybe my head was just too full from my week in Bellevue. One afternoon I had strolled the mountainous streets in the stinking heat, snapping photos of quaint old houses—some better kept than others but none so grand or upscale as those in big cities. The sense of time standing still was strong, harkening back to the days when Bellevue's mining economy collapsed. Somehow, folks found ways to make ends meet, perhaps by driving to wherever and whatever work could be found elsewhere. What I saw that afternoon: empty shops along the empty main street. Back alleys like those from my youth. Makeshift garages and rusting old cars. Kids' toys on lawns but surprisingly little sound of children playing, laughing. Maybe it was too hot to be outside, or maybe they were off splashing in a nearby lake. Far below, railroad tracks snaked their way across the valley, my vision limited to the rail line swerving from one mountain peak and another. Not a limitless horizon in these parts, just a skyrocketing of mountains in all directions—and the prominence of Turtle Mountain, the sheer cascade of falling rock like a scar on a murderous slope, the bones of those it killed long disintegrated into earth.

Colette drops me off at a coffee shop in Marda Loop. It's near my next destination, Michael Louie's home, in a neighbourhood of new, stately homes and manicured gardens. He disparagingly refers to it as 'Pleas-antville,' and it is—devoid of any hint of nature's disorder. Entering his semi-detached home, I'm struck by its clean lines, tasteful furniture, and sparsely decorated walls. Unlike my living space, it's free of clutter and satisfying to the eye, though I can't help but feel an emptiness here. When I leave a few days later, I clutter a kitchen windowsill with jars of fresh basil and instructions for Michael to plant any that grow roots.

I came with the intention of interviewing him about Michelle, if he's agreeable, but now that I'm here, I can't muster the courage to pull out my tape recorder. It feels like an invasion. A few weeks after we interred Michelle's ashes in August 2013, I wrote him a letter about my purpose, hopeful he would give me his blessing in time.

> Dear Michael,
> I appreciate and applaud you for doing all that you can to get on with your life. Michelle wouldn't have wanted it any other way. I know you've gone through hell and back, and the last thing I want to do is drag you through it all again. But the story won't just be about our loss or the tragedy of her death or the grief that will always be there no matter the passing of time and fading of memory. Writing about Michelle will also be about the fun-loving, vibrant, smart and compassionate young woman she was. It will be about her accomplishments as a journalist and the contributions she made—because no matter how the news industry treats its workers, she made a difference. I believe hers is a story that needs to be told, in part so her legacy lives on, and also to remind Canadians of the critical issues of our times and the role and sacrifices journalists make to ensure there is a record and that we can be informed about the world we live in.
> In my heart, I know I must do this. The story wouldn't be complete without your story of Michelle. I hope in time you'll be willing to trust me with it.
>
> Love, Auntie Catherine

I had hinted at the serious doubt I carried, too, whether I could do Michelle justice. Now, here I was in the home in which she might have settled, bringing colour and warmth to its rooms, her laughter mingled with Michael's as they snuggled on the couch and ate popcorn while watching a movie or talked about their day or read books or made love.

Over the coming days, Michael will let slip bits of memories or experiences. He's driving us to dinner at an Asian noodle house in his sleek, black VW sedan, and I'm aware of his masculine charm—a professional man nearing his forties, a cross-fit coach, at ease in his skin and with his Asian ancestry, a competence earned. He tells me about seeing a woman on the street the other day.

"She looked so much like 'Chelle," he says. "I had to drive around the block to find her again. I couldn't believe it. My heart was beating so fast, my mind racing as I searched for her on the street. Of course, it wasn't her, but for that short bit, I was convinced it was."

"I've had similar experiences," I say. "One time I saw a woman halfway along a table in a neighbourhood pub. She was the spitting image of Michelle, and I kept looking at her intently. Finally, she came over to ask if we knew each other, clearly puzzled by my gazes. The resemblance was uncanny."

Michael nods, both of us falling into thought. As with so much about loss, there's no way to explain. There isn't any logic to loss.

In the morning he leaves early for work, before I haul myself out of bed in the guest room. I tiptoe down the hardwood hallway and slip downstairs to make a coffee, though I've no time to dilly-dally. Michelle's editor from the *Herald*, Chris Varcoe, is picking me up soon. I'll spend the better part of the morning interviewing him and two of Michelle's other male colleagues.

We sit in the boardroom where they praise her work ethic and tell me stories—like the time Chris accidentally knocked a glass of water inside Michelle's brand-new designer handbag. She proceeded to make a joke out of it, letting him know in no uncertain terms that he owed her, poking as much fun at him as she dared.

I'm somewhat, though not entirely, relaxed interviewing these men, journalists who've taken time out of their day to talk about Michelle and the work she did alongside them. One recalled attending the 2009 National Newspaper Awards gala in Montreal when Michelle's reporting on health care for Canwest took the Beat Reporting category. But more than five years have since passed and details are vague. I'm left to imagine how ecstatic she would have been. I picture her in a sleek black dress, make-up tastefully applied, perhaps some sparkling jewelry around her lovely neck, as she mounts the podium, heart pounding, to face a crowd of her professional peers. No doubt she thanked her editors and colleagues, her fiancé and family, for support and encouragement given freely along the way. But in the end, it was her accomplishment, hard won through grit and determination. It's not difficult to imagine the confidence and charm with which she would have moved, like a gazelle, on her way to becoming a veteran of the profession.

When done in the boardroom, I say my goodbyes, thanking everyone for their time. I expect they see me as a bit odd, this woman nearing retirement age, still a reporter wannabe going through all the motions of "getting the story." In fact, I know I'm a bit odd, but it matters less as I age and I can't let it stop me from doing what I set out to do. But when I exit the building, I question what I'll do with the information I've gathered, hoping it wasn't a waste of their time or mine. I've already covered a good deal of this material with others, including how the newsroom scene went down the day they found out Michelle had been killed. But I still had to come here and do this, and nothing is lost by trying. Maybe what I learned will come to me in stages, glimpses of their abiding affection for their colleague and how good it felt to remember and talk of her freely once more.

A few hours later, I stand on the northern banks of the Bow River across from downtown Calgary. It's already early September and will soon be time to head home, to my husband and son, to process all things Alberta. But today, close to emotional exhaustion, I bask in the sun and sound of the running river. People come and go, some strolling, some cycling. Others sit with their Starbucks lattes on stones overlooking the wide sweep of shallow waves below gleaming skyscrapers.

Mercurial light radiates along the river's course, at once placid and turbulent. Miniature whitecaps peak in a white froth over riverbed boulders and rocks where currents race each other past the shore. Sunlight is golden against grasses bending in the breeze. I hadn't intentionally come here for solace. I came to touch Michelle's name on the soldiers' memorial again and revisit the steel wall along the riverbank. It towers above the Bow from Poppy Plaza, an 86,100-square-foot (8,000 square-metre) war memorial. The city retained an architectural firm to design the plaza around two functional features, one of which is the plaza's wooden deck, and the other is the steel wall which shields the deck from winter ice

REMEMBER / THOSE WHO
CANADIAN / INSIGNIA
G PEACE / AND SECURITY
ROUND / THE WORLD.

MICHAËLLE JEAN,
GOVERNOR GENERAL

ANCE / DAY GENERALLY FOCUSES... ON
OSE / FALLEN HEROES FROM THE FIRST
D / WARS AND THE KOREAN WAR, IT IS
TO REMEMBER THE SACRIFICES MADE
THOSE WHO HAVE SERVED AND DIED
THIS CENTURY, PARTICULARLY IN
PEACETIME.

-HOLLY BRIDGES

HER HEAD WAS SHAVED AND
HER WIDE BROWN EYES WERE
AT ONCE TIMID AND MISCHIEVOUS...
SHE SMILED BROADLY FOR A
PICTURE... SHE WAS GOING TO SCHOOL
—AT LEAST THAT DAY...

SINCE THAT TIME...(CANADIAN FORCES)
MEMBERS HAVE LOST THEIR LIVES... SO
DESPITE THAT DANGER... THERE REMAINS A
REALITY:

THERE'S STILL ONE LITTLE GIRL,
AMONG MANY, WHO JUST
WANTS TO GO TO
SCHOOL.

-KRISTINA DAVIS,
KANDAHAR

Poem by Kristina Davis cut into Calgary's Poppy Plaza, an 86,100-square-foot (8,000 square-metre) war memorial along the Bow River. Photo by Colette Derworiz

flows. The steel weathers naturally, darkening into a rusty brown. Quotes about war are cut into the steel all along the route.

I glance up to see the towering letters S-O-L-A-C-E cut into the wall. How could I possibly find solace, here or anywhere? The river's enigmatic curves and aquamarine clarity are sinking into my core, but solace strikes me as incongruous. It's as if I'm looking at myself from a height, grey-haired, and thin in my flower-patterned shorts and black T-shirt, feeling the power of this great river flow by, bereft of words that might ease my laboured unpacking of emotion. A kind of solace does come to me in the moment, like an afterthought or some small detail overlooked.

CHAPTER 13

YALETOWN

On a sparkling Friday in June 2017, I board a BC ferry at Swartz Bay bound for Tsawwassen. It's a trip I've made so many times over the years, I could probably do it blindfolded by now. But rather than heading directly to see family as is so often the case, I have an alternative destination this time around: Yaletown.

I read during the long, rumbling bus ride from Tsawwassen to Richmond, every now and then stopping to gaze out the window at agricultural land that stretches, row upon row, all the way to the southeastern horizon. Birds of prey—red-tailed and Cooper's hawks and bald eagles—perch on fence posts as traffic flies by at 100-plus kilometres an hour.

The snow-capped Coast Mountains skirting the northern horizon remind me that I'm not on the prairie, but here, where the Fraser River delta has created some of the best farmland in BC and where the Tsawwassen First Nation signed the second modern-day treaty in BC, an event I attended during my days in treaty negotiations. If I could block out the mountains to the north, it would feel a lot like the Big Sky country of southern Alberta where Colette and I travelled almost a year ago. When the packed, caterpillar-like bus finally enters the terminus where the SkyTrain takes over, I'm ready for the day's journey to transport me underground where traffic is no longer an issue. It was Expo 86 that brought the first rapid transit to Vancouver, the city where Michelle grew up. She was eleven the year Vancouver showcased its spectacular setting to the world, the same summer I had my first job as a community newspaper reporter on the southern Gulf Islands and a time when the character of Vancouver began to change more dramatically—for better and for worse.

At the Yaletown-Roundhouse SkyTrain station, I emerge above ground to a perfect day in an upscale mini-city that's completely foreign to me. Since moving away from Vancouver in 1977, I rarely have had occasion to do more than pass through Yaletown on my visits. I vaguely recognize what part of the city it's in, aware that the original Expo site isn't too far away. But I can't for the life of me remember what this area looked like in the 1960s and '70s, except as a dirty, semi-industrial area with dilapidated old hotels on its edges. We are, after all, not far from Vancouver's infamous Downtown Eastside where impoverished and traumatized folks have long populated these streets. Close also to the Classical Joint coffee house in Gastown where I went as a young woman, listening to bands like Pied Pumkin. I remember heading home one December night, my head still swinging to Shari Ulrich's voice belting out "Fear of Flying." I waited for over an hour at a bus stop above the cenotaph at Victory Square, past midnight, snow pouring down through pools of light from streetlamps. Who knows how many folks lived nearby, shivering in their bug-ridden beds while I stood there stamping my feet? Alone and in my early 20s, I was oblivious to everything except the cold and the uncertainty of whether a bus would ever come to take me home.

Now I cross the busy street from the SkyTrain station, enjoying the gentle breeze and aesthetics of this perfectly groomed community south of that same Victory Square. I pass the Roundhouse Museum, where a polished black CPR steam engine on display triggers thoughts of my father and his railroading days. In just one very long lifetime—my father's—this glorious metal beast has become a relic of history.

Silver chrome and glass windows on skyscraper condo buildings gleam in the late afternoon sun, and pedestrians stroll beside planters festooned in ferns and shrubs that curve with the flow of arched streets. Turning, I realize I'm going the wrong way and walk back a block to the condo tower where Sarah Noble has invited me to a gathering of her and Michelle's high school and university friends.

I step inside behind a young girl in a pink T-shirt with a thick, curly, nut-brown ponytail down her slender back.

"Hello, I'm here to see Sarah and Sanjay," I say to the concierge.

He calls over my shoulder: "Katie, wait. You have a guest," pointing me toward a spiral staircase that winds its way up the glassed-in stairwell.

"Hi, Katie," I say. "I'm here for the party with your mom and dad."

Katie is pretty, like her mother. Her unblemished tanned legs glow as she bounces up the stairs ahead of me, her ponytail flipping up and down. At the top, she holds the door open, and some four hours after leaving home, I've arrived. A handful of men are shooting the breeze around a coffee table in the middle of this party room, while Sarah walks over from the kitchen area to greet me. Her wide blue eyes shine in the dim light, but I sense her angst as we hug. Michelle was like a sister to her.

"I miss her energy and having her bounce into our apartment," she once told me. "And her complaints about her mom's red car, which she called 'the tomato.' That was *so* Michelle, and I'll never find another friend like her. She was the only person who knew everything there was to know about me."

Sarah is a physician now, a wife and mother of two children, and Michelle was her rock during early university days when she floundered through a liberal arts degree before switching to science and medicine. They held each other up as they overcame barriers along the way: in Sarah's case applying to med school three times before being accepted; in Michelle's case leaving Vancouver for small hick towns to get the reporting experience she needed before landing a job with a big city newspaper. Even though they were miles apart, they stayed close—phone calls and visits as often as they could. Shopping sprees on Robson Street became a ritual whenever Michelle was in town, the two of them practically running into Starbucks after their purchases to don their new upscale apparel. What would be the fun in waiting until they got home?

"I'm so glad you could come!" Sarah says, as I put my purse and knapsack down.

"Thanks so much for organizing this, Sarah," I reply, turning to meet her clutch of friends. A super busy woman with a lot on her plate, she's gone to considerable effort to bring us all together for an evening of reminiscing about their high school and university days with Michelle.

Lily Kamarn arrives with her husband and two girls in a matter of minutes, but I'm already in the thick of a conversation with Tyler Foley, a Delta Hotel sales manager in grey dress slacks and a light blue shirt. Later, perusing the photo albums, I see him as the joker he must have been in his late teens, holding sway at the end of a banquet table with girls standing around and behind him, Lily one of them. Michelle isn't in that picture, but as we pore over the albums, it's soon clear that she was very much at the heart of this crowd. Tyler points to a photo of Michelle wearing a black dress that hugs her waist and a neckline that reveals a modest bit of cleavage. She and another glamourous friend, eyelashes thick with mascara, are hugging and smiling for the camera.

"That's the New Year's party at the Hyatt Regency," he says, and everyone concurs. Soon they're all babbling about this special occasion. I'm sipping a nice red wine by now, enjoying myself maybe a bit too much. Twenty-some-odd years their senior, I'm eager to let them know that my teen years were every bit as rowdy and wild, though I didn't have a boyfriend quite like Michael Yu, Michelle's love attraction during her early years at SFU. They car-pooled to campus in his VW Passat, the same one he'd drive at a screaming pace so he could "catch the air" on the bumps of a super steep hill.

Michael is also here tonight and claims he's a good guy now, settled with a young family and wife. I can see why Michelle liked him—good-looking, confident and sexy, his voice smooth when he tells us that she liked carpooling with him because she thought his little Passat had a nice yuppie look to it. "I remember her always being really well-dressed. I mean, she had these great legs. She knew it, so she'd wear nice dresses. She was never one to go to school in sweats. Back then, I liked reading GQ magazine, so she used to walk across campus, carrying her fancy bottle of Perrier water and the magazine. She felt so yuppie," he says with a laugh. "It used to blow me away how smart she was."

It's a side of Michelle I never got to know. Although I've seen some of these photos before, I've not heard the stories that went with them. I didn't live in Vancouver during those years, but when visiting, I recall Michelle flying out the door to connect with friends, to go shopping or dancing or hiking. I felt a tad jealous, wanting to spend time with her, foolishly wishing she'd want to spend time with me.

Soon I'm ensconced on the couch next to Lionel Grannis. He points to more photos as others pile round us, stacks of albums scattered across the coffee table. Pizza has arrived and beer and wine continue to flow. I wonder if my tape recorder is catching anything in the din; I wonder if I can keep my brain on task.

Lionel is a good-looking guy, slim and fit in his jeans and T-shirt. He's already jokingly introduced himself as Brad Pitt's look-alike, and there's no doubt he's pretty cute. As the evening wears on, though, I sense a sadness in him. Maybe the loss of his parents, each to cancer when he was in his 20s, brought home the reality of what really matters in life. I don't know, and I don't pry.

One photo of him and Michelle stands out. It's the after-party of Sarah and Sanjay's Indian wedding reception, standing by the serve-yourself bar. Lionel, dressed in a red T-shirt, lips plastered against Michelle's cheek, swivels his eyes from her face to look at the camera as the flash goes off. Michelle's hands rest on his shoulders, and she's giggling irrepressibly, her nose crunched up so much that her eyes squint. I can almost feel her giggle, delight bubbling to the surface.

I've seen that smile before. It's her beaming smile, the one that says to the world: I absolutely love life, and I'm so very happy in it. As much as it hurts that she isn't anymore, I'm comforted by those who knew her from these carefree, fun times, who loved and laughed with her as they raced their way toward adulthood.

So far, I've yet to meet any of her friends who shared her love of literature, but Lionel tells me his father did. David Grannis, a bookstore owner with a PhD in English, "tutored" Michelle during her fourth year at SFU. Or perhaps it was less a student-tutor relationship as a fatherly friend with whom she'd share her essays for discussion and feedback. Sadly, David will never impart his memories of Michelle to me. He died in 2003.

Lionel's brother Matt comes to sit beside me. Matt was Michelle's first boyfriend, and she, his first girlfriend. Like his brother, Matt is good looking, but not in a Brad Pitt look-alike way. He's got curly, cropped brown hair, deep brown eyes, and a muscular frame. Wearing a short-sleeved grey shirt, he slings his arm across the back of the couch, leaning into me as we talk. He confesses that he didn't always treat Michelle with the respect she deserved, that he played too many games. Oh, youth.

"I really loved her," he tells me, wistfully.

Matt is less certain of himself than the others. I recognize his insecurity, not unlike my own in youth, jealously watching peers carry on conversations with casual ease. But tonight, after much coaxing, he tells me a story that involved Michelle's brother Cam. He's reluctant to spill details but soon dives into storytelling mode, revealing salacious bits and building momentum as he sets the scene in the spacious basement of the Langs' home on Cypress Street. Clearly, they were teens up to no good.

Guzzling beer and joking around, Matt and Cam were an odd match. A brash, outwardly confident guy, Cam could hold his liquor well while Matt just didn't have the same sway. So when Matt spotted a workout bench in the room, he decided to pump some weights to dispel his jitters. Seems that the weights were jury-rigged in some fashion. When one end spun loose and went spinning across the white carpet, all Matt could do was watch in sickening terror as the wheel smashed head-on into a glass vat of red wine that Michelle and Cam's father, Art, were brewing.

Matt could hear an exclamation erupting upstairs: "What was *that*?!" And then he heard thundering steps stomping down the stairs. Art appeared at the threshold of the room, aghast at the river of red wine oozing into the carpet, as Matt looked wildly from side to side, frantic for something he could begin to mop up the mess with.

"The next day I knocked on the door with a bottle of Dom Pérignon," Matt says. "It's not to say it's the batch of red wine or anything, but at the time it was a lot of money for me. And he forgave me and still invited me to future breakfasts after that—a class act, all the way."

Matt turns to me: "You know the phrase 'rolling on the floor laughing'?" I nod, smiling and anticipating what's to come. "But have you seen a person actually do that?" Matt asks. "When Michelle got home and found out what happened, she literally laid down and rolled on the floor laughing out loud for a long time. She asked me to tell her again and again what happened—and just broke up every time. She wished that she'd been there and got the whole thing on video, and wanted me to re-enact the whole thing. She wanted every detail. She bugged me and Cam and her father. Like, we all just wanted to let it go, but she just kept rubbing it in each one of our face's individually—and telling all her friends. It just made her whole week."

I learned a few other things about Michelle that evening that helped me understand the breadth of her fun-loving ways. One of those new bits of background revolved around a popular TV show in the 1990s: *Beverly Hills 90210*. Evidently, Michelle went about assigning the male characters from the show to her male friends, and they'd all get together to watch it, pretending that her friends were these hot guys on the California scene who lived and played at zip code 90210.

I watch a short episode and imagine Michelle taking her high school drama classes to heart, transforming the teenage characters of these cut-out, good-looking, sexy dudes, poking fun at her peer group, poking fun at all things American and cliché and shallow.

I also learn a few details about her altruistic side, things I perhaps ought to have known as her aunt, prompting me to ask: where the hell was I during those years? Clearly, not in the loop. One summer, Michelle and her Grannis brother friends, Lionel and Matt, signed on as volunteers at a camp for disadvantaged youth on Gambier Island in Howe Sound. She no doubt enjoyed the freedom away from home, but Lionel remembers that Michelle enjoyed working with the children, too. Years later in Regina, she became a Big Sister. All part of the picture, revealing to me seemingly unrelated but colourful swatches of what made her tick. That night in Yaletown I got to see her through the eyes of close friends—Michelle with a fully developed capacity for compassion and kindness but also irrepressible zest and a wicked sense of fun.

Four years after my evening with Michelle's friends, I find myself in a corner of my studio peering at an orange Nike shoebox that sits on a shelf along one wall. It contains condolence cards and letters, as well as other memorabilia: a flag someone was flying on an overpass above the Highway of Heroes when Michelle's casket sped below in a convoy of limousines; a CD of the repatriation ceremony in Trenton from which the convoy had come; the ribbon wrapped around the bouquet from Governor-General Michaëlle Jean at Michelle's Vancouver memorial. There are some things I've not wanted to rush into. Her parents have entrusted me with these irreplaceable items, and I take my responsibility with them seriously, sometimes with angst. I've had them for almost ten years now, in my mind a rich, unplumbed source almost too tender to pry open. But I lift the shoebox lid and begin sifting through its contents in earnest.

One of the condolence cards is from Sarah. Michelle's confidante during the ups and downs of her love life, Sarah knew intimately how difficult one particular relationship had been, a man who "checked all the boxes," but who undermined Michelle's self-esteem. Sarah felt her friend deserved someone who would treat her with more respect, someone who had her best interests at heart.

When Michelle and Michael Louie found each other, Sarah was thrilled, but she also supported Michelle as she struggled with her decision to accept the Afghanistan assignment. As a physician, Sarah understood the tension of setting a loved one's needs aside to fulfil her professional ambition. Sarah was there for Michelle, telling her how proud she was when she finally decided to go.

Words betray so many genuine, heartfelt efforts to express profound sadness. As I finger the cards in my hands, I feel the bond between Sarah and Michelle, and remember the intensity of my own high school friendships, so all-important at the time. In cursive handwriting, Sarah tells Michelle's parents how their daughter understood her and her vulnerabilities in ways no one else did. She could tell Michelle anything because she knew her friend would never judge her—or, later, her husband, Sanjay. A soft-spoken man, with deep brown eyes full of warmth, Sanjay recalls how they could hang out as a couple with Michelle, someone who didn't harbour any jealousy toward him or their relationship.

The last time I saw Sarah and Sanjay was in November 2019. It was a Remembrance Day service at their former high school, Magee Secondary, where a plaque was unveiled in Michelle's honour. I spoke at length about the young woman who was my niece and Sarah's best friend. Following the event, reporters hovered around me while those I met that night in Yaletown moved past.

But Sarah and Sanjay stopped briefly, a look of concern in their eyes. It gave me pause, as if they were questioning my motives. Was I doing this for Michelle or for me? Was my ego tainting their memory, their steadfast love of someone so dear as Michelle? I know that same doubt, wrestle with it often.

CHAPTER 14

THE LOON'S CALL

Thunder. Mostly flash lightning, though I'd seen a fork crack upwards from the horizon when I left the airport earlier. Now a squall of rain. I stand at the sliding back door of my Saskatoon Airbnb, sipping peppermint tea and watch the wind play with patio furniture on the deck. It teases the chairs, moving them sideways, reserving its full strength for another time.

The rain is steady, visible in the halo of the streetlights here, a newly built enclave where homes back upon each other void of alleyways, shrubs or trees. It's not at all like the neighbourhoods I remember when I was a little girl. Another rolling crack splits the night sky, this one more distant. Another cloud opens up. A steady pitter-patter diminishes to a fizzle while a louder crack breaks and then subsides into a dull rumble. Thunderstorms very much like the ones I remember from my childhood. Wild and exciting, charged with energy and drama.

It's August 7, 2017, and this is my first taste of Saskatchewan in about fifty-seven years, save one brief train stop in Melville in January over two decades ago. I could barely contain the thrill I felt when I disembarked onto the train platform in the early 1990s. Freezing air shot up my nostrils. Sunlight sparkled on hoarfrost that covered prairie grasses rolling across the plain. Hours later, I fell into a dreamlike state as I gazed outside my compartment window and watched the train's locomotive ahead. It rounded a bend in the tracks, pulling passenger rail cars along as we chugged into a violet sunset that swallowed farmhouses and surrounding fields whole into a deepening twilight.

Not the province of my birth, but the one which holds my earliest memories of childhood. It's the sound of thunder that returns most vividly to me as I stand and stare out the back of the Airbnb, and I ponder the impermanence of all that has gone before. Homesteaders who survived hard times. Drought. Fire. Bitter cold and blinding blizzards. Where are their farms now? Paved over for row houses in suburbia, like the one in which I stand? Or back further still, to the undulating bison herds that once roamed the plains, sustaining the lives of Northern Plains Indigenous peoples for thousands of years? Until, that is, us colonizers arrived. Are their ghosts roaming through the heavy cloud or flying with the gusts of wind while I stand here tonight, listening for whispers from my past.

Tomorrow I will drive to points north with friends of Michelle's— the reason for my journey to Saskatchewan. But in this infinitesimal speck of time, rain falls softly. Crickets chirp. And another rumble of thunder rolls along like a train from my early youth.

I'm travelling with two of Michelle's former colleagues from the *Calgary Herald*. Robin Summerfield, Colette Derworiz and I have been planning this trip for months now, though Colette has done most of the heavy lifting. After picking Robin up at the Saskatoon airport, she and I will drive to Prince Albert and join Colette. From there we'll travel to La Ronge and overnight in a motel before driving another 600 kilometres along a gravel road to Points North Landing. After that, we'll hop on a chartered plane to Lang Bay on Burnett Lake in northeastern Saskatchewan. We have our fingers crossed that the pilot will be able to get us onto the uninhabited shoreline, though there are no guarantees.

Robin works for CBC Radio in Winnipeg. Her husband, Mike O'Brien, was one of Michelle's best friends from her reporting days at the *Regina Leader-Post*. A deadly sarcoma killed him in 2015, leaving Robin completely bereft. She continues to grieve her complicated losses on this pilgrimage and breaks down frequently, while her seven-year-old son is safe at home with her parents.

Colette is no longer at the *Calgary Herald*. The last of Michelle's close friends from Calgary's flagship newspaper, she took the buy-out she'd talked about the summer before when we travelled to Crowsnest Pass. Colette is single. Love interests come and go. It calls to mind all those years I searched for love, battling loneliness and depression, before I met Bruce.

At sixty-four, I'm about twenty years older than them and almost seven years into the research for this book. I've left my husband and son in Victoria for the three weeks I'll be here. At times, I battle decades-old demons, hoping I'm not intruding and that my age isn't a barrier to the three of us being friends. Doubt, my constant companion.

All these points in my journey. I am criss-crossing parts of Canada just like my father criss-crossed the Prairies when he worked as a civil engineer for the CNR in the 1950s. Back when we lived in Prince Albert, smack in the middle of Saskatchewan. Is my journey to learn more about

Michelle also about experiencing parts of Canada that I long to know? A way to quench my suppressed thirst for travel and knowledge? An urge to be a free spirit on the road again? Getting to know Michelle is paramount in my mind. It's while writing that I see it has also been a journey to reclaim the young woman I once was.

As Robin and I drive north, I recall the first time I met her at Michelle's memorial service in Vancouver on January 11, 2010. She was pregnant with her son, Will Lang O'Brien. It's clear from stories and photos of him that he's full of beans and a comic, just like his father. But Robin quietly but persistently worries about her son, though perhaps he's faring better than she is since Mike's death. The loss still so tangible.

"I'm afraid of flying in small planes," she confesses as we motor along. "I'm worried about what will happen to Will if anything happens to me."

My hands on the wheel, I glance at her profile. Her thick dark hair falls neatly to her shoulders, worry pulsing at her temples.

"I've flown on lots of small planes into remote places, Robin," I say. "Most pilots are very experienced, but I understand why you worry."

She glances in the back seat to make sure all her gear is still safely tucked away. When the trip is over, she'll produce a radio documentary.[13] She's anxious about that too, and wonders aloud why she is doing it. Questions I haven't thoroughly thought through myself. It's difficult for me, but nowhere as heart-wrenching as for her. Almost seven years since Michelle was killed, I have a measure of acceptance. But for Robin, Michelle was not only a best friend but also the one who introduced her to Mike.

We drive at a good clip along the highway. It's flat, of course, but I love the wide-open sky, and it's hot and sunny. We slip in and out of silence, still feeling our way with each other, somewhat but not entirely at ease.

I don't recognize P.A., as we called it when my family lived here all those years ago. Colette is staying at her sister Carmela's, in a neighbourhood much like the one I stayed in at the Airbnb in Saskatoon—a brand-new subdivision with backyards on top of backyards. Colette's ice blue eyes greet us at the door. Hugs all around, shoes by the front door. Carmela comes to usher us upstairs, her dark hair a contrast to Colette's blonde mane. We slip into a mercifully cool living room and sink into a brown leather couch. After dinner we relax on the back deck around a gas fireplace, cuddled in blankets, drinking wine and talking into the night. As the sun sets, layers of lemon yellow and tangerine melt into a deeper crimson before slipping deeply into an indigo night sky. I long to sit here and star gaze for hours, but I tire before the others and shuffle into bed around midnight. Before we head back to the highway and get on our way tomorrow, we will drive to the street where I once lived and, with luck, find my childhood home.

Carmela is at the wheel of her four-by-four, driving the streets of P.A., rounding corners like a pro. I pause to wonder how these sisters chose their respective careers—one a reporter and the other an RCMP officer. I don't know if she ever met Michelle, but given her profession, she's no stranger to violent death. Driving with her reminds me of the time I accompanied an Aboriginal liaison RCMP officer, on the beat as a reporter for the *Ladysmith-Chemainus Chronicle*. Police cruiser shocks allowed her to drive bumpy alleyways just like that smooth ride I want to have through life.

But Carmela is off-duty on this August morning, driving Colette, Robin and me around the downtown streets of P.A. in her dark green Ford Expedition. It's still a small city by today's standards, with one-floor squat buildings lining one main street. Windows are papered up where storefronts used to sport mannequins, shoes and office supplies. Many, but not all, have gone out of business.

"Times have been hard since the pulp mill closed about ten years ago," Carmela says, slowing down when she spots some folks milling about a short distance away.

"There's Marlene Bird," she says.

I look over to see an Indigenous woman in a wheelchair, surrounded by people hanging out, shooting the breeze, hooting with laughter. Somehow, she survived the savage beating, sexual assault and burns that covered her body after her assailant set her on fire. Long strands of salt-and-pepper hair fall over her bent face. For no reason, a vision of the tooled-leather handbag my mother brought home from the federal penitentiary comes to mind, my small fingers caressing the floral sworls carved into bronze leather. Even then, I was vaguely aware that an Indigenous man created it, though I was yet to learn why disproportionate percentages of Indigenous inmates populated the prison nearby.

We leave the downtown core and head to 11th Street East and the modest white stucco home where my family lived from 1954 to 1960.

Along the way, Carmela drives past a lush, green park, and I get a glimpse of the North Saskatchewan River. I long to walk alongside it, perhaps as far as the confluence of the North and South Saskatchewan Rivers about thirty kilometres east. Time to think and process.

Suddenly we're on "my" street, and I hold my breath. I need not have feared, instantly recognizing the white picket fence and front porch, beckoning me back to a simpler time. The foliage on lofty elm trees offers patches of shade as I step onto the street. The house, garden and fence are in immaculate condition, clearly well-maintained and in order. The street number is prominently displayed on a wooden window box, adorned with black mondo grasses. Two elongated red bird houses, each with three perches, bookend the window box. Grey shingles on the roof offset a fresh coat of white paint on house and chimney. The bungalow practically sparkles on this modest plot of land.

Colette takes photos of me squinting into the sun by the front gate. I'm an older woman now, a lifetime removed from the little girl who once ran through the gate to sprint up the street, my faithful black Lab Rocky romping along at my side, to play with my friend Janey Kalmakoff. In summertime, we played in her backyard playhouse for hours, time spent in imaginary worlds much like the ones that Michelle created for her brother Cameron and friends across the back alley from their Kerrisdale home in Vancouver.

I walk up the street to the Kalmakoff's house. If this were Kerrisdale, the odds of finding the same houses on this street some fifty-seven years later would be diminished, yet here they both are: ours a model home while the Kalmakoff's looks like it hasn't seen a coat of paint in years. The railing on the front steps is barely intact, and the concrete steps are crumbling. The irony of the state of our respective childhood homes hits me. The matriarch of their family, Beth Kalmakoff, was a striking woman of considerable intellect, a towering presence next to my mother. Many years ago, she died of a brain tumour.

I look for the lilac bush that Janey and I brushed past as we chased each other in a game of tag. Alas, it lives only in memory now—that of perfume enveloping me in a cloud so lovely that it wafts over me still.

The happy little girl I once was. The happy little girls Janey and I both once were.

Back at Carmela's house, Colette, Robin and I load our gear into the rental SUV in the early afternoon. The heat is bordering on stifling when we climb into the sparkling clean vehicle, Colette at the wheel. Our destination is La Ronge. Colette has booked a room at the Harbour Inn on the shores of Lac La Ronge, where my father once fished for pike and walleye—the freshwater fish of abundant prairie lakes.

I can feel the road opening beneath us as we cruise out of the city and head north. Seven years into my quest to learn about Michelle, I'm on a parallel journey to satiate my thirst for travel and discovery writ large. Going places where few have been before, every step of the way stitching the fabric of my country, Canada, more deeply into my psyche.

La Ronge will be our first overnight stop before we reach our penultimate destination: Burnett Lake in northeastern Saskatchewan, named after a Regina RCAF pilot who was lost over the English Channel in 1944. Close to both the Manitoba border to the east and the Northwest Territories to the north, the lake is one in a land dotted with hundreds, carved when glacial ice scoured the Canadian Shield before retreating millennia ago.

In 2015, the Saskatchewan Geographic Naming Committee named one of the bays on the remote lake after Michelle because she had worked as a reporter at the *Moose Jaw Times-Herald* and the *Regina Leader-Post* and also because she was a casualty of war, serving, if you will, to bring home the stories of Canada's mission in Afghanistan.

Initially, the three of us talk about what is prompting us to make this journey and how it came to be. In February 2015, Colette had written a *Calgary Herald* article about the naming of Lang Bay and Goddard Lake,[14] after Nicola Goddard, the first female Canadian soldier to die while on patrol in the Panjwaii district of Kandahar province in May 2006—the same area where Michelle also took her last breath.

"When I wrote it, I thought how cool it would be to go there," Colette says. "Having Michelle die in Afghanistan changed me, changed how I think about life, how I think about journalism, how I think about just being, and I'm trying to grow from that. For me, it just felt like another step. One of our friends said, 'Well, I don't know that I need to go there because it doesn't hold any special memories of Michelle.' And I said: 'Yeah, but why wouldn't we make it have that, then'?"

Colette pauses and continues: "To me, it was that this place has been named after her, and that holds some significance. I've always thought I'd like to go to Afghanistan, but it's not safe. This felt like something we could do, and we could give it some special significance by visiting it. First, I talked to my brother-in-law, who said we'd need a float plane. Then it seemed like it might not be doable after all, because it was about $10,000 for a float plane from La Ronge." But Colette didn't give up, eventually locating a pilot associated with Points North Landing, a bulk fuel and transportation station, halfway between La Ronge and our destination.

"I'm pretty stupidly organized," she says, and we all laugh. Later, talking about Michelle's persistence in sleuthing out a Canadian connection in New York City when 9/11 happened, Colette adds: "Yeah, I guess we all channeled Michelle in some ways by making this happen."

Persistence. Yes, I think to myself, remembering the time Michelle parked herself in the emergency room at a Calgary hospital. She waited hours, hoping to make a connection to a man recovering from being mauled by a bear, all for the sake of story. On a hunch, she followed a woman out to the parking lot and introduced herself. It was the man's wife.

We bump further north along the dry, dusty road when Robin asks me what Michelle was like as a child. I tell them how shy she was, painfully so, but also how full of fun—all the mischief she got into with neighbourhood friends and her penchant for creating imaginary characters for her brother and friends to act out. Maybe she liked the idea of being a producer/director. It gave her a stage to play with.

Of course, we also dive into the topic of her work and theirs—namely, journalism and journalists. The sacrifices made, the vicarious trauma, the importance of reporting to shed light on abuses of power, to raise awareness of women's rights, human rights. What it meant to Michelle and how motherhood might have shifted her passion. And we share uncanny events that each of us has experienced since her death—like the soldiers that Colette and another colleague met after the 2010 Remembrance Day service, one of whom was a medic who flew in by Black Hawk helicopter after the incident. "She didn't suffer," he told them. Afterwards, they leaned against a wall together, reeling from what felt like a chance encounter. How was it they would meet someone who knew this intimate detail, right after the Remembrance Day service, their first since Michelle died?

We're nearing the end of the day's journey and munch leftover goodies from Colette's family: Rice Krispies squares, puffed wheat squares, chocolate chip cookies and gingersnaps. On the road for about two and a half hours, we have finally talked ourselves out.

One of the first things I see as we dip down to the lakeshore in La Ronge are children splashing and diving under cerulean blue water. Mothers sit on blankets in the sand, passing the time of day, their faces raised to the sun. The children's backs glisten in the sunlight, their black hair plastered to their skulls as they laugh and squeal in the breeze. It's a place I'd like to return to, my summers at Waskesiu Lake north of Prince Albert, where I scuttled along the sandy bottom, deeper and deeper into the cool clean water and lay prone in a dead-man's float.

After checking into the motel, we watch breaking news: Trump and Kim Jong Un are in a turf war as to who could annihilate the other with nuclear arsenals first. I turn my back from the screen and a world that seems so distant. Stepping outside, down the dock, I feel the lake slapping against the bottom boards like a softly rocking cradle. A pelican flies overhead and I follow it with my eyes until it's a white pinpoint that soon vanishes altogether. A float plane skids along the surface and chugs towards a nearby dock. Two men, their bodies silhouetted against mercurial light, bend forward and haul on lines that pull the plane into the dock. They secure it—a choreographed dance, a rhythm to their simultaneous movements along the sun dappled shore.

I write in my journal: *feet in lake, surprisingly warm. A stillness. A calm within.*

The central and more northerly part of Saskatchewan is unlike the flat expanses of open prairie in the south. The next morning, we head out and drive for hours through boreal forests, some of which have been ravaged by wildfires.

I write: *A small rodent skittering across the gravel road, then a baby beaver, baby rabbits, two ospreys in a nest and ravens at every turn.*

The terrain is hilly at times, and other times meandering streams cut across marshland. The road is an undulating ribbon of washboard that allows occasional glimpses of lake vistas from high points along the way. It has one thing in common with the more southerly landscape—dust. Just like the big semis that leave us momentarily blinded when passing, the wheels of our SUV also create dust clouds in our wake, perhaps much like those that LAVs generated on the terrain of Kandahar province. With a shudder, I remember a poem, or rather one stanza, in Kanina Dawson's book *Masham Means Evening*.

> *And farther up on the ridgeline overlooking all this*
> *the Pakistani journalist and his Taliban hosts*
> *would have stood, watching a Canadian convoy*
> *approach in the distance, raising dust clouds a mile long.*

North of La Ronge, we stop for fresh air at a bridge over the churning Churchill River. I hoist myself out of the back seat and find myself by a wooden cross, on top of which is a faded, framed photo of a boy, Clarence Richard McDonnell, 1971–1983, and the inscription: *Gave his life to save a friend*. I gaze through trees to the river below and imagine him jumping in, mindless to the immense power of moving water. It was a force I felt when swimming off the Atlantic coast of a Canary Island during the year this boy was born. Waves tossed me about like a pebble, but luck was with me. Between surges, my head bobbed above surface. In that split second before being pulled under again, I caught my breath and stumbled onto the sandy shore minutes later, shaken like I'd never been before. But Clarence was not so lucky. His photo reminds me of Michelle at that age, both in the springtime of their lives, full of hope and promise. Robin walks over and her face falls, both of us wondering if tragedy will stop following us. As we stroll to the middle of the bridge, we snap photos, knowing they can't possibly capture the power of frothy whitecaps skimming at breakneck speed below. They flash over boulders until the water calms just as it nears a widening arc at the river's bend. All blue. All roar.

We drive onward, the thunder from the river lingering in my brain as Colette reflects on her feelings about losing someone close. "People think: 'Oh, it's been a year. All the anniversaries are done. You've moved on, right?' But people don't move on. They move forward. They keep living, but it's always there.

"Michelle really appreciated nature," she says. "I think it's so appropriate that there's a bay named in her honour. It doesn't bring her back, of course, but it acknowledges what a huge sacrifice she made. I feel like by going to it, we honour it."

"It's like she's forever stamped in a place of beauty," Robin adds.

I understand the northern part of the province where we are headed hasn't always been dotted with rivers and lakes or a swampy no man's land. Some hundred million years ago, sea turtles swam in what was then an inland sea stretching from the Gulf of Mexico to the Arctic. It's hard to imagine how that could have been when we arrive at Points North Landing about six and a half hours and 600 kilometres later. Barren and yet rich in intangible ways—wilderness in every direction and the abundant resources that bring folks to these places, to mine, log, fish, hunt. It's no place for pretense; there's a kind of raw energy in the mostly men who work and return to the camp to shower, eat, sometimes brawl and then bed for the night.

I think of my father as I scan the landscape. He probably camped in more primitive digs while earning his university tuition as a hard-rock miner in the 1930s. Much later in life, he recalled those days fondly, days when he was so strong of body and mind. I've brought some of his ashes with me. After all, as Michelle's paternal grandfather, he might lay some claim to the bay named after Michelle. Arthur Lang, veteran of the Second World War and former Saskatchewan resident.

I've tucked his ashes into a corner of my luggage, now parked in my Atco trailer room. It's sparse, but neat and clean, furnished with a single bed, bedside table and sink. There's much to explore on this industrial expanse of gravel and dirt: trailers, machine shops and arena-like dome buildings. Robin, Colette and I eat a late dinner in the cookhouse, served by Alice and Eleanor, two gutsy women who are proud of their joint nickname: The Hoodlums. They lean into each other when I snap their photo, grinning as all get out.

We wander around after eating, wrapped in thought about what tomorrow will bring. At this latitude in August, the days are long. The shadow I cast is like a Henry Moore sculpture, a tiny oblong head, an elongated body with one arm raised in a semi-circle to snap a photo of a large transport bus, McClean Lake Operation emblazoned on its clean white side. A flaccid orange-and-white windsock marks the end of the flat, packed earth, beyond which is a fringe of stunted forest.

Pickup trucks, a Kodiak four-by-four, stacks of oil drums, rows of oil tankers, hills of sand, gigantic rolls of cable, fresh heavy tire marks swirling in the dry earth and hydro poles black against the big prairie sky as daylight begins to turn dusky. We approach a rusted orange barrel drum on an outside edge of the base behind the cabins. "Jacky's Bear Barge" is painted on its side in capital white letters. Nearby, we see bear scat full of berries, and fringes of purple fireweed growing nearby. We gather a handful, a small bouquet to leave for Michelle at Lang Bay tomorrow.

At the towering inukshuk near the entrance to the base, I frame a photo of Colette and Robin. Colette is leaning into the boulders, one leg hung up on the corner of a supporting slab. She's wearing black pants and a short-sleeved black T-shirt that nicely sets off her longish blonde hair and pretty features. The look in her eyes is far away, the kind of look I imagine model photographers seek. Robin leans against the structure, her hands comfortably clasped in front of her navy-and-blue-striped sweater. She bends her dark head ever so slightly into the camera, her mouth twisting into a lighthearted smirk, a mischievous playfulness so much like that of her friend Michelle.

I wander off on my own, kicking up dust as I stroll toward the lake. This quest we're on together, to write or produce our version of events, to get at the heart of why we're here, is on my mind. My thoughts are interrupted when I spot a man behind the wheel of a dusty pickup parked on the dirt.

"Are you waiting for someone?" I ask, stepping forward to greet him.

"Yeah, my sons and I are here to pick up my brother. He's a fishing guide on Hatchett Lake, flying in from his latest trip. He's supposed to be back soon," the man replies, tapping his fingers lightly on the steering wheel and smiling.

"Nice place to wait," I offer. "Where are you from?"

"Stanley Mission," he says.

"Oh, I remember seeing the highway sign when we drove up this afternoon from La Ronge."

One son, on the cab's rooftop, smiles sweetly at me. I notice his cleft lip and ask how his summer is going, but he's super shy. Slipping off the roof, he makes himself scarce. The other son (both are teens) slouches in the passenger seat, his baseball cap pulled low over his forehead as he scrolls through his phone while his father and I talk.

"My name is McLeod. We're Woodland Cree in this part of the province."

"Nice to meet you. I'm Catherine, from Victoria, BC. Tomorrow I'm taking a float plane with two friends to a bay named after my niece—Lang Bay, on Burnett Lake. She was the reporter killed in Afghanistan."

"Yes, I remember hearing about that," McLeod says, nodding. "Sorry for your loss."

Without skipping a beat, he starts talking about his people's ways and the importance of family, the generational sacredness of taking care of one another. I'm lulled by the cadence of his voice as he offers to say a prayer for Michelle tomorrow.

Colette and Robin saunter over, and I introduce McLeod. He extends his arm outside the truck window as Colette and Robin step forward.

"I was telling McLeod about our trip tomorrow," I say. "He's from Stanley Mission."

"I've never been there," Colette says.

"Not many even know about it, let alone visit," he responds, chuckling. "Stop by any time and my boys and I will show you around."

Then he switches to Cree. Like a soft cloud descending, his voice spills over the lake surface. Drifting off in my cozy room later, I take comfort in his kindness. I can't think of anything more fitting than a Cree prayer for Michelle. Perhaps it will place her spirit properly in this ancient land, her sacrifice honoured by descendants of those who came before.

The next morning our pilot, Dave Hanson, stands by while we board a Turbo Otter floatplane at the dock. Robin heads for the cockpit, while Colette and I hunker down in the back. There are enough seats for at least four more people, so the space feels cavernous as it rattles around us.

We cruise above swaths of stunted forest and muskeg. Below, plumes rise from smokestacks at a mill in the distance and one long dirt road veers into a Y, punching its way through the forest for miles. I turn my gaze inward at the instrument panel while Dave answers Robin's questions through headphones. Maybe he's explaining how to pinpoint one small lake in a land covered with hundreds.

With the engine roaring in my ears, I ponder how Michelle wrestled with her predicament during the long flight to Dubai and then on to Kandahar Airfield. After saying goodbye to her fiancé at the Calgary airport, did she curse herself for being so driven, wishing she could be content with her regular beats at home? Maybe she craved one last embrace as she whispered in Michael's ear: "Don't worry, baby-cakes. The time will fly and, before you know it, I'll be home." Was her heart on that flight heavy, like mine is now, tempered nonetheless by the adventure that awaited?

In less than an hour, Dave begins circling above a lake before landing smoothly in the bay. Robin's shoulders drop, softening with relief as we motor loudly to the rocky shoreline. The lake surface is calm, reflecting a mix of grey and blue from the sky above. It's approaching ten o'clock. Closing my eyes, I hope McLeod is pausing before he begins his prayer. I want to be ashore, where I can listen in silence, receptive somehow when his voice tumbles into space.

Dave lashes lengths of yellow rope from the plane to a short, sturdy tree, stomping through muskeg in his knee-high gum boots before helping us ashore. Swatting mosquitos as we go, we trudge through brush and muskeg to a large boulder. Robin lugs her recording gear, while Colette leads the way, clutching a plastic bottle of white wine for our toast.

Robin Summerfield (L) and Colette Derworiz at "Michelle's Landing," Lang Bay, Saskatchewan. The province's geographic naming committee named the remote northeastern bay on Burnett Lake in Michelle's honour. Photo by Catherine Lang

"We made it! It's Michelle's Landing," Robin shouts, referring to the boulder where we stand and survey the lake.

Just then, a loon's haunting call echoes around a bend.

Without a word, our pilot retreats to the cockpit to give us privacy. It's a sweet, unexpected gesture, and one for which I'm grateful when I take a plunge later. I haven't come all this way not to swim in the bay, even though the day is not as hot as I'd like and I've forgotten my bathing suit.

Waist deep near the shore, I sprinkle some of my father's ashes. My fingers dance lightly over the lake's surface as I release soft, silky ash into the clear, cool depths, thinking of how much Dad and Michelle would've loved this northern lake. Whispering their names, I summon them to join me: *Arthur. Michelle.*

Ducking under, through murky, green water, I surface and swim to the middle of the bay in my underwear. Cold but not frigid. The cleansing ritual of immersion, a sweet balm to anxieties large and small. Turning back to shore, I see Robin leaning heavily into Colette, head on her shoulder, weeping, and catch a glimpse of the mauve fireweed bouquet beside them. Colette a stalwart comfort, an arm wrapped tightly around her friend. I push my arms through water, forward and apart in a slow circular pattern, not wanting to intrude. This private grief they share, not just for Michelle but for other deep losses, one on top of another.

Wading over rocks along the lake bottom, I stumble ashore on a small boulder to warm up and sit for a time when Robin calls me over.

"It's time to interview you guys, so get on over here, will 'ya."

On Michelle's Landing, Robin holds out her microphone. I've memorized a stanza of Christina Georgina Rossetti's poem "Remember" for the occasion, mindful of Michelle's love of language, mindful also of her mother's startled response when she discovered the poem in Michelle's handwriting. It's been four years since my brother read it beside Michelle's grave in Vancouver.

We toast Michelle to the heavens. I listen again for the quiet in this wilderness, contemplating how magical and fierce it must be under a sky lit by aurora borealis in winter.

Timeless moments. Timeless concepts. That's what I seek. I find them in the loon's distant call as we turn to leave. It lingers in a sound chamber of my mind, reverberating in our wake.

CHAPTER 15

NORTHEAST TO SOUTHWEST

The engine roars in my ears as I feel the aircraft lift from water to air. A reluctance to leave this silent land settles in my heart. I stare out the window at the passing sweep of lakes cast askew over the landscape, like giant jigsaw puzzle pieces tossed from afar. My mind drifts. I've touched this place where change is embedded in geological time, shaped by forces of nature beyond human comprehension, though regrettably not beyond human intervention.

In no time, the aircraft floats down onto water, and Dave motors to the dock at Points North Landing. Robin, Colette, and I disembark, saying our farewells. Minutes later, we settle our bills and hit the road. Robin climbs into the driver's seat of our dust-caked vehicle, remaining at the wheel for the duration of our trip south. It gives her a focus, something to batten down the grief as we speed along the rough, dusty road for hours again.

At La Ronge, we stop to visit Robertson's Trading Store, a large family enterprise established in 1967. A sandwich board outside welcomes us in Cree: *Mithoogee see gun see.* (Have a good day!) Inside, I wander up and down aisles, snapping photos on my phone, fascinated by the eclectic collection of wares—clothes, kitchenware, groceries and the most comprehensive array of camping, fishing, hunting and guiding gear I've ever seen. Bundles of braided sweet grass in one corner, snowshoes in another; gold pans on shelves near heavy-duty long-handled axes, while an assortment of iron animal traps and moose and bear trophies hang on cluttered walls below the ceiling.

A few men negotiate the price of pelts through a cubby hole at the back of the store. The surrounding display shows a booming business. Select items are priced, like the beaver fur and moosehide gauntlet gloves at $400. I stare at circular racks of Prairie long-tail weasel, squirrel and larger racks heavy with wolf, wolverine, lynx, and beaver pelts. Running the palms of my hands down the thick piles of fur, I wrestle between brain and heart to reconcile this traditional Indigenous trade with the brutality of lives taken—for survival, yes. Nature in all its splendour. Nature in all its suffering. Humankind included.

Outside, Colette and Robin present me with a beaded poppy. I bring it up to my nostrils to inhale the sweet smoky smell of deer hide backing and admire the crimson poppy rimmed in tiny black beads—each one skilfully sewn onto the hide. I stand awkwardly for a moment, touched by their kindness. It's a keepsake I'll wear proudly on Remembrance Day over the coming years, a reminder of our time together as well as our shared loss.

Driving on, we hit pavement again and detour off the road north of Prince Albert to Waskesiu Lake, where I played in the 1950s just like the children swimming in Lac La Ronge now. I have no recollection whatsoever of the forested drive to the national park entrance, which we breeze through since it's Canada's sesquicentennial and park fees have been waived.

But the Waskesiu of my childhood is a bustling resort town now, with a promenade of modern shops and espresso cafés. We join the throngs of vacationers and wander along. Across the street, I spot a small cabin on display, an artifact of my generation. It reminds me of a photo of my sister, Margie, posing on the little porch of one such cabin. My memory of her in shorts and a crisp white sleeveless blouse: beaming, her face uplifted to the sun, her chestnut brown hair tied back in a short ponytail. Basking in the hot sun, leaning against the fence around the tiny porch as if to say "Summer's here, and we're on holiday!"

More throwbacks to the past are on display over there, including a small museum and a log cabin that Grey Owl lived in. Grey Owl, the Englishman who falsely assumed an Indigenous identity, writing romanticized stories of his life on the land. We poke around for a bit, but just like when I was a kid, it's the lake that beckons. Tracking across hot sand beneath a modern playground, we scope out a space on the crowded beach.

"There goes our water baby," Colette says, as I throw down my towel and wade into the lake.

Dads and daughters and sons and mothers laugh and splash about as I plunge under. It's no longer a solitary immersion in remote wilderness and also much warmer when I sink below the sweet silky surface. Blue below and bluer still above.

The three of us will soon go our separate ways. Our journey to Lang Bay in the rear-view mirror, we've completed our goal of stamping Michelle in the northern wilderness. Robin and I drop Colette off in Prince Albert. She'll head home to Cranbrook, BC. At the John Diefenbaker airport in Saskatoon, I drop Robin off for her flight home to Winnipeg. But I'm not flying anywhere yet, only halfway through my days in the hot, bleached Land of Living Skies. First to Regina, then to the farm.

A grain elevator draws me off Highway 1 into small-town Saskatchewan in the south, on my way to Regina. I spot Craik and its white clapboard tower rising into a brilliant sky, a smattering of rail cars with "Saskatchewan Wheat Pool" emblazoned on their sides. Not a soul in sight, the air still with dry heat. I wander the tracks and ponder helter-skelter piles of railroad ties, some gleaming with creosote, tossed aside to rot. I let the stinking heat penetrate my bones. I listen to the symphonic clack of crickets and smell dry grasses. No breeze to dip and bend their slender, bleached-white stalks. Could Michelle have stood in a place such as this, I wonder, feeling the same heat in her bones?

I discover the Craik museum, deserted but open "on request." It's a smattering of charming white buildings, the size of sheds. Signs inform visitors: "Pioneer house" and "News office." I contemplate what news they cranked out in this one-room building—perhaps of livestock and grain prices, weather patterns, maybe even government relief in hard times. All the buildings are like one-room schoolhouses from a pioneering era. The only structure that's open inside is an old-fashioned washroom with a functioning toilet, faded, flowery wallpaper and a tiny sink and mirror.

In my wanderings, I find remnants of the prairie Dad knew intimately when in charge of various railroad spur lines. Decades after quitting his job, he sketched the geometric patterns of a rail network and scribbled the names of towns in his illegible handwriting, a gesture to preserve fragments from his past. I inherited his copy of *Prairie Branches: Canadian National Railways in Southern Saskatchewan*. Craik is one such town, and the book, a relic of a bygone era when air travel was too expensive for most.

The nostalgia I feel for a simpler time is as intense as the heat. Some twenty years later, when Michelle skipped across her back alley to play with her friend, my life was less simple. I'd moved abruptly from a childhood of carefree innocence to one of anxiety and insecurity after my father quit his CNR job. When we landed in Vancouver following two difficult years in Winnipeg, I was ten. For Michelle, home remained in the tony Vancouver neighbourhood where she grew up until, at twenty-four, she took her first reporting job in Prince George in 1999.

My gracious host in Regina, Betsy Kalmakoff, is the oldest sister of my childhood friend Janey. She beckons me inside her spacious condo on McIntyre Street, within walking distance of the Saskatchewan legislature.

"You haven't changed much, Betsy," I say, looking into her black eyes. "How many years has it been since we saw each other?"

"A lifetime ago, I'm sure," she says.

Betsy's shoulder-length dark hair is greying, but I still recognize her from the Hallowe'en newspaper photo in a long-ago family album. She was the tallest of three adolescent girls, my sister included, all with wide, toothy grins, clutching their trick-or-treat pillowcases at someone's front door.

Almost right away, we're into long, in-depth conversations, remembering our parents and our years in Prince Albert, as well as where life took us when our families moved away.

Regina is my home base for several days. I have research to do in this city where Michelle worked as a reporter, but I'm also here to explore and have some fun. At night, Betsy and I head across a city park to the Regina Folk Festival on the dry, packed earth. By day, we wander into the Regina Art Gallery, staring at huge canvases of other-worldly paintings—abstract images, bold colours, all mystical images of a visionary artist. Alex Janvier, a Denesuline man from Cold Lake First Nation, a residential school survivor whose talent was recognized by nuns but who nonetheless didn't escape the trauma embedded in those walls.

Out into the bright sunlight, we process the impact of his body of work and stroll around Wascana Lake, pausing before a bronze statue of a starving girl child. Clutching scant stalks of wheat, she's a memorial to the Holodomor, Josef Stalin's murderous campaign in the Ukraine in the early 1930s. Certainly, terrorism of one form or another predates our times.

One afternoon, I arrange to meet Cliff Walker, a retired brigadier-general, at the Saskatchewan war memorials on the legislative grounds. Walking around the site, he begins by pointing to Michelle's name among those of fallen soldiers who served in Afghanistan. He's proud of the fact that the memorial site committee didn't hesitate to include her. I pause to consider this, wondering how, as a journalist, she might have felt. He escorts me around several monuments that make up this installment to the fallen from Saskatchewan. It took arduous coordinating efforts to research and contact families in order to create these bronze plaques, their lengthy columns dating back to the Boer War. Lists

Michelle's mother, Sandy Lang, wipes a tear from her eye following the unveiling of an Afghanistan memorial plaque at the Saskatchewan War Memorial in Regina, October 2010. Photo courtesy Postmedia

of Saskatchewan's dead from the First World War, Second World War, Korea and Afghanistan also include those from peacekeeping missions over the years. Finally, we stand before a towering, creamy-white pillar on top of which is a statue of a World War 1 nurse. Turning to me, Cliff shares his memories of the day it was dedicated to nurses on the front lines of "The War to End All Wars."

After we part, I find a quiet spot to decompress. Amidst all the carnage of the past hundred-plus years, Michelle's name is one of few civilians—just a reporter, embedded with soldiers, doing her job.

One morning, I head out to interview Colleen Silverthorn at her summer home on Echo Lake in the Qu'Appelle River Valley. Another colleague of Michelle's from the *Regina Leader-Post*, Colleen plans to make me lunch. But I learn the hard way that the flat prairie doesn't lend itself well to orienting myself in the right direction. Hours after setting out, I discover I've been driving in circles on the south side of Regina when I should have been driving northeast.

Arriving at Colleen's, I'm exasperated, embarrassed, hungry and very late. I dig into the food she's set aside, explaining that after countless stops for directions and finally heading north, a special constable rescued me on the last stretch into the valley. He escorted me along a gravel road, past sparkling watery marshes as a golden eagle glided by at eye level.

Colleen laughs and recounts a few stories, easing my anxiety.

"Michelle skidded into her two-year stint in Regina in the middle of a prairie blizzard and late for her first day of work. Her car had died on the side of the highway, and she'd hitchhiked into Regina from Moose Jaw in a CBC news van and arrived late for her first Agribition news conference.

"This was after she'd gotten the job in the first place by arriving half an hour late for her job interview at the Hotel Sask, driving right on by Regina's landmark hotel and ending up on the other end of the city.

"She was so obviously a rising star that she still got the job," Colleen says, pulling out notes from the eulogy she wrote for Michelle's memorial.

"And this one cracks me up, too. She once came back to work complaining about the stupid city planning in east Regina where drive-through windows were on the wrong side of the car—because she had to lean over the passenger seat to get her food.

"We explained to her that she'd actually gone through the drive-through backwards."

Oh, Michelle. You loveable, sometimes scatterbrained, smart and funny woman. I laugh and wonder if I channelled her today. Was she out there someone, holding on to her tummy and giggling at my frantic efforts to point the car in the right direction?

Sitting at a picnic table in her garden, Colleen and I talk for almost two hours. Her husband, Sean Frisky, and her dark-haired daughter, Allie, listen in. Allie is twelve, full of curiosity and energy, lean and pretty. She bounces around, hitting her tennis ball against the paved patio stones. Sean is quiet while Colleen speaks, a rapid-fire rush of words and memories. He knew and loved Michelle too. Perhaps he's reflecting on the good times when Michelle sat alongside them, passing long, slow summer days by the lakeshore.

Their oldest daughter, Sam, fourteen, shows up, her long blonde hair backlit by the summer sun. She remembers Michelle and speaks in a small voice that belies her tall grace. The youngest daughter, Syd, appears as well. About ten months old when Michelle was killed, Syd has no memory of this friend her mother speaks about with such passion.

It's a small world, this clutch of reporters whose lives keep criss-crossing. Colleen and Colette went to university together. Colleen met Robin through Mike, who was her colleague at the *Leader Post*. In the Regina newsroom, Colleen, Mike and Michelle were a hard-working trio, partying just as hard when the work day was done. Now they're both gone, while the memories remain deeply lodged. She reveals why she didn't come to Lang Bay: "I worked really hard to process Michelle's death. I almost had a panic attack at the thought of going there."

Between stories about wild nights out, dancing and cruising the bars, Colleen talks about her close-knit bond with Michelle as a colleague. They scrambled to get stories and meet deadlines, sitting side by side at their desks.

"Michelle and I just clicked. Intense situations sometimes breed strong connections, good friendships. We were both trying to break stories, and we were each other's cheerleaders, working crazy deadlines, high stress. Michelle and I never had a sad moment together, except for covering September 11."

As the newspaper's political reporter, Colleen went to the legislature to get then-Premier Lorne Calvert's response. Back at the newsroom, she found Michelle frantically working the phones to find a Canadian eyewitness in New York City.

"I don't even know how you do that. You just start phoning people. Somebody knows somebody who's in NYC. A lot of phone lines were down and not as many people had cell phones then."

But Michelle was persistent. Hours after trying to reach someone who worked in downtown Manhattan, she finally got through.

"She talked to a man who watched the trade centre collapse. She held it together on the phone, of course, but afterwards she was sobbing," Colleen recalls. "I remember going into the bathroom with her. I basically had to hold her up for a long time. She was so traumatized. In a way, it was that day that ultimately led to her death, too."

Later, I research the article Michelle wrote. On September 12, 2001, she shared a byline with other reporters, under the headline "I'm not getting out of this inferno."

Seconds after Grant Harder heard the hijacked plane hit the first World Trade Center building, he looked out his office window to see a single red baseball cap floating through the air among bits of ceiling tiles and chunks of wall.

For the former North Battleford resident, it was the first sign of the tragedy that was taking place at the World Trade Center, located across the street from where he works.

It wouldn't be the last.

"To put it in human terms, a girl I work with, her friend's fiancé called her from the 100th floor and said good-bye to her. He said 'I'm not getting out of this inferno'."

I pause to soak in the irony of how things unfolded. Michelle traumatized by a stranger's story: a co-worker whose friend was saying good-bye to her fiancé while watching the towers burn and collapse before her eyes. Michelle, no longer the objective reporter and not even a decade later, a casualty of the War on Terror herself.

Talk of her crazy escapades with Michelle and Mike slip away as Colleen recalls the hysterical phone call from Colette that broke the news about Michelle. In a fog, Colleen had handed her baby to someone, who exactly she can't recall. Frantic, she rushed headlong into the frozen world outdoors, breaking the night silence with her screams.

Sean asks if I'd like to go for a boat ride. "Absolutely," I say. It has been intense, listening to his wife reminisce. I follow them along a path to their dock. We board a pristine white motorboat, and Sean soon gets the engine purring. I lean back in the comfy cockpit, lifting my glass of red wine and smiling at Colleen, while Sean motors out to the middle of the lake. It's long, with cottages along one side and a mostly uninhabited dry embankment on the other—much like the Okanagan terrain where Michelle and her brother Cam played on their summer holidays. Sean pulls close to the opposite shore, and we face a plot of land where a dilapidated tuberculosis sanatorium treated patients from 1912 to 1971. It was also home to the Saskatchewan Summer School of the Arts, also known as the Sage Hill Writing Experience, where prominent Canadian authors gathered over the years.

"Michelle and I used to come here and walk around," Colleen says, gazing at the tangled mass of prairie grasses and shrubs, sand-coloured and wild.

"We could feel a presence. It wasn't frightening, but it was very eerie. It was like we could feel old spirits crouching in the tall grass as we stomped around, looking for remnants of the former buildings and conjuring up spirits of the dead."

I listen to the silence. The lake cradles us, rippling water lapping against the boat's waterline. The heat of the day rises from the shore, warming my bones like sun on a stretch of flat lava. I search for a place to step ashore. The land is level, then rises slightly up a hill, beyond which I cannot see. I concentrate on the criss-crossing of twigs, shrubs and grasses in a hollow where perhaps white-tailed deer and antelope lie at night.

Maybe it's a mix of fescue, blue stem or buffalo grass? Or a mix of common yarrow, showy milkweed and meadow goat's beard? I love the sound of native plant names, but I've absolutely no clue. We're not close enough to shore to see fine distinctions—shapes, textures, smells—nor do I know enough to identify whether these are native to this land. I sink deeper into the quiet. It's fluid and warm, filaments of light stirring a grove of cottonwood trees as the lake rocks gently against the hull. I feel an urge to walk the land, sit on its rises and ponder the meaning of life and of death, of loss and my own journey through it.

Maybe I want to believe that Michelle's spirit rests here occasionally. It would be a perfect place to watch over Colleen and her family. Colleen, who learned of Michelle's death while suffering post-partum depression and who remains fragile almost eight years later. Colleen, whose back is wedged into a corner of the boat's cockpit, her cropped blonde hair and pretty blue eyes scanning the lake. The grand vista of this coulee rising, the breadth of a blue whale, slumbering between both sides of this valley as far as the eye can see.

"Echo Valley Resorts bought the property from the government a while back." Colleen says, turning to face Sean.

"Yeah, we're afraid for its future," Sean replies, his hand resting on the engine throttle. A good-looking man of few words, he watches: there at the ready should Colleen need him. The day's light is beginning to fall, and with it, the temperature shifts a notch. Sean starts the engine, though he puts it in the lowest gear. We glide southwards, the bow slicing the water in one long uninterrupted arc. Silhouettes ripple as we circle the shoreline around to the west end. A patchwork of houses—some cottages, many well-kept permanent homes—with water views and the accoutrements of summer living: docks, skiffs, canoes and kayaks, swimming ladders and water toys. Fluorescent pinks, greens and oranges all akimbo on front lawns. It's notorious gang country, too—Indian Posse and Native Syndicate—Colleen tells me. There's much more to this gentrified place than meets the eye.

Soon after, we step ashore and say our goodbyes. At least I know my way back to Regina, though a part of me is loath to leave.

Earlier, Colleen told me: "It's funny. I've forgotten so much, Catherine."

In the days to come, I fear she may have remembered too much.

Chapter 16

UNCLE AXEL'S FARM

This journey of mine to learn about Michelle's life is a quest to better understand her, to somehow fill in the pieces I missed when she still walked this earth. In doing so, I'm getting closer to the many lands in this nation of ours. I already knew the Vancouver where she grew up. Part of my growing up years were there, too. But while my family life took me from east to west, hers went the other way, and in looking for the places she went as a young adult, an ambitious and talented woman embarking on a promising career, I see how she was burrowing her roots deeper in the provinces of my birth and early years.

When Michelle got a job at the *Moose Jaw Times-Herald* in 2000, she often went to my great-uncle's farm in nearby Herbert. She was the newspaper's agriculture reporter, a topic she knew little about. Her cousins three times removed had solid working knowledge of the difference between a free-enterprise wheat pool and a government-controlled one, and she wanted to know every little detail, what made some things work and what made other things complicated. Therein often lay the story she sought to etch from facts and figures, bringing a human element to her reports wherever possible.

It was her first job at a daily newspaper, one she hoped would be a stepping stone to a major daily in a big city. In the early months after moving to Moose Jaw, I imagine her sitting in a diner, tumbleweed rolling down a lacklustre street, wondering about her future. She rests her head on to the table and sheds a few tears. Maybe she's homesick or sad about the man she left behind in Prince George. Or maybe she fears forever getting stuck in small-town Saskatchewan, almost 1,500 kilometres from home.

On August 20, 2017, I follow Michelle's footsteps to the farm east of Swift Current. Herbert is a typical Prairie town with a quiet breed of people who came from all over as settlers to the "World's Choicest Wheat Lands," as government ads once boasted.

I stop for gas in town before driving the dusty grid roads to the farm, trying to follow directions from my father's cousin, Ken. I'm sure he could find his way home in a blizzard or a dust storm, but it's like a maze to me. "Take the road to the first four-way and turn right. At the next stop, turn left and go about a mile. At the next grid, turn left again." And so on. I'm completely baffled within a few minutes, so I call him on my cell. He talks me past a few stops until I finally spot steel silos with the name NELSON—an anglicized version of my great uncle's surname, Nilsson—rising above the horizon. The sprawling property is where the paternal roots of my family began in Canada. I never met my great uncle. He immigrated to Canada from Almhult, Sweden, followed by his seventeen-year-old sister—my grandmother—and built the farmhouse that Ken lives in some hundred years on.

Today, two houses sit on the property, along with scattered heaps of rusting farm equipment as well as equipment still in use—all John Deeres. The house to my left looks semi-abandoned, with a six-by-six chunk of wood set up as a step to the front porch. A white Great Pyrenees dog is in front of the newer home to my right, so I approach the older house and peer inside. Piles of dust-covered, broken furniture are strewn about haphazardly. A "Red Indian Motor Oils" poster hangs prominently from one wall, crimson on one half of a diagonal line and black on the other, it frames a red-faced "Indian" chief with braids hanging below his headdress.

No one lives *here*, I think to myself. I've got to try the house next door, so I look for a way to slide past the wary dog when a tall, lanky man steps out the front door.

"You must be Catherine," he says, extending his long arm to greet me. "I'm Shayne. C'mon in. We're waiting for you."

I step inside to meet my second cousins, my great-uncle's sons, Ken and Don. Don's wife, Sharon, holds a toddler, Sierra, on her lap and waves an arm at a plump boy named Asanee. He's wide-eyed and grinning. I grin back and wonder if Sierra, whose black pigtails stick out on top of her head, is Asanee's sister or cousin. I sit down at the kitchen table, and we begin to get acquainted.

Day three on the farm. The wind blows hot, so I sit in shade outside the house that Uncle Axel built in about 1912. I doubt it was ever like this when he and his Norwegian wife, Anna, lived here, although no doubt there were lots of flies even then with all the butchering and livestock and manure. I'm acclimatizing, but slowly, reluctantly.

Day four on the farm, Don, Ken and I scatter the last of Dad's ashes on a lookout in the pasture above Shayne's farm. We crouch on our haunches to tuck them into a hollow beneath a boulder where a petro-glyph is carved into an ancient lichen-covered stone. Later, I wonder if my relatives ever asked their Indigenous friends about the significance of this petroglyph. Was it a marker for ceremonial gatherings? Or a strategic point for scouts to scan the landscape?

The farm is where Dad wanted to live out his final days, but it was just one of countless wild ideas he had in life, for he was far too frail to go anywhere at the end. Now I like to think of his spirit resting alongside other prairie folk—ancient ones who were the first peoples of this land and the more recent settlers, all of whom shared a deep love of the wind-blown prairies.

I study the rolling fields of wheat, golden and carved in elegant lines and curves as four giant green combines work in sync to harvest the grain, plumes of dust filling the air as they cut and slice with enormous spikes on rake-like lengths of steel, up and over the hills and down dips in the plains, while little birds fly suddenly skyward to avoid the steel teeth, flit-ting to another spot and then another. How much has changed since Dad came here as a youngster, I wonder, thinking of the faded, milky photo of him and his siblings standing by a hay wagon, a pitchfork in his hand.

"Those little birds don't stand a chance," Dave, a twenty-five-year-old Hutterite man, tells me one day, his voice gentle. "Once the birds reveal their location, hawks will swoop down for the kill."

I'm sitting aloft in the super high-tech cab of his combine. It's air-conditioned, fitted out with GPS and video cameras ahead, below and behind. Was it as high tech in 2000 when Michelle went for a similar ride?

I glance at Dave's profile. He's very cute and easygoing, confident as he shares his knowledge about life on the land, his sentences punctuated with "You betcha." We chat about how the combine works and wheth-er Hutterite women operate them (they don't, but other women do, and Dave thinks they're better at it than men). It's "the farm boss" who decides which fields and what crops to harvest, not a job he wants. "Too much pressure," he says, nodding his head toward the gravel road below where the boss is leaning against a dusty pickup and checking his pocket watch under suspenders. When I step outside the air-conditioned cab later, I feel a wall of heat shrink-wrap the skin around my bones.

On another stifling hot day with no breeze, Ken and Don drive me to the Hutterite colony. They know their way around because they do business there, and Ken is hopeful we might get an invitation to a sit-down meal in their hall. But the vast complex is empty outside, save for one lonely boy walking the length of the mammoth steel-sided hog factory, kicking stones in the dust as he paces back and forth. Ken suggests it's this boy's job today, guarding the building for long, stinky hours at a time. He can't be more than nine years old.

We drive around, about to give up, when we see a man digging in the earth, a gaggle of children around him, playing and running down a ridge of dirt. He walks over to greet us. Ken and I get out of the car to shake hands with him, the children's teacher as it turns out.

Arne is swarthy, handsome and welcoming. A man who is proud of his place in this community, he says: "I teach them old German."

"Really?" I ask. "What is old German? And why do you teach them that?"

"It's our custom, our history, our culture," he replies, explaining that the children aren't in school right now, but they are still under his care out here.

They straggle shyly forward in twos or threes, boys with black-peaked caps on their heads, ever so curious about us. Then two little girls creep forward. The face of the smallest is almost obscured by the long brim of her grey-blue bonnet. She dares a faint smile when I try asking her name. None of the children says a word. They simply stand and stare.

I suppress my instinct to take their picture, this little gathering of children living a life from another time and place. I fear it would be rude, and it probably would be. They are people, not curiosities, after all. Still, it's a piece of this prairie mostly hidden from view. The scene is reminiscent of the children watching Canadian soldiers huddled around Afghan elders in Hosi Aziz, Michelle pictured towards the back, head down, scribbling furiously in her steno pad. Did she have a second to look over at them and smile, wishing she, too, could take their picture to capture a world beyond our knowing?

I glance over to the rows of houses in straight lines. It must be brand-new, for there are no trees or grassy areas to speak of. A woman wearing a bonnet steps out her front door to fetch a child playing in the dirt yard. I wonder if she'll be joining other women in a communal hall somewhere, cooking or sewing the hours away. And again, I'm reminded of the similarities with the lives of many Afghan women—isolated in their homes except for when they gather in groups to cook or sew, far from the prying eyes of the outside world.

Ken, Don, and I say our farewells to the teacher and children and drive onto the dirt roads that crisscross each other in a seemingly endless fashion, over undulating hills and stands of Cypress trees along ridges. An old wooden home sits alone in a large field, almost tilting with the grade of the slope, casting an elongated shadow across the land.

These fields surround the town of Herbert, where Ken, Don, and Sharon take me out to a Chinese restaurant, one of two eateries in the town and the only one open in the evening. The other serves homemade pierogis at one end of the museum where a CNR station once operated, but it's only open for lunch. I can count on one hand the traffic that rumbles through Herbert, both vehicle and pedestrian, on a busy day.

This tiny town is Ken's domain. After twenty-five years on Herbert town council—eleven as a councillor and fourteen as the reeve—he knows everyone. And given how Ken loves to talk, he remains the consummate farmer-cum-politician in this town which, like so many around the grid roads of southwestern Saskatchewan, is a step back in time. I walk its streets, the main road through town and the residential cross streets and wonder: how long can it survive? The grain elevators by the highway, once stocked with harvests destined for export across Canada and beyond, weathering under the breathless summer sun and whistling winter wind. Maybe Michelle thought of writing about it, never having enough time after all her day's assignments.

For when Ken's generation of farmers pass, the Hutterites will remain and also a handful of family members who, like Shayne, will continue to work the land, raise livestock, fix farm equipment and houses and outbuildings, not to mention carry on the requisite wheeling and dealing of grain and cattle markets, about which Michelle once wrote while on the agriculture beat less than twenty years before.

One morning, Ken and I sit across from each other at the table, piles of papers scattered here and there. I turn to look out the window, sunshine streaming in. Vehicles are spread across the dry, packed earth behind which are towering, gleaming silos.

Turning back to Ken, I say: "Tell me about Michelle."

"Well, we were always excited to see her, of course. She was so lively and asked so many questions," he replies. "And she had the best questions, things I hadn't thought much about for a while."

"Do you have any special memories of her?" I ask.

Ken pauses. "Not that I can think of right now. I mean, she was always thoughtful and nice to spend time with. We always wanted her to stay longer than she could. Of course, we got her up in a combine, too. She loved that!

"We missed her when she moved from Regina to Calgary," Ken says.

I nod. "She wasn't here long before the *Leader-Post* scooped her from the Moose Jaw paper and then she got scooped again. I bet she missed you guys too when she left for Calgary."

"I suppose," Ken says, looking out the window. "It was a real shock when she was killed. And very sad."

We sit for a while without speaking. Soon we make our way outside.

I want to hold onto the spell of the wide open, stunning plains but know it will inevitably fade with each passing hour and day once I'm back in a city where people's lives revolve much more around pretense and urgency of time. Here I'm learning to sit and stare into nothingness and let the pace of life fall into a slow unravelling of moments. I'm not always at ease, though.

The flies (incessant). The clutter and piles of junk (everywhere). The dust (embedded).

I wonder if Michelle felt as overwhelmed by the flies as me. I acclimatize as the days pass, trying to set judgment aside and accept things as they are, just as they accept me for who I am—a family member, variously introduced to townsfolk as cousin or daughter of cousin by Ken, the scrappy, wiry guy with his thick, grey hair askew and eyes as sharp as a sleuth.

Sharon, the mother of all, her body bent, wayward somehow as she moves her heft and occasionally barks at the kids, mostly at Asanee whom she takes to Bible school. She talks in an easy stream about Juanita, their adopted daughter, now gone, dead at forty-one from alcoholism. She arrived in their home at the age of three, having already gone through two or three foster homes.

"She never felt like she belonged," Sharon tells me, while Juanita's daughter Abigail walks around with a wild, side-to-side lopsided gait, smiling brightly at me, her dark hair sprung out in frizzy curls at the sides of her wonky face. Shayne is feeding cereal and homemade applesauce, spoon by spoon, into her mouth.

Don sits quietly at the table or hobbles to the car to accompany Ken and me—out to the fields and into town, to the Presbyterian cemetery where our relatives lie in rest. He points out this and that on the land that is his expansive backyard, knowing it with his hands and body and brain in ways I never will. A seeming blankness in his big, sad blue eyes, except when he smiles and a deep-seated kindness surfaces.

Ken is the stubborn one, determined to go his way but apologizing for the state of affairs not being more "presentable," saying he's going to do any number of things, like take Max, the chocolate brown, arthritic spaniel, to the vet after he gives him a bath. Max's fur is matted and a lump protrudes from his belly, but he wags his cropped tail and lies by Ken's feet, following his master wherever he goes. Ken also plans to get around to the jury-rigged light fixtures and bulbs hanging down, electrical cords springing out from sockets, as well as install the sauna he bought at an auction for $800. A well-made unit, it's stuck in a corner in a back room off the tiny kitchen.

Beautiful, heavy wooden furniture is at every turn—cabinets and chests, an old wooden phone. Antiques galore, inside and out, hidden amidst the rubble. The half-finished railing on steep, narrow stairs that lead to a landing on the top floor, on one side of which is an unfinished room, access blocked by more junk—an old metal walker and stacked up paintings and pictures, one an aerial view of the farm when it was tidy and freshly painted and the yard around out-buildings was green with grass.

Am I so different? I live in a townhouse with screen doors and a husband who can't abide houseflies, but I have yet to let go of stuff I've carted from here to there throughout my life. I tell myself it's because I don't have time or energy, which is partly true. But it also involves letting go of attachments, like my portfolio of clippings from my reporting days. In truth, that's the real reason why I have stuff stashed into every possible nook and cranny in my home, too.

The room I sleep in is likely the master bedroom, with a brass bed-frame and faded handmade quilt, built-in floor-to-ceiling dark wooden cupboards across one wall, two chests of drawers, one decorated with hand-carved elephants and antelopes from an African savannah. When I ask about them, Shayne tells me that his grandmother—my great uncle's wife, Anna—took him and his brother to Kenya to see the wild animals when they were young.

There are wild animals in these parts, too. The herd of bucks that move away from us in the pasture. When we stop to look, they stare back from their prairie hill, antler racks pointing skyward, silhouetted against the light-diffused sky. One set of antlers bigger than all the rest, the dominant male, sentinel.

On another occasion, we spot a small herd of pronghorn antelope in tall grasses. Even more skittish, their hides a smooth blonde brown, white markings on their rumps. I hold my breath, hoping they will linger. But no. The moment is gone. I hear my father singing a song from my childhood. *Home, home on the range, where the deer and the antelope roam... and where seldom is heard a discouraging word and the sky is not cloudy all day.*

When I return to Regina and Betsy's home, I ponder how I'm changed. From northeast to southwest and places in between, I've witnessed the landscape shift from rock and forest and lakes to the silent small towns with abandoned grain elevators and piles of decaying railroad ties, dust blowing down empty streets, small businesses shuttered or clinging to a bygone way of life. With their strip malls and brand-new suburbs, the cities draw the young and some oldsters away. Gone are the back alleys of my youth, where my friends and I played kick the can. My mother, watching on from the backyard, where the porcelain tub of her wringer washer jostled in the summer grass.

The old downtown cores of Prince Albert and Moose Jaw with tired, old buildings that have long lost their shine. Regina and Saskatoon are thriving though, at least the parts that I see. Their downtown cores are vibrant with culture, universities, art galleries and museums as well as parks and waterways, well-maintained neighbourhoods and old, wooden three-storey houses—places you can escape to with a view above the canopy of a tree-lined street and a sense of being outdoors in the comfort of old floral couches and wooden rocking chairs.

Yes, I'm nostalgic for a time when rushing was less pervasive and distractions far fewer. Where there was time to watch a breeze flutter kitchen curtains and stare at nothing in particular at all. Time doesn't stand still, but I can on occasion.

How fortunate I am to know that wealth can be measured by abundance of experience, companionship and nature—the timelessness of the prairie sky or a herd of domesticated bison staring from the ridge of a rolling field, their dark brown hulk rooted against a late afternoon golden glow. Where glaciers cut into the Canadian Shield to create boulders and rivers and lakes. Where Cree, Dakota, Assiniboine and Dene made their mark on the land, carving petroglyphs, creating middens wherever they went. Where ancient burial grounds gave way to pasture and crops of durum wheat, lentil, canola, barley and flax, where homesteaders—my ancestors among them—built a new life. Sadly, it was often without regard for those who came before.

Heading from Regina to Saskatoon yesterday, I felt a deep sense of having truly been out and of the land. I will depart in moments, sufficiently brown as a berry, ready to take flight for the west, my home. About to board the plane, I turn around and call a simple image of Michelle to mind, envisioning her as she went about her way in this place, so far from home for the first time in her young life. Before she went to Calgary where she got her dream job, where she found her soulmate. Before she went to Afghanistan, hoping to meet women and children getting an education while war raged around them. All she ever wanted, I think, was to keep learning and grow from it, while also writing to inform and cultivate compassion.

I duck my head inside the aircraft, thinking as I stroll down the aisle to my seat. I came to learn about Michelle and to see for myself the mark she made on this province. I also came to rediscover the province I knew as a child. Looking out the airplane window, I mumble: *What a fine adventure I'm on.* Although deeply sad that Michelle isn't alongside me, I take comfort from meeting the folks she crossed paths with as she went on her way—a reciprocal remembering of her endearing self.

April 7, 2018

Dear Michelle,

I've met the parents of Andrew Nuttall a few times, the soldier who died while on foot patrol in Panjwaii district one week before you were killed. One of your colleagues told me that you were afraid you were going to cry during his ramp ceremony. You were afraid because you had a job to do—to tell the story of a fallen Canadian soldier to the Canadian public back home. It was the only ramp ceremony you reported on.

His parents live here in Victoria. I bumped into his father, Richard, four months after returning from Saskatchewan. We were in a church in Cordova Bay for a pre-Christmas bluegrass festival, of all things. It felt a bit uncanny at the time because while the John Reischmann quartet was taking a break, I walked away from the buzz in the hallway into the church library set off in a quiet, little alcove. The uncanny part was that I headed directly for a bookshelf, as if drawn there by an invisible tether. A handful of books were perched along the top of the bookshelf. Reaching out for one, I found myself looking at the cover photo of Andrew on top of a mountain, his arms stretched wide as if to say *life is good, live it every day, do good in the world, seize all possibilities.* I leafed through it at my leisure before returning to the hall for the rest of the concert. That was when I spotted Richard sitting along the back wall near the entrance.

"Hello, Richard," I said, extending my hand. "I'm Catherine Lang, Michelle Lang's aunt."

"Oh, yes. I remember," he replied, taking my hand into the warmth of his palm.

"I just saw the book on Andrew in the library," I said.

"Did you? Oh, let me show you," he said, instantly on his feet to guide me back to the library. He picked the book up and pointed at Andrew's face, his fingers gently smoothing over the cover.

"This was Andrew's church, you know."

"I didn't know that. The book does a great job of capturing how much Andrew loved life," I said.

"Thank you, Catherine. He did so much in the time he had. We were very proud of him."

We walk back to where the music was beginning again and parted ways, each of us to our own seat.

It goes without saying that Richard misses his son terribly. I saw it in the slump of his shoulders and in his eyes—a fracture in his heart. But there we were, doing perhaps what both you and Andrew would have wanted. Living in the moment, listening to the sweet and sad mix of fine musicians, their gifts spilling from mandolins, banjo, guitars, bass and voice. As the sound filled our heads, our bodies swung in silence and the longing that lingers dissipated. Despite sorrow, the rhythms of life, the joy of it all was ours for the moment.

I don't know the back story, but it was Richard Nuttall who made sure that Victoria had its own memorial to commemorate our mission in Afghanistan. Evidently, the granite monument, inscribed with 160 names of Canadians who died serving in Afghanistan, travelled thousands of kilometres to its permanent home behind Victoria's law courts. A few weeks before the unveiling in September 2017, I saw a picture of Richard in the local rag, the *Times Colonist*, but I already knew about the event. Everyone came over for it, including your Michael, and of course Bruce, Sam and I were there, too. I could see Richard from a distance, and I spotted Andrew's mother Jane in the crowd, but the afternoon unfolded according

Catherine Lang points to Michelle's name on the Afghanistan Memorial in Victoria, September 2017. Photo by Gisèle Bentley

to a predetermined script, so I didn't connect on that occasion.

Her Excellency Shinkai Karokhail, Afghanistan's ambassador to Canada, spoke. Though difficult to understand her English, she had the bearing of a noblewoman, standing at the microphone and speaking directly to all those assembled. I think you'd have been impressed by her, too. When she remarked that the Afghan people will not forget Canada and the sacrifices made by Canadians, I felt a mix of pride and humility. Countless more Afghans died and families suffered terrible loss, yet they remember Canada for stepping forward to help in the fight for democracy? Something about that feels unreal to me, though there's also truth to it. Those who went—you to witness and report, the soldiers to serve—demonstrated courage beyond my grasp.

Lieutenant-Governor Judith Guichon also spoke, and even though public speaking isn't one of her strong points, I was moved by her remarks. She said that while the general public have short memories, "those days are seared forever into memory" for the families and for those who served. Premier John Horgan spoke. Very briefly. He lost a friend in Afghanistan, Myles Mansell, and choked up as he said his name. When I visit the memorial, I look for Myles' name now, too.

A whole raft of military and political dignitaries surrounded the podium during the speeches, including Walt Natynczyk. Every time I think of him, I see you sitting side by side, grinning widely, all helmeted up in the back of a LAV. Must have been when you accompanied him and the others on the tour of forward operating bases around Christmastime. Anyway, I digress.

Before the speeches, I shook hands with the soldier whose image is etched into the memorial slab. He came all the way from Cape Breton, if I remember correctly, to lead the military parade that wet September day. The image is based on a photograph of him leaning to the right, his arm outstretched to grasp the hand of an Afghan boy. Like the majority of servicemen and women, he was there to provide a measure of security to this little boy whose future was so uncertain. As I write this to you, I wonder how old that boy is now and whether he's still alive.

During the ceremony, I sat alongside Art, Sandy, Cam, Sandra, their two children—the niece named after you and your nephew, neither of whom knew you, or you, them—and your love, Michael Louie. Bruce and Sam stood strong beside me. Family, once again. Ours among many—Memorial Cross Families—all of us having lost a brother, a husband, a son, a daughter, a mother, a sister, a niece or nephew. Art introduced me to a father whose son didn't die in combat. He fell into a deep irrigation well in a field, and despite his comrades' valiant efforts, they couldn't find a way to lift him out. His father stood in front of me, and as I stared at his back, I wondered how he keeps on. Does he wake in the morning imagining his brave son stranded deep in the earth, hoping against hope for another chance at life?

Near the end of the ceremony, he stood beside your father and the other Memorial Cross fathers, all of them assembled in a small circle before the brand new memorial slab. Richard Nuttall remembering Andrew in that sad gathering, too. Rev. Jim Short, a military chaplain who served in Afghanistan in 2008, led them in prayer, paying tribute to the nineteen men who died during his deployment and his promise to remember them every day.

"May the words I speak now connect us as a community with a common purpose. May this sacred stone, this hallowed ground, be a place of remembrance, of inspiration, of comfort, of reflection, reminding our country of those who have served," he said.

If I close my eyes, I see your dad, head down, legs slightly apart, arms loose at his side. Not being religious, I sensed his discomfort during the prayer, stoic in his nicely tailored suit, a light lustre in the fabric. Droplets of rain, more like a mist, settled on his sloping shoulders. What went

Former Premier John Horgan, flanked between Lt.-Gov. Judith Guichon (L) and Her Excellency Shinkai Karokhail, Afghanistan's ambassador to Canada, during the Afghanistan Memorial unveiling in Victoria, BC. Photo by Gisèle Bentley

through his mind? Was he thinking of the last time he saw you, hugging goodbye at YVR before you flew back home to Calgary, weeks before you'd be flying to Dubai and Kandahar Airfield? Or maybe he thought about the times he coached you in baseball or nagged at you to do your homework. Maybe he saw you reading your favourite books over the years—Jane Austen or Kazuo Ishiguro or Lucy Maud Montgomery. Or playing on the floor with Humphrey or bossing your brother around. Diving head first into Okanagan lakes. Skiing the slopes of Grouse Mountain.

Ah, well. Just as Richard and Jane are remembering Andrew, we have these memories of you. They come and go, but I think for your mom and dad and Cam, Michael too, they're more private. Remembering you as we learn to let go, learning to let go as we remember you.

Now I sit by my upstairs window gazing at the fresh canopy on the Japanese maple in our backyard. A hummingbird alights on top of the wine-coloured leaves, then lifts only to alight again on a nearby branch. She pokes her head down at the leaves, and I wonder if she's eating invisible bugs, though she stays still for no more than two seconds. Third time now, she whirs her wings and circles to the top of the canopy when another hummer flashes into view, speeding directly toward her, swerving, as does she, to avoid colliding at the last nanosecond, the two of them an aerobatic flying duo. Straight up and away, they arc in tandem, the male to the right, the female to the left. As suddenly as they appear, they're gone from view.

Love, Aunt Catherine

PART III

And when we are gone to ground and all our structures have crumbled back to dust, the river will become again just the place where light and water and sky find each other among the trees.

Margaret Renkl[15]

CHAPTER 17

LANGUID LIGHT

Bushra Saeed-Khan is petite, her black hair pulled tightly into a neatly coiffed bun at the nape of her neck. I notice a few grey streaks around the black-and-white trimmed bandana that frames her fine-boned face. It's a warm day in July 2019, and we're meeting outside a busy Moka House on Victoria's Cook Street. Victoria is her last stop across Canada with her husband, Adil, and their six-month-old baby girl, Jahan. It's characteristic of Bushra to embark on this journey on this tenth anniversary year to visit the families of those who lost loved ones in the blast that killed Michelle and four soldiers in December 2009. Bushra sat across from Michelle in the back of the light-armoured vehicle, one of the five who survived the improvised explosive device that Taliban operatives detonated beneath them.

Bushra and I embrace under the canopy of large chestnut trees that line the street. I look into her dark eyes and feel the warmth of her smile envelop me. Adil stands quietly by, as he often does, a gentle man who has been by Bushra's side every step of the way along her difficult and painful recovery. Jahan, sitting wide-eyed in her stroller, is adorable. I instantly want to cuddle her, but instead just smile and wave my hand to see how she reacts. She giggles, and I'm smitten by her cherub cheeks and wondering eyes.

This isn't the first time I've met Bushra, but I've been anxious about seeing her again. I know she has struggled with survivor's guilt, and I want to acknowledge her courage even as I wrestle with self-doubt. I'd met her in Ottawa only a few years after she lost half of her right leg as a result of that deadly explosion, our first encounter tentative and fragile. At the time, I didn't know where she was in her long medical journey[16] or how much was still to come—fifty surgeries to repair her insides and also to learn to walk with a prosthetic. I didn't know about phantom pain either or how desperately she wanted children.

Her story is remarkable, though it's not really mine to tell. Colin Perkel at Canadian Press and others have featured her in articles, and always, she comes across as gracious and strong. Her memory of the day of the blast distilled into one unforgettable moment: looking up at a clear sky after she was pulled from the LAV. Most everything else was a blur, but even in the chaos, she knew those clear skies had been to the Taliban's advantage, not hers.

On this sunny afternoon in Victoria, Bushra and I stroll from Moka House to the Afghanistan Memorial sandwiched between the law courts and Christ Church Cathedral on Quadra Street. Despite a slight limp, Bushra keeps pace. Pushing the stroller, she confides how having Jahan has allowed her to turn over the dark pages in her life following the incident. She doesn't dread the month of December as much as before, for it's the month when Jahan came into the world—in the same hospital where Bushra spent years recovering. I focus on sweet Jahan when we reach the grey granite memorial etched with names. Adil balances his daughter comfortably in his arms as they circle the monument, pausing to reflect and find Michelle's name and those of the soldiers she died with.

Jahan fills up the space with all the exuberance and joy of a well-loved, deeply nurtured infant. Black hair and eyes like both her parents and a smile that bubbles. Bushra tells me about all the different kinds of bears she calls her baby daughter, reminding me of Tomson Highway's song "Oh Little Bear," a tender lullaby about the Little Dipper and Big Dipper constellations. Later, when I read about Anishinaabe baby carriers, a tikinagan,[17] it calls to mind how this bond between Bushra and Jahan seems akin to an Indigenous worldview, one which holds that babies are close to the Creator. She holds Jahan tightly, close to her beating heart.

Bushra's sister, Hanaa, brother-in-law and their children join us at the memorial. We begin talking about the day it happened and how their lives changed. Hanaa is also beautiful, dark hair framing her glowing face. She describes the minutes, hours and days after the attack. How Bushra clung narrowly to life for a time as the family held its breath and prayed. How she and another sister bathed Bushra's foot and washed her hair in the intensive care unit at the Ottawa hospital. I can see the news photos in my mind as she speaks: multiple tubes criss-cross and attach Bushra to medical machines. I see green walls surround her, her tiny frame swallowed up by a mass of equipment, her black hair splayed across the starched, white pillowcase. Was it then that Hanaa had a recurring dream, one in which Bushra was running flat out on both legs?

I know from reading the features by Mr. Perkel that after Bushra was stabilized at Kandahar Airfield, Canadian Forces flew her to the military hospital in Germany and then to Ottawa, where she continued her long journey to recovery. A civilian and policy analyst with what was then the Department of Foreign Affairs and International Trade, she was embedded with troops and therefore given the same level of care as the other injured survivors of that blast. It strikes me that there are some things the military does right: they pull out all the stops to save those injured but fall short when meeting many veterans' long-term needs, which are plenty.

Hanaa hands me her baby boy, Baraak, and tells me his name means "blessing" in Persian. I learn that Jahan means "universe." Cradling Baraak in my arms, I comment on how lovely this cultural tradition is—to name one's children after concepts large and small. A wise tradition, it seems to me. We sit perched along the length of a short concrete wall beside the memorial and continue to chat while Bushra's older nephew romps around.

"Our grandmothers in Pakistan used to go shopping in Kabul in the 1960s," Hanaa says. "It was akin to a shopping trip in Paris for westerners." I wonder about the lives both women might be living if in Pakistan, with its complex history and relationship to Afghanistan, Taliban tribes on both sides of the porous border.

Soon both Bushra and Hanaa are breastfeeding their babies, and I snap a few photos, hoping against hope to capture the loveliness of these moments. I cast my gaze at Adil from time to time and wonder about his journey throughout this long ordeal. He's a tall, thoughtful man, with a softly expressive face, ever so gentle. I can see why Bushra loves him, and he, her.

In a month's time, we'll cross paths again at the next stop on my journey: the rededication ceremony of the Kandahar Cenotaph. When the Department of National Defence unveiled the cenotaph in a private ceremony earlier in the year, veterans and their families were deeply disappointed and upset at government's failure to include them. Bad press forced DND to do the right thing and arrange for a similar ceremony for Afghan veterans and families of the fallen. Characterized by one reporter as the "remnants of a decade of war," the cenotaph was built by and for soldiers at Kandahar Airfield. DND put enormous effort into making the rededication as memorable as possible.

For my sister, Margie, and me, it's a bookend to our trip to Trenton for the repatriation of Michelle's remains from Kandahar almost ten years before. Now we're travelling to Ontario with Michelle's parents, Art and

Sandy, in summertime, the heat soothing our bones as time and memory have begun to patch the hole Michelle left behind in our hearts.

After landing at the Ottawa airport on August 16, we're met by Capt. Gareth Newfield, our family's escort. He's a slightly rotund, serious middle-aged man who nonetheless makes us all smile and relax with a remark that the military chose him as our escort over "a twenty-five-year-old who eats bullets for breakfast." He summarizes his upbringing as "just a poor Ontario boy." Now a father of a young daughter, he considers this assignment his solemn duty, inviting us to contact him at any time of day or night. "I'm here for your comfort," he says, "and if you need to visit the memorial at 2:00 a.m., just call me."

I glance at Art and Sandy, sitting beside each other at the table in this private room inside the hotel lobby. They nod and smile politely at Gareth, but we're unaccustomed to this sort of attention. I can't imagine Art or Sandy needing to visit the memorial at 2:00 a.m. It strikes me that they mostly need each other in the privacy of their hotel room, where Art will sip his scotch and perhaps read the newspaper while Sandy will reach for her novel. But to know this man is willing to set aside whatever he might be doing, including getting much-needed rest, is rather remarkable to us.

There's an interesting history to the Kandahar Cenotaph, not the least of which is that it kept growing over the decade of our combat mission. Its dismantling and removal to Canada in 2011 was not an easy task.[18] But of course, the military is superbly good when it comes to matters involving operational logistics. Sigh. If that were all it took to win the good fight, we wouldn't need military forces anymore. I digress.

According to a Canadian Press story, the cenotaph was "so heavy that only the world's largest transport aircraft could fly it from where it stood at the Kandahar Airfield." I first saw the display when it came to the legislature in Victoria. It was a beautiful sunny day, early summer if I recall correctly, and Bruce and I were seated in a row of chairs in front of a line of military officials addressing the families who lost loved ones.

During that ceremony, I looked across the green expanse of the legislative lawns, dotted with perfectly tended annual plantings. Perhaps they were bright red begonias at that time of year, framing the majestic line of deciduous trees that edges the grounds on the eastern perimeter. Sunlight was dappled and a breeze blew, the rustling foliage like soft waves.

Stepping out of bright sunlight into the building, I remember darkness overtaking me. When my eyes adjusted, I saw the memorial: rows of black plaques mounted on white marble. A photographic portrait etched on each of the 160-plus plaques inscribed with basic facts of life and death: rank, full name, age, birthdate, date killed, regiment, task force and where killed. A heavily bound book sat open on a sturdy podium at the entrance. Bruce and I stepped forward to look for Michelle. I met eyes briefly with a handsome officer who stepped up to help us find her. And there she was, one of over 160 who didn't come home from Afghanistan. Hair in a ponytail, she smiled and stared intently into the camera. I ran the palm of my hand across the cream-coloured paper, smoothing the photograph while studying the all-too-familiar details of her death. The sole Canadian reporter bound between the book covers.

On this muggy August afternoon in Ottawa, Art, Sandy, Margie and I disembark the transport bus that has delivered us to the National Defence Headquarters. We aren't the only civilian family here, but I speculate that we're vastly outnumbered by families with solid military connections. As we begin walking to our destination, Sandy and Art see Bushra by a path and stop to chat. She's radiant, wearing her silk black-and-red poppy scarf and pushing Jahan in a stroller. I know who she got the scarf from—the parents of twenty-one-year-old Zachery McCormack who died in the blast. My eyes fall to the medals pinned above her left breast, the Canadian Sacrifice Medal and the Canadian General Service Medal for South-West Asia. Years before, I'd seen them on display in a glass case in Ottawa's War Museum. But today, their significance comes to life, and I recognize this day is important for her in ways I can't possibly know.

We part ways and fall into line with those strolling along a path that skirts one side of a man-made lagoon, edged with tawny grasses and bulrushes. Wearing a calf-length skirt my mother bought me in the 1980s, I think of her when the silk in this taupe-and-cream-coloured skirt brushes against my hips and thighs. But today, beneath the silk, it's my mother's slip caressing me—the one she wore under her wedding dress in November 1942, some seventy-seven years before. Tiny as a songbird back then, her smile soft and radiant, a bouquet of red roses tucked between arms covered in white satin.

The night before today's ceremony, I had carefully laid the slip onto my hotel bed to show Margie—both of us reminiscing about our mom and the difficult circumstances she faced when her husband went to war

Bushra Saeed-Khan and husband Adil Khan, following the Kandahar Cenotaph Rededication ceremony in Ottawa, August 2019. Bushra, a federal policy analyst for Global Affairs Canada, suffered life-threatening injuries in the December 30, 2009, Taliban attack. Photo by Catherine Lang

so soon after they wed. The wedding had to be moved up by four months because my father had been called for engineer officer training before deploying to Europe during World War II. Leaving his wife may have been difficult for him, too, but he was full of purpose.

Today, our escort takes us to our seats and lets us settle in. We face the sloping façade of the Afghanistan Memorial Hall, gleaming like polished onyx, reflecting wavy images of people and the wreaths lined up at its base. Hidden from view inside the walls of the hall, the Kandahar Cenotaph awaits.

Art, Sandy, Margie and I are seated together close to the front, surrounded by strangers on rows of chairs stacked up on a raised plywood platform. The air is buzzing—families visiting other families and friends. Most, as far as I can tell, are grateful to be here. I glance behind and see a media tent where a flank of tripods holding heavy cameras points over the crowd. I approach the tent, hoping someone I know will be here from the *Calgary Herald*. But no, the *Herald* sent someone from the *Ottawa Citizen* to represent Postmedia, a woman I've not met before. I ask if she'd like to meet Michelle's parents, and she nods enthusiastically, following me through the rows of guests. I introduce her to Art and he stands, stretching out his hand as they smile and chat for a short while. He seems genuinely pleased to meet her, an editor of a major daily newspaper with her hand on the pulse of events. His talk is animated, and as I stand by, I wonder if this is my role now, ensuring a connection between the press and our family. I turn to the *Calgary Herald* wreath at the base of the memorial hall. It's prominent among the other wreaths, but I feel an absence. Michelle's colleagues ought to be here, I think to myself and sigh.

A military band is playing off to one side, all decked out in their red serge finery. I listen to the brassy music amidst the cacophony of people mingling and then shuffling back to their seats. The ceremony begins with a video montage on large screens intended to highlight Canada's contribution in Afghanistan during our mission there. A part of me aches inside. I desperately want to believe that although Canada didn't provide the foundation for lasting peace, at least we accomplished some good.

The montage ends just as a rush of heightened energy ripples through the crowd. Everyone stands as an emcee announces the arrival of our Commander-in-Chief. Governor General Julie Payette steps onto the platform, surrounded by other dignitaries. I crane my neck to see her wild blonde hair, but it's not there. It's under a white CIC cap, a single long braid falling between her shoulders. Golden ropes embellish the left epaulette of her startling white jacket, a row of military medals pinned above her right breast. She addresses the crowd with immaculate poise, offers words intended to inspire, perhaps to give solace, to make us proud as a people. And I think we are. At the same time, I detect an almost cheeky mirth as she pauses in her speech for effect.

When Chief of Defence Staff Jonathan Vance comes forward to make his remarks, I think, *he's the real top soldier, the one who has seen battle.* He chokes up as he talks about how the cenotaph in Kandahar and now here in Canada triggers heartache and pain but also brings comfort—a conduit through which we can talk to those we've lost and let them know we're still here, that we think of them during our living moments and carry their memory with us wherever we go.

Afghanistan ambassador Hassan Soroosh steps up to the microphone, and I scan the crowd briefly, wondering where Bushra and Adil are sitting. Though I can't spot them, I wonder what's going through their minds as the ambassador begins speaking. This small, modest man tells us that Canadians are an "indelible" part of Afghans' consciousness as much as Afghans are part of ours. He remarks that now it's time for Afghans to do the heavy lifting and carry on the work that international security forces began. He talks about the schools that Canadians built, the education that Afghan children are getting because of our efforts, more robust Afghan police forces and maybe something about clean drinking water. I've heard about these accomplishments before and lose my focus, thinking they're only part of the story. No one speaks the unblemished truth, the dark and complex reality on the ground. The day before, eleven people were killed and more wounded by a suicide bomber at an Afghan wedding in Kabul. Yet the dignitaries repeatedly say: "Canadians did not die in vain." I stand and listen and know I would not necessarily say that, though I don't want to dwell on it now.

When the speeches are done, we stand as a chaplain offers a prayer. A lone bugler plays the "Last Post," and its mournful, soulful lament takes me back to the freezing Trenton tarmac when the impact of Michelle's death unleashed a torrent of grief and shock in our family. Today, almost ten years later, standing in the muggy heat under a sun that is beginning to break through the clouds, my heart beats steadily. We stand for two long minutes of silence.

A roar comes out of nowhere. Faces turn upward. It's a flypast—four black birds of prey approach, slicing the sky above. The elongated hulks of Black Hawk helicopters obliterate the sun's rays for a brief moment, flying in a missing man formation,[19] an aerial salute with a gap between planes signifying an absent comrade. I study the rotors whirring these beasts through air, let the vibrations sink down through my core, imagining myself on the ground in Kandahar, rooted to the spot by the ominous sound of war. For the soldiers among us, what memories does it stir?

The chaplain offers a parting benediction—his closing reference an acknowledgement of what Canadian Forces tried to accomplish and the goodwill and hope inherent in that effort. Yes, this speaks truth to my sense of why we're gathered here, honouring and mourning our fallen, our unwitting sacrifice. Even if in vain, that goodwill and those efforts were something. I reflect on the "ordinary" Canadians around me, how we carry it with us and how blessed we are to be able to extend generosity— of spirit and promise. Alas, also of young blood and unfulfilled dreams.

A tall Indigenous man in uniform steps onto the platform. Under his green beret, a dark braid falls down his spine. He holds an eagle-feathered staff high as he escorts faith leaders into the memorial hall: a chaplain in a floor-length, white robe; a rabbi in a kippah; and a woman mullah with a mauve headscarf. We follow their movements into the inner sanctum on huge TV monitors. I catch myself holding my breath as they congregate around the large boulder that is the centrepiece of the cenotaph—a boulder originally transported from a site where two Canadian soldiers died in 2002 and into which is embedded a bas-relief image of an angel caring for a dying soldier. I think of the viewing that André Gauthier presided over at KAF following Michelle's death and those of the soldiers who died with her. Solemn. Sacred. Transcendent.

The Indigenous soldier sweeps sweetgrass smoke that spirals upward. The chaplain, rabbi and mullah recite passages from the Old and New Testaments and the Quran. Though we're not in the sanctified air of the room yet, I watch the ritual in a dreamlike state. And then it's our turn to enter the memorial hall, to see Michelle's plaque once again. Sandy comes alongside me, and I caress her rounded back as she bends down, her daughter's eyes staring back at her. My eyes fall on the bracelet around her wrist, a gift from the soldiers who had them made to commemorate their comrades and Michelle. It's inscribed with the initials of everyone killed that day: GM, GC, ZM, KT, ML. KIA. Dec 30, 2009.

We mingle with others for a while in this space that's been blessed, though the sweetgrass smoke barely lingers. Bushra comes forward to greet us and we all hug briefly. Soon after she introduces us to Renée Filiatrault, a petite woman in a navy dress, her chestnut-brown hair cascading over service medals pinned above her left breast. I've seen her face before, marching toward me from the front page of newspapers almost a decade ago—a grim-faced pallbearer, a civilian staffer, and liaison between the military and press. Of all six pallbearers on that day, she was the only civilian supporting Michelle's flag-draped casket on the Kandahar tarmac onto the cargo plane destined for Trenton. As Bushra introduces Renée, none of us are quite able to find words. So Renée speaks of Michelle, describing her exchanges with the *Calgary Herald* reporter who wanted to tell humanitarian stories instead of always running with the pack to chase down the controversial stories of the day.

When we've filled our hearts and heads with our memories, Art, Sandy, Margie and I head toward the reception hall. I feel a lightness carrying me along. I see the tall eagle staff and the swirling haze of sweetgrass smoke, the incantations from people of faith ringing through my head once again. Stream after stream of folks from the ceremony stroll along either side of the manmade lagoon, our reflections wavering in one relentless wash of movement, the colour of our clothes and shapes of our bodies merging into the languid light of late afternoon.

CHAPTER 18

A HIGH SCHOOL REMEMBRANCE

I'm wearing a knee-length black pencil skirt and my orthotic black leather shoes when I step onto dry pavement and slip out of Sandy's Nissan sedan. It's overcast, but not so cold for November. My red-felted vest is keeping me warm. I scan the parking lot. There's not a soul in sight, probably only until teenagers start spilling out of classes. Ducking my head under the car roof, I lean into the back seat for a wooden-framed box about the width of a small coffee table.

Lifting it out, I cradle it in my arms as carefully as I possibly can, for it contains a precious flag, folded meticulously by a soldier I do not know. I like to imagine he or she practised the proper way to fold the flag many times, and that when they folded this one, they held an image of Michelle in their hearts and hands, knowing it had draped her casket during the ramp-to-repatriation ceremonies, as well as during memorials in Vancouver and Calgary. It has been undisturbed since then, on a shelf in a bedroom closet.

I can see the flag's red-and-white banners through the glass-covered top, which is framed by the rich amber glow of wood—a weight in my arms to be sure, but it's not a struggle to carry it into the high school Michelle attended in her teens. It's entirely possible that I once loitered here myself when it was still hard-packed earth or grass—long before the new school was built on this property, back when I attended Magee in an old brick building standing small and squat in surrounding school fields.

I don't have particularly fond memories of my time at Magee high school, but standing here today with the weight of this box in my arms, I feel a sense of accomplishment in my life. I've travelled a distance to arrive here, and for a few brief moments, I'm self-assured and calm, a sense of purpose drawing me forward into the halls of the school.

It's November 7, 2019, and I've come to give a speech during the school's Remembrance Day service. I've worked diligently to prepare remarks that I hope will reach the students, though doubt niggles. Will I strike the right chord with this teenage audience? Most are from upper middle-class families. Privileged, for sure.

Today, Magee is unveiling a small plaque donated by Canadian Pacific Railway, inscribed with Michelle's name and the years of Canada's combat operations during the Afghan mission: 2001 to 2011, during which some twenty-five journalists, foreign and local, were killed while covering the mission. Several reporters are here, as is the independent Member of Parliament, Jody Wilson-Raybould. A few years ago, I approached her at a treaty signing event to remark on her speech about Indigenous self-government. I mention this to her today because I want her to know something of who I am. Almost involuntarily, she tilts her head ever so slightly, looking intently into my face. She doesn't recognize me, not that I expect her to, but we connect ever so briefly and I'm grateful she is here.

I'm comforted by the fact that many of Michelle's friends, those I met at Sarah and Sanjay's in the summer of 2017, are also here. We hug in the reception area, and I thank them for coming, knowing they've taken precious time from their jobs to attend. This is their alma mater too, and I wonder how it feels to be once again in the high-ceilinged, open-space foyer where they hung out on classroom breaks—one of many such clutches of teens, Michelle at the core of their laughing, fun-loving and also angst-ridden huddle.

My sister Margie is here with her two-year-old granddaughter, who's literally sticking to her grandmother's side. Her blue eyes sneak a peek at me from under her shaggy blonde bangs, inching even closer to Margie.

"Thanks for coming, Margie," I say, hugging her gently. "I wasn't sure if you'd make it."

"Well, little missy here didn't make it easy, that's for sure," she replies, putting a hand on her granddaughter's head to tousle her hair.

I nod, realizing with a start that the first time we came together to remember Michelle was before all but one of her four grandchildren were born. Art and Sandy's two young grandchildren are here too, along with Cameron and his wife. They sit in the front row of the large auditorium next to Michelle's parents as students begin to file in, filling the auditorium to capacity.

During the event, a *Vancouver Sun* photographer snaps a photo of Sandy and Art.[20] Sandy's profile is in sharp focus, looking up at the stage, a faint blue light over the crown of her head, her blue eyes clear, one hand by her mouth where her index finger curves softly over her lips. The beaded poppy from the trading store in La Ronge is on her lapel. It's as close as

Sandy will ever get to the bay named after her daughter in northern Saskatchewan. Beside her, Art's profile is fuzzy, out of the lens' depth of field and almost ghostly, a longing in his upturned face, his cheek slightly hollow, a line of grief, but perhaps also pride, carved into the set of his chin.

This is the second time this year, the tenth since Michelle was killed, that my family is together to remember her more publicly than usual. A mere three months ago, we attended the rededication of the Kandahar Cenotaph in Ottawa. Before this year is out, I will travel to a legion in Edmonton, where I'll join a tenth anniversary gathering of families and friends of the soldiers who were killed by the same roadside bomb that killed Michelle. In many ways, these events are bringing me closer to the end of my journey of remembrances for my niece. Not that I will stop learning about and remembering her. Perhaps like the Canadian flag that draped her casket, I'll fold up this decade of roaming our country and begin a wandering into other unknown places.

Sandy, Art and I have been working for weeks with the school's vice-principal, Kelly Egilsson, to contribute to today's Remembrance Day service, compiling photos of Michelle as a child, a teen, a young woman and a reporter. Kelly is going to great lengths to ensure a memorable event. Is it because he, too, has been touched by war? His friend, Trevor Greene, the Canadian soldier who survived an axe attack during a *shura*, can't attend the service because of other commitments. But I'm sure Kelly carries his friend close to his heart as he labours to coordinate and finesse the program—the piper, flag party, speakers, slide show, concert choir, wind ensembles and string orchestra.

A week before the day of the service, I visit my alma mater, Langara College. A ten-minute drive along 49th Avenue from Magee, Langara still has its journalism program, and I'm drawn to return, thinking perhaps a journalism student might cover the event for the student paper.

The campus has grown in the thirty-plus years since I won the Penny Wise scholarship to attend J-school. I bristle past new buildings and find a security guard, who points to the main entrance. Strolling through the foyer, I feel at odds. An outsider now among preoccupied students scurrying to class and unknown futures, I find the stairs leading to the journalism department. Everything is changed. Reception areas don't exist anymore, but there's a sign for the photography department where an instructor reluctantly stops what he's doing to lead me down the hall to a hidden suite of offices. I pass a closet of a room where a dark-haired woman sits at a computer. She looks like a student to me, but no, it turns out that she's an instructor.

I introduce myself as Michelle's aunt, and she springs up to shake my hand.

"I met Michelle," Peg Fong says, smiling warmly and taking my hand in hers. "I was on my way through Calgary once and got to hang out with *Herald* reporters. Up in the newsroom, I found myself surrounded by my long-time friend Robin Summerfield, Michelle and other colleagues— Colette Derworiz, Kelly Cryderman, Renata D'Aliesio, Gwendolyn Richards—swinging a hula hoop around my waist and laughing uncontrollably. I was so jealous of them," she says. "They were such a tight-knit group of fun and dedicated reporters."

"I can't believe you knew her. Small world," I reply. "I thought you must have been a student when I first passed your office." As we speak, her byline pops before my mind's eye, scratched to the surface from a recess in my brain. Later, I send her an email telling her I sometimes think Michelle is orchestrating various serendipitous encounters wherever I go. And it's true. I do feel that sometimes—as if Michelle has thrown a line of rope in my direction, drawing me in and out of the journalism profession.

I tell Peg the reason for my visit, and light flickers in her black eyes. "One of my students would be perfect," she says. "I'll ask her this afternoon. Her name is Kristen Holliday, and she's top-notch."

"Thanks so much, Peg. I think it's fitting that the journalism students here know about Michelle, so this means a lot to me."

"Of course," she replies. "If I can, I'll try to come as well," adding, "I can tell how much journalism still matters to you."

Soon enough, I'm walking back down the hall to the staircase, satisfied that I followed my instincts. This upcoming generation of reporters are the important ones now. I'm probably overestimating my influence, but I indulge a sense of playing a small part in passing a torch. Not to mention letting Langara students know about the high school student down 49th Avenue who went all the way to the top to cover the war in Afghanistan.

As it turns out, Kristen is the Penny Wise scholarship recipient, a small blonde woman who's well-spoken, confident and focused. Best of all, she's passionate about the profession she has chosen, just like Michelle, just like me. I tell Kristen about the Michelle Lang Fellowship that Postmedia established in Michelle's honour, encouraging her to apply. Small ways in which to contribute to Michelle's legacy. At least, that's my hope.

A week goes by and I'm standing at a podium on stage, staring into a night-black void. The light is on me, and save for the first few rows, the 500 guests below are shrouded in darkness. I begin my prepared remarks, lifting my eyes and peering into this silent, cavernous space, pouring my heart into every single word I've written about Michelle. About her personality, her sense of fun, her dedication to journalism, about the impact of war on our family. I end with "she was one of you," hoping that will land with at least some students.

When done, I return to my seat and calm myself by breathing deeply. The subsequent musical interludes are elegant but haunting, lifting me into reverberating sound, where wind ensemble, trumpets and the "Piper's Lament" clear my troubled mind.

When the service is over, a few folks come to greet and hug me, including Ms. Wilson-Raybould. I feel my heart cracking when she closes her arms briefly around my back. A few salty tears roll down my cheeks and my heart churns. I whisper: "She was so special."

Later, Sandy and Art drive me to the Tsawwassen ferry terminal where we say our goodbyes. I hug Sandy through the passenger door and grab my suitcase from the trunk. I look at Art and recognize his emotional exhaustion. We hug, and I say: "It went well, but I'm glad it's behind us now." He nods, our eyes meeting. "Definitely," he says, the relief in his voice palpable.

And then he ducks in behind the steering wheel, already pulling away as I turn and walk to the departure area, always coming together and moving away. I roll my suitcase past the ticket gate, up the escalator and onto the smooth flooring where my suitcase glides all the way to the boarding gate, my mind calm. It's late afternoon and surprisingly bright on the platform outside the waiting area. I sit down to watch light descending, the approaching ferry a dot in Georgia Strait. By the time it nears the dock, the ship is silhouetted against a deepening gold and tangerine sky.

CHAPTER 19

COMING TOGETHER, TEN YEARS ON

I leave Victoria on the last Friday of 2019, once again via ferry, en route to the Vancouver airport where I'll be catching a flight to Edmonton, the city of my birth. I'm going there, rather unexpectedly as it turns out, to be with the families and comrades of the young men who died alongside Michelle ten years ago.

Gazing out the ferry window, I sip my tall medium roast as we motor past Piers Island, the colour of the sea ever changing with light, tide and currents. I pull a Ziploc bag from my belongings and stuff homegrown dried oregano into herb jars. I love this tangible task, stripping tiny green leaves, herb oil staining my fingers, fragrance rising to my nostrils as my forefinger and thumb rub the length of twig that once held roots into my poor clay-like earth. Oregano, that lovely Mediterranean herb, which grows in the poorest of soils, spreads over the edges of garden beds, pops up in random patches. A way for me to balance the fraught nature of this journey and bring a measure of calm to my soul.

I also check my texts and copy links of the *Calgary Herald* articles—Robert Remington's and mine—and post remembrances of Michelle out into the wide virtual world beyond this steel vessel that carries me past the mossy green boulders of Beaver Point on Salt Spring Island, the navy-blue grouping of islets, Selby included, where my husband Bruce wants his ashes scattered into the truly translucent waters near Active Pass, a favourite anchorage during his sailing days and where Japanese Canadians from Chemainus once jigged for abundant rock cod. Each point along the way part of my history, part of my unremarkable journey through infinitesimal time.

I note the landmarks I've come to know so well from countless trips along this route—the dock at Otter Bay, for one. Some thirty-three years ago, I came and went from Pender Island over the summer I worked for the *Gulf Islands Driftwood*, reporting on news and events on the Outer Gulf Islands. Now, gazing at the lay of the forested islands, I ponder the journeys my mother took across Canada in her long life and how she was already in her mid-thirties when she first left her hometown. I don't think she'd gone farther afield than Grand Beach on Lake Winnipeg when she followed her husband to Alberta, where my father's job took them. By then a married woman with a young son, my mother was typical for her generation, never questioning whether to follow her husband.

I don't know anything about their journey from Winnipeg to Edmonton, but I imagine Mom felt sad to leave her parents and siblings behind in order to fulfill her responsibilities as a wife and mother in an unfamiliar part of Canada, a place where she'd learn how to fit into a new neighbourhood and make new friends. Was it with a mixture of excitement and apprehension that she stepped from the platform onto the train, her small son holding her hand? I'll never know, but now that I'm on my way to Edmonton, I wonder about these things.

For me, Edmonton is just a place name on my birth certificate, while a handful of old Brownie-box photos trigger memories for my siblings: there I am in my snowsuit, my sister standing beside me, our snow-covered neighbourhood behind us, nondescript and humble as 1950s neighbourhoods tended to be; my brother sitting on a backdoor wooden step, his hand on the glossy black fur of his beloved dog, the gleeful smile of a happy boy following an afternoon's play.

But it's not my intention to go to Edmonton at the tail end of this calendar year to seek out the hospital where my sister and I were born. My imperative is to take part in a collective remembrance of those who made the ultimate sacrifice in war ten years on—an opportunity to remember not just those who died alongside Michelle but also to be with those seriously injured and others who walked away, their bodies intact but their psyches altered forever.

From Remembrance Day on, I suppose, I anticipated that this tenth anniversary of Michelle's death was going to be different from the more private remembrances of years past. Partly, I've been wondering why ten years is any different from two or six or seven. Michelle's absence is still felt keenly in our family no matter the anniversary. By virtue of being a more public remembrance this time around, it's definitely more pronounced—not the loss per se but the attention being paid to it. I'm not sure how I feel about that. But I'm pleased that the *Calgary Herald* ran an opinion piece I wrote about Canadian–Afghan connections,[21] giving me a platform to express my views about why those connections are significant.

I want to remind Canadians that Michelle's belief "in the power of journalism to effect change was what led her to Afghanistan to cover

Canada's military and humanitarian mission. She wanted to report on the lives of Afghan civilians and find out if things that we take for granted in the western world—education and health care, for starters—might improve as a result of western intervention."

In addition to my thoughts about the personal loss our family experienced, I wrote that 2019 was also the tenth anniversary of the year that four women from the Shafia family were murdered by family members in Kingston, Ontario—a horrific instance of honour killings in Canada. Like Michelle, I wanted people to care about what happens to women everywhere just because they are women.

The *Herald* is also publishing the first of Robert Remington's three instalments on this milestone anniversary,[22] recounting Michelle's time in Afghanistan. Robert shared a desk with her and often berated her for working too hard, staying long after other reporters had left the newsroom. He once told her she should wrap up and head out into Calgary's night life.

"If you spend all your waking hours in here, you're going to end up single," he quipped.

With a gleam in her eye, she retorted: "Uncle Bob, I'm too young to be lazy like you," and they both laughed.

The camaraderie was palpable, the somewhat wizened veteran of the trade, a tall, gangly but robust man, some twenty-plus years her senior, with a sharp brain, a journalistic instinct honed over time and a matching ability to write. She probably loved being his cubicle mate most for his zest and self-deprecating humour, not to mention the stories he could tell.

So today, Michelle will be front-page news again, her shy smile below Robert Remington's byline and the headline: "Remembering Michelle Lang: 'Worst news' from Afghanistan is confirmed." The *Herald* commissioned him, a former trusted colleague, to write the series, and it accomplishes what I probably couldn't have, though I know the details by heart. Robert's feature series hits the mark on every count. Fact-based but personal.

For me, it's almost as if my writing is a vain attempt to resurrect her. But how can my journey to get to know her more ultimately accomplish what we all wish for the most—to have her with us again, a middle-aged woman now, with a busy life juggling work and family? Her death woke a restlessness in me, to go where she had connections, scouring up bits of information and getting glimpses into the life she was living. Then again, perhaps it has been a way for me to postpone the letting go of her and of my own youth.

Will this trip to Edmonton be the end of this journey? Will it at least help bring some closure, a more solid reckoning with the truth that she isn't coming back, that she will always be a young woman approaching the pinnacle of her career? After all, that's how we'll remember her, and I will get on with my life. Except that this is my life. Puzzling my way through a multitude of predicaments, fumbling in the dark more often than not. Trying to get at what lies underneath, the meaning of life and loss, the seeming inevitability of war and its tragic consequences, the connection between purpose and worth.

I disembark the ferry and find my way to the Vancouver International Airport. Some hours after leaving home, I board the plane for the short flight to Edmonton, my energy waning. But adrenalin kicks in again when a stocky and jovial guy called Wolfi picks me up at the Edmonton airport. He's an eager young man, ready to pull out all the stops so that I lack for nothing during my stay.

Wolfi is short for Wolfgang, so named by his mates, among whom is Jodie Densmore, a medic who served in Kandahar, though not the medic attending to survivors of the blast that killed Michelle. I first met Jodie in 2011 when she gave a presentation to university women about her deployment to Afghanistan. Following her talk, I introduced myself and we became good friends. After all, she was there in Kandahar on December 30, 2009, a day seared in her memory forever as well.

About two weeks before the tenth anniversary reunion, we talked, struggling to make a decision about whether to go. She longed to catch up with the guys with whom she served, and I knew this particular opportunity wouldn't come my way again. After much humming and hawing, we both decided we couldn't not go, hustling our butts to make it happen at the last minute.

Wolfi hauls my luggage into my Airbnb, a squat condo building on 109th Street SW, within walking distance of the High Level Bridge, and leaves me to settle in. I unpack quickly, hanging a few clothes in my small but bright and airy room. By one of the two large windows, one facing west and the other north, there's a comfy upholstered chair and a small desk. The queen bed takes up most of the room, which is just fine by me since all I need is a warm, snug and private space. In fact, it comforts me, this containment of sorts. The walls are a pale blue, and the light filters in generously.

Now midday, I decide to venture out for a few groceries and get my bearings. There's nothing fancy about the neighbourhood. If anything, it's more like the neighbourhoods from those old Edmonton photos—squat stucco houses from a different generation and sagging old garages. But 109th Street SW is a busy thoroughfare, and neighbouring streets have newly built houses among the older ones. Grand old leafless trees line the boulevards, and even though it's the dead of winter, it's surprisingly balmy. I don't need the extra layer of mittens that I've brought, but I tread gingerly, carefully avoiding ice on the sidewalks and streets. Unlike when I was a kid, I might break something if I fall now.

I get my groceries and a bottle of wine and head back to my room. Light will soon be fading, and I've got tomorrow to explore. The sunset is all pink and orange and purple. I sit on my bed and stare at it intently until the colours dim and dusk slides deeply into an ink-black sky.

The next morning, the day before the anniversary, I wander about the neighbourhood again and discover a busy, pedestrian street. It turns out I'm close to one of Edmonton's oldest and most funky neighbourhoods, Old Strathcona. I head into a coffee shop to satisfy my addiction to strong espresso and watch people. It's a vibrant mix of young singles and young couples, smiling and relaxing with their lattes just like at home. I've brought newspapers and my journal, and this near-perfect combo is not lost on me. I'm stepping outside my domestic life and the responsibilities that get in the way of simply being out in the world with nowhere especially to go and no one to account for. Unencumbered, as it were, and I like it a lot.

I call Michael Louie. To my surprise, he's in Edmonton too.

"Hi Auntie, I wish I'd known you were coming. I'm taking my nephew to a hockey game, so I don't have time to meet."

"Oh, that's too bad, but I understand. It was a last-minute decision to make this trip, and I forgot that you might be here visiting family."

"Yeah, I usually come to see my folks and sister at this time of year. What brings you here?"

I tell him the reason for the trip, and he pauses. "I wish I'd known ahead of time that Remington was writing those articles on 'Shelle," he says. "A bunch of friends and colleagues called to ask if I'd seen them."

My stomach churns. "I'm so sorry, Mikey. I don't know why I didn't think to let you know."

We say goodbye, and I take a few deep breaths. It had been niggling at me, whether to call and warn him about the upcoming coverage. A part of me hoped someone else would do that, shirking the responsibility to remind him of what he'd lost, how it would be all over the newspaper again. I remember how Sandy once opened a newspaper to see one of the last photos taken of Michelle, standing beside Bushra during a briefing before their convoy headed out. She wished someone had warned her, too. I ought to have had more guts.

After coffee, I stroll further down Whyte Avenue, stopping to admire the Princess Theatre and its beautiful marble façade and heavy wood-panelled doors, gleaming in the sun. Opened in 1915 during the silent movie era, this grand old dame of a theatre has since gone through various incarnations as cinema itself changed. At times threatened with demolition, it was finally designated a heritage building in 1976 and is Edmonton's only surviving historic theatre. I crack a door open to peep inside, but the bill on today is a horror movie so I keep moving. Seems that Old Strathcona is thriving because of small businesses that have transitioned through the decades, retaining some history while also changing with the times.

I spend the afternoon exploring farther afield. I can see the Edmonton skyline in the distance to the north and set my sights on crossing the High Level Bridge across the North Saskatchewan River. It's sunny and still balmy, possibly minus five degrees Celsius, but not the minus twenty-five or minus thirty that I expected. I begin snapping photos as I approach, intrigued by this massive two-level bridge built between 1910 and 1913. A plaque set into a steel beam tells me that the chief engineer was a Phillip Motley, and I wonder if the *Calgary Herald*'s chief editor, Lorne Motley, is a descendant. It was Lorne who had to tell the newsroom that Michelle had been killed. As one of the newspapers executives who offered Michelle the chance to go to Afghanistan, he carries the burden of knowing she would jump at the chance. But I know it's not likely I'll ever ask Lorne if he's related, if his family was a prominent one as far back as the previous century. Connections and single-digit degrees of separation.

I think of my father too, and realize how, as a civil engineer, he would have loved this massive steel-truss bridge, built for trains and electric cars on the upper level and for cars, bicycles and pedestrians on the lower level. Crossing over, I peer far down at the North Saskatchewan River snaking in both directions, huge gaping holes in the frozen surface, the frigid water running swiftly below textured ice sheets that stretch as far as the eye can see. Behind and below is a large wintry sports field that flattens out the terrain along the southern shore of the river, while the dome of the Alberta legislature comes into view ahead.

I'm almost across this mighty 2,500-foot (762-metre) bridge, the sun still shining. I'm beginning to peel off layers as I leave the bridge behind to explore the legislative grounds, feeling my heart accelerate when I spot a skating rink and hear kids squealing with delight. I make a beeline for it. I haven't seen an outdoor skating rink in so long. Lamenting the fact that I don't have skates with me, I enjoy it vicariously anyway, watching adolescents hunched over and screaming past each other, the swish of their skates cutting into ice as they swoop sideways and round corners. I step onto the ice myself, jacket wide open now, and gingerly sweep my legs forward, imitating the skating motion to not much avail. I stand for a while, letting others skate by, remembering how I skated for hours in the cold and came home breathless, fingers too numb to untie my laces, calling out to my mother for help.

I wander the grounds and approach a bronze statue depicting a Ukrainian pioneer family. The mother holds a baby in her arms, while a small child is partially hiding behind her skirt. A third child stands against his father's legs, head back, a look of deep unrequited longing on his face. All of them are barefoot, this statue in the snow, except for the father. Husband and wife stare intently into each other's eyes, and I wonder if he's leaving, to find work, to find food. These figures are part of a diorama displaying a sheaf of wheat and various farm implements, and I wonder about Alberta's settler history and the legacy this imparts. Like the statue of the starving girl child representing the Holodomor at the Regina legislature, the history of Ukrainians runs deep in these Prairie cities. Elsewhere on the grounds, a giant bronze statue of a railroad official in a top hat and long black coat drives a spike into the railroad, another iconic image of this country. But I don't see anything that acknowledges the Indigenous people of this region, the Nehiyaw (Cree), Denesuliné (Dene), Nakota Sioux (Stoney), Anishinaabe (Saulteaux) and Niitsitapi (Blackfoot) nor the Metis. Strangely, a Haida totem and a Kwakwaka'wakw one, both Pacific Coast tribes, are on the grounds. I think of Michelle and wonder if she wondered about these things, lamenting the fact that there was never the opportunity to discuss topics in depth that we cared about. The plight of women in Afghanistan, literature, journalism, her half Haida cousin, Ellen, family writ large.

Back on my hunt for a coffee shop, I stride along block after block, past a mix of old brick buildings that have seen better days and skyscrapers, their golden windows gleaming against snow. The new is gradually taking over the crumbling old. A modern university campus, MacEwan University, looms ahead, and I think "where there are students, there's bound to be coffee." But I can't smell any dark roast aromas when I arrive, and pedestrians are scarce. I stroll past wide, well-used back alleys, the Crash Hotel where Jodie will be staying when she arrives later today, makeshift metal fences around construction sites. A row of flashy, 1950s-style neon signs poke out from brick buildings, one after the other along a street I cross.

The day is wearing on as I come to Rogers Place, the sunlight bouncing off the sweep of its curving façade. It's a glamourous beast, this building, and I wonder about its destiny as a major sports league arena. Why not an opera house instead? I'm not ashamed about my lack of passion for our national sport, but I'd be kicked out of town were I to say so out loud. Then a memory: straddling my ten-year-old brother's upper back while he laid on the worn area rug in our living room, riveted to his beloved *Hockey Night in Canada*. At five, I was full of energy, bouncing up and down on his back while he stared at our dinky black-and-white television.

Finally, I round a corner and voilà—an open coffee shop. I've been walking for almost three hours, and I'm more than ready for a sit down. It's a bright, cozy space in the heart of Edmonton's Ice District. A mirror and turquoise walls offset the chic white tables, and for a while, I'm the only patron. Sipping my Americano, I glance across the street. A silhouette: a man in a tailored suit pushing his suitcase across a glassed-in skywalk, the sky behind him falling into a deep cobalt blue. This side of the world, so posh and elegant in this moment, where sparkling white Christmas lights spiral around pillars upholding the porte cochère of the Marriott Hotel. A sleek black Porsche glides forward, passengers step out and into the hotel lobby while a valet whisks their vehicle into a heated underground parking lot. Or so I imagine anyway. It's a distant world from Afghanistan and the Timmy's at Kandahar Airfield where Michelle may have grabbed a morning coffee before heading to the media tent, the world outside the airfield full of unknown dangers, where ordinary Afghans went about their days in the city and in tribal villages.

The light is right for walking back the way I came. It's probably safe for me to do so, unlike when Sgt. Jimmy Collins made the decision to turn the two light-armoured vehicles under his command back the way they'd come. After meeting with village elders in Hosi Aziz, he made that impossible, haunting decision. I wonder if I'll meet him at long last tomorrow. I wonder who else I might meet, once again going outside my comfort zone, still unsure how I'll fit in with military families and veterans with direct experience of war.

I step outside into the twilight. When I reach the legislative grounds, they're alive with young families, parents wandering with their children, pointing at bright, festive lights glistening in their midst. It's a child's view I see ever so briefly, that wonder of lights sparkling against blankets of snow under a night sky.

On the morning of the anniversary, I wake early, lifting my torso from the comfort of a warm duvet and turn to my reflection in the closet mirror. The face looking back at me is like the one in that photo when I was twelve, holding our dachshund mutt, Baron, in my bedroom on 47th Avenue in Vancouver. Not so long ago, I found a picture of Michelle at that same age, and it struck me how we could've been the same adolescent girl, on the cusp of our turbulent teens, mine perhaps more so than hers, though I don't know that for a fact. I only know she got a grip on life sooner, addressing her anxiety and insecurities by making healthier choices while I undermined my confidence and esteem in self-destructive ways. A moment later, I hear her voice ringing in my ears. "Oh, Auntie Catherine," she is saying. It occurs to me that she probably understood me in ways I wasn't aware of. Then again, maybe she could see something of herself in me too—a mercifully lighter version. Her voice floats in again, and I hear a slight teasing reprimand. "You're taking yourself seriously again."

As I dress for the day, my thoughts turn to Afghanistan and the knowledge that I'll never be able to go there. To Kabul perhaps, but not likely to Kandahar, the Taliban-controlled region in southern Afghanistan. I'm reading passages of Michael Elcock's *A Perfectly Beautiful Place* that describe his travels through the battlegrounds of the First and Second World Wars, where Canadians fought and sacrificed their lives. Tens of thousands of lives. Crosses like corn stalks in Flanders, was it? No, I cannot make a similar journey, not likely in my lifetime.

So instead, I journey across our country to places where Michelle had some connection. Sgt. George Miok and Cpl. Zachery McCormack are the connection now, and that's why I'm here. To pay my respects to them and their loved ones, to share our grief, to represent our family.

How many times have I scoured pathways in my brain, details of what happened, who the players were, the sequence of events—all ending up at the same place, a void as big as the hole in the ground that the blast had made? Large enough, Padre Gauthier said, to hold a bus. The day had afterwards dawned with a magenta sunrise. My medic friend Jodie was there, part of the clean-up crew deployed to the site. We were sitting in her Kelowna living room one afternoon when she described how Michelle's notes floated by on the breeze. How could it have been, I wondered, that pages of Michelle's notebook survived, and she didn't? Those hand-scribbled notes represented her livelihood, the raw material with which she planned to write three articles, her first encounters with the ordinary Afghans she had travelled so far to meet, to gain an inkling of understanding about the lives they led. The notes that fluttered in the chill wind of Kandahar in December.

So many sensory details that aren't mine. I know of them only second-hand, and that's hard to reconcile. As if by being there I could make sense of this tragedy, this war, the smell of the earth bloodied and thick with mud. It had rained, making big puddles above earth. Clay, perhaps much like the clay in my garden, does not absorb the water in that part of Afghanistan. Instead, it pools, though once it evaporates, dust returns.

I venture outside around 1:00 p.m. to buy a newspaper with Remington's final piece about Michelle's last days in Kandahar. I know I can and will get it online, but I want to hold it in my hands, clip it for my files. I panic a little when the gas station only has an *Edmonton Sun*, though for all I know, it carries the story, too. I can feel my nerves catch me up, my gut lurching as I cross the ice-crusted street to check out the Shoppers Drug Mart. They're sold out, but I breathe a sigh of relief at Safeway where two copies of the *Edmonton Journal* are on the stand. I buy both and scurry back to my home away from home. It turns out that Colin Perkel has also revisited the event ten years on,[23] writing a feature about the survivors and families who lost loved ones, but I won't read his article today. I haven't the stomach just now.

It's time to get ready. Apprehensive about the evening ahead, I lay my black wool pants on the bed, along with the top that I bought a few years ago while shopping with Sandy in Vancouver. She knew right away that it would look good on me, with its paisley-like pattern on sparkling gold and red swirl across a black background. Though I'm thin and my shape is intact, I feel my age. I'm applying some blush and lipstick when I hear the intercom and hurry down to let Jodie inside.

"I need to borrow a needle and thread," she says as I welcome her and a guy named Dan inside the building. "Goofy Dan popped a button off his shirt."

I meet eyes with a young man of medium build, with dark hair partly spiked and an easy smile, wearing a white T-shirt. Jodie is holding his blue-and-white checkered shirt in her hands. After fetching a needle and thread, I escort them into the condo building's community room where we can sit down, the late-afternoon sun streaming in through sheer curtains. Jodie deftly sews his button back on, her blonde hair falling over the shoulders of her lemony yellow blouse. She's wearing tight jeans with a bit of a bell bottom flare, excited, I think, to be back in the company of the men with whom she once patrolled through Afghan villages.

"Jodie, when you get that button back on, can you work on getting me another kidney?" Dan jokes, saying something about a blast.

"Yeah, right, Danny," Jodie replies, lifting her face and grinning.

I'm puzzled by this exchange, but now isn't the time for questions. I'll research the details in the months to come and learn how, while under supervision and following orders, Wolfi set up and detonated a Claymore mine in a training exercise, dispersing hundreds of small steel balls over the practice range. The steel balls that tore through Wolfi's forearm were no doubt excruciating, but the ones that spit into twenty-four-year-old Cpl. Josh Baker's chest were fatal. And their mate, Dan, one of two others seriously injured, lost a kidney, immediately whisked away for life-saving medical treatment, recovering elsewhere and separated from the camaraderie he so desperately needed. Meanwhile, the leaders in charge—those who had failed to ensure the soldiers were behind cover or far away from the firing—faced military trials and some convictions,[24] a heartbreaking legacy all around.

Jodie's friend, Nick, is waiting outside in his black SUV. I scramble into the back seat with Dan and soon we're speeding along 109th Street, through the downtown core to the James Curry Jefferson Armoury in north central Edmonton. It's getting dark when we arrive in the industrial-sized parking lot and make our way inside a large, squat building. We're led up a flight of stairs to a brightly lit banquet-sized space where about forty to fifty folks stand or sit around long tables of food. I scan the room, looking for faces I might recognize.

A slight, fair woman with a tray of food passes by, offering me a slice of pizza, and I thank her. She smiles graciously and keeps moving. A few moments later Anna Miok, George Miok's mother, enters. A short woman with beautiful plump, rosy cheeks, Anna sees me as I walk toward her and calls: "Catherine." We embrace briefly. Tears in her eyes, she explains her husband Eli is recovering from surgery in the hospital. I can see that she's worried, but soon others come to greet her, and I retreat to a nearby table. One of her other sons enters, Laszlo, a smart-looking man with dark hair and soft handsome features. She tells me later how George's brothers didn't want him to go: "'You've done your service to Canada, George. Don't go again,' they told him," Anna says. "It was his third tour of duty, once to Bosnia and then to Afghanistan, the first time in 2002."

I shake my head and look into her eyes. As a reservist, he didn't have to go. But words fail me, so I rest my hand on her shoulder. She never tires talking about George, her smart, beautiful and caring son, remembering how it pained her to leave for work when he was small.

"I took a cleaning job at the hospital from 7:00 p.m. to 11:00 p.m. so that I could be at home during the day with my boys. When it was time for me to go, George would crawl to the door and cry as I left. I cried, too."

"Oh yes, I understand," I reply. "I remember having to leave my son Sam in daycare where he was the only child. I can still see his head bent slightly, his little hand barely waving goodbye as I turned to go. The large play room seemed to swallow him up, along with a deep sadness. But I had to leave. I'll never forget how hard that was." Anna nods. Though I don't know the pain of losing a son to war, I have a mother's heart, and, for a moment, I grasp her loss: those inner moments when we felt we had failed, unable to save our boys from harm, however large or small.

A little overwhelmed, I cross to a table near a window where Laszlo Miok is leafing through a photo album with pictures of his brother, George, and his buddies. We stand on either side of a bar table and speak haltingly. Neither of us can think of much to say, a haunting sadness in his dark brown eyes. All around us, people are talking loudly, boisterously, drinking beer, and sampling the fare. We drift away from each other, and a little while later, I scan the room. He's gone.

Craving a moment to myself, I sit next to a fellow named Lance. He's sipping beer quietly by himself, and I wonder if he's alone because he's not interested in the back-slapping joviality of so many of the guys milling around. The brotherhood.

"I was in Bosnia, in defence and security—mostly of buildings but sometimes protecting people," Lance says. "I saw guys leave bases and go into enemy territory, into the indiscriminate killing fields of land mines. The psychological stress of not knowing whether they would return was too much, but my superiors wouldn't deploy me with battlefield troops. They said I was too old."

I look at him, a man perhaps in his early forties, strong and fit. I'm skeptical, but what do I know? It's why he didn't go to Kandahar, though he was Zachery McCormack's trainer, the twenty-one-year-old whose parents are hosting this anniversary event, the boy who was engaged, like Michelle. Just moments ago, I saw his picture in the photo album, cuddling a puppy he named Napoleon after saving it from local children who were swinging it high in the air on the end of a rope. Zach, as his friends called him, traded a granola bar and a pencil for the puppy. Of all the soldiers killed that day, he looks the youngest, as if barely out of high school, except when in his orange-tinted goggles and full combat gear, giving the finger in jest to George Miok on the morning of the day they went out.

Lance seems to be carrying a burden beyond my reach, so we sit in silence for a few moments. Then Zach's father, Robin, a fit, diminutive man, comes by and escorts me to a window, pulling the curtain back to show me the illuminated "bubble" over the back of a red GMC truck, Zach's prized possession.

"Zach's mother and I wanted to do something to preserve the truck and also bring awareness for his life and the lives of all the soldiers who gave their lives for the well-being and safety of others," Robin tells me. "When we went to the unveiling of the Afghan Repatriation Memorial in Trenton in 2012, we saw one of the Canadian Heroes vehicles and, with their help, we now have an amazing tribute to him and the three other soldiers we lost that day." He points at the photos and names of the soldiers painted along the side of his truck. "We wanted to put Michelle on there too, but her family said no." He turns his head from the window to look at me.

"Oh," I say, flummoxed. "I didn't know."

"We could still make up a decal to put on there," he says, "if your family is willing."

"I'll ask her parents the next time I'm talking to them," I offer.

Robin's grandson, Carter, is zipping around with some other children. He's about three and very cute, springing all over the place just like Tigger in *Winnie the Pooh*. Robin and I watch him for a bit, both of us cheered by his antics. Next thing I know, Carter is singing "O Canada" at the top of his lungs. Evidently, he learned it at hockey games, along with the "Star-Spangled Banner." His mother, Zach's sister, is here, but on the far side of the room. A petite woman, she has jet black hair and skin as white as seashells.

Kirk Taylor's mother, Tina, is standing nearby, a fun-loving woman with shoulder-length dark hair and a wide smile. I learn that she lives in Arizona, which is where she was when Kirk was killed, a story in itself because, like our family, the military couldn't reach her directly. I can tell she's a tough cookie and like her a lot. She's come all this way to be with those whose sons shared the same fate as hers, to talk about their grief and how they're coping ten years on. I overhear them chatting about Garrett Chidley's mother, Sian LeSueur, expressing regret that she couldn't attend. I stand on the fringe of this tight-knit group of women, not because they keep me at arm's length but because I know my loss isn't the same.

But later, when it's time for a photo, someone goes out of their way to include me, and I'm touched. Unexpectedly, I find myself in their midst—women who lost their sons in the same incident that killed Michelle and the woman who lost her brother in the accident that cost Dan his kidney. With arms around each other, Tina, Anna and Zach's mother, Armande, smile for the camera. Armande hadn't known who I was when she offered me pizza earlier, but now she takes my hands in hers and thanks me for coming. I remember catching my first glimpse of her. A slight woman of eminent grace, she meandered through the gathering to make sure her guests had everything they needed.

I'm on the far right, next to Heather Middleton, the youngest among us. She's smiling brightly, her dark brown hair falling softly over her shoulders. I learn that Michael Louie's sister taught her children in grade one. On the day she'd flown to Kandahar Airfield to visit the cenotaph, her mother-in-law explained why Heather wasn't dropping the kids off at school. It was yet another uncanny connection to Afghanistan. Heather's brother, Josh Baker, killed in Afghanistan six weeks after the brother of her children's teacher had lost Michelle, his soulmate.

"There was a whole lot of pain in that room, but there was also a whole lot of healing before the evening was finished," Tina told CBC reporter Alex Cooke later. She also told the reporter something she told me: how she encouraged all her children to go into the big, wide world and "shake it by the tail."

"Because of what I'd said to them all, I had to stand by Kirk's decision even though I knew he'd be walking into danger," she says. I nod, thinking of Michelle's mom and the kick in the gut she felt when Michelle told her about the Kandahar assignment—not to mention the near-constant anxiety Sandy felt once Michelle had left to report on war.

I stroll off to leave Tina mingling with Armande and Anna. There's another person I do and don't want to meet. My gut churned earlier when I heard him introduce himself as Matt Chinn, the emcee, at the microphone. He was a master corporal in the LAV Alpha that was leading Charlie along that muddy road ten years ago. Like many of the guys here tonight, he's stocky and muscular, with a crew cut and gregarious manner as he makes announcements throughout the evening. When I introduce myself near the bar, he straightens up almost imperceptibly and chats about scuba diving, telling me how he trains recruits for Corrections Canada now. I'd like to mine his memory for details about that fateful day, but he clearly doesn't want to go there. I'd also like his permission to use his photos—to my knowledge, the last ones taken of Michelle. I'm grateful for them—of her at work, on the assignment of her lifetime. I've probably already described the photo: her hair in a ponytail, head bent over her notepad, scribbling like mad while surrounded by soldiers, some Afghan children on the fringes of the gathering along the length of an irrigation canal and semi-nomadic dwellings and structures. The ground and air the colour of Afghanistan: a light sandy brown.

Jodie catches my eye and calls me over to a bar table where she's laughing with some guys. In her element here, she's with those who had her back and whose backs she also protected from harm. Sort of like connective tissue in our bodies, I think, this sinew-like substance that ties them together, putting their lives on the line every time they went outside the wire. A village patrol, marching along a labyrinth of narrow streets in the forty-five degree heat, one hundred pounds of kit on her back, eyes straight ahead while men stared, hostility fierce in their eyes, and children peered from doorways of their mud-brick dwellings. Eyes on her mate's back as they marched, she focused her mind with each and every step.

But tonight she introduces me to her friends, and I realize how much they love her—the only woman here tonight who served among them. The photo that I want of them, goofing around and grinning, is right there at my fingertips. I pull out my phone and point my camera. Click. Click. Click. I'm out of practice and on edge. Somehow the lighting isn't quite right, the glint in Jodie's chestnut-brown eyes amiss, the results blurry.

We're standing in the corner near the bar and I soon find myself talking to Barrett Fraser and Fedor Volochtchick, two of the soldiers seriously injured in the blast. I'm fidgety, increasingly ill at ease. I don't really know what to make of these men and I suspect they don't really know what to make of me—a sixty-something woman with grey hair and a pleasant but anxious demeanour. Neither has visible scars. Barrett is tall with brown hair and an easy smile. Fedor—his mates called him Volvo or Fed—is almost dwarfed by Barrett, with small bones and kind hazel eyes above high cheek bones. Both Calgary reservists, they had their sights on a career in the military.

"I really wanted to go on another deployment," Barrett says.

"And that wasn't possible?" I ask, searching his face.

They both look at me, a bit stunned. I'd forgotten the details of their injuries—for Fedor, a cracked jaw, broken vertebrae and partly torn off buttocks; for Fraser, multiple surgeries to repair his nose and feet. With his chin resting on his rifle, his face and feet took the brunt of the blast.

"Oh, I'm sorry," I say, wanting to reach out and comfort them. But I'm not a close friend or relative, so we say goodbye quietly, politely. Drifting away, I wonder if their physical wounds now pale in comparison to their mental ones. I'm a stranger to these men, uncomfortable with probing the raw grit of memory, living with injury, necessarily cultivating a steely strength to go on.

I'm walking away from the bar when Matt Chinn's voice bursts from the microphone again. "Hey folks, time for these soldiers to meet in the breakout room. Grab your favourite bevvy and see ya' there five minutes MAX." A line of guys and Jodie file past a room divider and disappear. I know it's out of bounds, but I itch to be a fly on the wall, my reporter antennae instantly alive and twitching. When they come out twenty minutes or more later, I rush over to Jodie, hoping for a teeny crack I can slip through. But no. She's tearing up, her lips sealed. At least right here, right now. Suddenly, we both jump, startled at the sound of a very loud crack. On the other side of the room, a tall, muscular man is hurling a chair hard against the floor, and Jodie is gone from my side in a flash. He's shouting something unintelligible. The room freezes for a split second when a number of guys jump into action, restraining him, talking to him all the while.

I've no clue what it's about, though I speculate it has something to do with the private briefing in the breakout room. The moment passes and everyone resumes what they were doing—sitting or standing around in clusters, nibbling and chatting, drinking beer and laughing. Then it happens again, and once more, we all stop and stare. This time the guys are nearby, and without further ado, they escort him wrestling from the room.

It must be after 10:00 p.m. by now, and I'm done. I stand on the edge of the crowd, watching the dynamics between Wolfi and others and wonder how he's really doing tonight. He and Dan are side by side when I glance over—Dan's complexion a bit off colour and his face drawn. The effort to stay upbeat all night long is wearing on him.

How do these folks do it? I don't think I'll ever understand how military families and friends greet one another heartily and strengthen their bonds. The unspoken stories between them and the raw intensity of it all. The chair-throwing incident a mere half-hour ago a crack revealing some of the rage that must burn underneath, then swept from view ever so swiftly.

I pause to remember the investigative series in the *Globe and Mail* by Michelle's former colleague, Renata D'Aliesio.[25] Called "The Unremembered," it laid bare the stores and statistics of veterans who returned from duty only to take their own lives. Renata's reporting led the military to formally recognize these men and women as casualties of war—an example of how journalism can effect change. But here and now, I stare at Wolfi's back as we go down the stairs and outside into the black Edmonton night, both of us lost in thought.

Jodie and I meet at the airport the next morning to check in for our flights to Vancouver on New Year's Eve day. With an hour or so to spare before departure, we find a Starbucks near the gate. She points to a table near the floor-to-ceiling window overlooking the tarmac and I pull up a chair. By now, I'm desperate for a coffee. Jodie slips up to the counter and orders two grande-sized cups of steaming hot java. I gratefully accept this small pleasure, eager to chat about what went down the evening before when a short, barrel-chested man walks up to the counter behind us, his companion a pretty woman with shoulder-length, curly brown hair. Jodie turns, recognizing him instantly.

"Jimmy!" she calls out.

He looks over his shoulder. "Hi, Jodie. Thought I might bump into you here." He and his fiancée stroll over to our table and sit down. He fixes his intense blue eyes on me after a short while. "I'm sorry I didn't get back to you," he says. "There was a lot going on."

I nod, eager to let it go. He's Sgt. Jim Collins, the man in the light-armoured vehicle designated Alpha, ahead of Charlie, the LAV carrying Michelle. Collins, the soldier with his head outside the turret, watching everything go down as if he were living the opening scene in *Hurt Locker*, shock waves rippling 360 degrees around him. In the early years after the incident, he responded briefly to my emails and then stopped. But here we are now, face-to-face, a decade on.

No doubt saying "there was a lot going on" is putting it mildly. All the characters in this drama, I meet them as fellow human beings, want to know how they're doing, want their stories to somehow help me patch up missing bits. So, it's a good moment when Jimmy tells Jodie about the neurotherapy he's undergoing to heal his brain from the concussive effects of the blast. Seems like he might just have hit on something that's actually working after ten long years.

He drops the names of soldiers, those killed and wounded, trying to come to terms with his loss, the different pieces of the puzzle that his brain is struggling to work its way through. Suddenly, he looks straight at me and says: "You must think I'm crazy. This must be hard to relate to."

"No, actually," I reply, looking straight back. "I can totally relate. It's exactly what I'm trying to do by writing, as if it'll help solve a riddle and make some sense of it all." Like those wounded men I met last night, Barrett Fraser and Fedor Volochtchick, I too have had to reinvent myself, set different goals, and keep going. A decade on, still puzzling my way through the emotional trauma of losing Michelle in the way that we did, along with the regret of setting aside a career as a reporter, the profession that surely was my calling just as it was Michelle's. Now I'm a writer, wandering into unknown territory where finding my way turns into a game of not finding my way a lot of the time.

The conversation turns to the semi-declassified information they were privy to during the briefing in the breakout room the night before. I'm all ears as Jimmy swears about terrorists outside Afghanistan getting paid very big bucks to build the bomb. The knowledge that some of those responsible are probably still alive gives me pause. Within days of the incident, an allied force targeted the compound where the bomb was detonated. But they didn't get those who made the IED in a neighbouring country or the higher-ups who mastermind such killing.

But for Jodie and the guys, the anger they experienced at learning this and other details was mixed with a measure of relief. Whatever it was that they were told, they came away with renewed understanding not to shoulder blame.

Ten days after I walked across the High Level Bridge and gazed at the North Saskatchewan River far below, I stare numbly at strings of light illuminating the dark outline of the same steel-trussed bridge against a night sky. The image flashes across our television screen over and over again. It's January 8, 2020, the day that Iran fired anti-aircraft missiles in error at Ukrainian Airlines flight 752,[26] believing it to be an American counterattack in retaliation for killing a top Iranian general.

As I watch the news, a familiar sense of powerlessness and rage comes over me. A majority of the victims had ties to Canada as citizens or permanent residents, and many of them lived in Edmonton—professionals, university students and a dozen children. My god. Days later, I listen online to a stream of grieving classmates and associates at a University of Edmonton memorial. Tearfully, they remember how friends, students, classmates touched their lives, describing aspirations and accomplishments in medicine, engineering and science that died with their loved ones. How dearly they will be missed. How they will never be forgotten— like Michelle, lost to us for all time. On it goes, and some days later, I read Anser Daud's tribute to a friend, pinching hard at my heart. "There is no measure for the nourishment that their love provided. There is no metric by which to weigh their lost potential."[27]

In an effort to cope, I pick up a pen, but the impact of this tragedy on the heels of my Edmonton journey is too close—as is my anger at the West's twisted complicity in global affairs. I grasp for words that will resonate, that will give shape to so much loss, and I falter, remembering my sister once saying: "They're only words."

I drop my pen and take the dog for a walk. It's late morning as I enter a fern grove, letting sun-filtered forest light wash over me. *But there is beauty in words, too*, I say. *Beauty and meaning.*

CHAPTER 20

FROM KANDAHAR TO CALGARY TO MONTERREY

Over the years of researching this memoir, I couldn't bring myself to ask Michelle's parents to talk about the day they found out their daughter had been killed. Would diving into the details of what transpired trigger the trauma all over again? Some eleven years on, I eased my way in by first talking to my nephew's wife, Sandra Benavides. She began by talking about the day before Michelle died.

"I think it was the last time I saw Sandy truly happy for a long time," she said during a phone call.

Her future in-laws, Sandy and Art, had travelled to her hometown of Monterrey, Mexico on Boxing Day to meet her family. It was a happy occasion, with relaxed and lively conversation around Tecate beer and excellent Tequila. Sandy couldn't have been more thrilled about the bridal shower planned a few days after their arrival.

Now, there are few things that Michelle's mother loves more than to dress up and go to a party for such a once-in-a-lifetime event. I picture her folding her sparkling black party dress and putting away her patent leather flats afterwards, reliving the day's highlights. I bet she was itching to tell her friends back home all the details—the elegant and beautifully decorated home, the lovely and thoughtful gifts given to her son's vivacious and accomplished fiancée, and the magnanimous laughter of Sandra's aunties and sisters, not to mention a household of nieces in party dresses and nephews with haphazardly strung neck ties weaving their play in and around the guests.

"Sandy was meeting all my aunts and other people, and you know how much she enjoys that," Sandra said. "It was a very happy day for me, too, because I got all these lovely presents, and I was with my mother and all my siblings and their daughters and my aunts. We were laughing and talking and laughing some more while the kids played around us."

My brother Art was having a good time as well, getting to know his son's future father-in-law, a respected lawyer and raconteur, and his gracious and kind wife, Malena. Lounging around a table and shooting the breeze or eating fine Mexican cuisine, Art was relaxed and happy. In four months' time, his son would be marrying into this cultured, delightful family.

The day after the bridal shower, Sandra took her future in-laws and fiancé through the Museo de Arte Contemporáneo de Monterrey. She remembers being in the museum's huge lobby when Cameron got a phone call from Michelle's fiancé. When she saw his face fall, she knew it couldn't be good. Her memory is that they initially learned there was an incident in Afghanistan involving Michelle and another woman, one of whom had survived. Later, when I talk to Michelle's parents, that's how Sandy seems at first to remember it, too—that they didn't know right away whether the woman who survived might have been Michelle. But Art is firm, unequivocal even. No, he said. They were told right away that Michelle had been killed.

The discrepancy in how it unfolded gives me pause. The fog of memory, the trauma and disbelief pulled each into their own peculiar void, a moment of irrevocable change. The vast geographical distance that the news travelled is not so distant in today's digital world, but the reality on the ground prevented a split-second 'hit-the-presses' call. As it turns out, the confusion was matched by those in the *Calgary Herald* newsroom that morning as Michelle's colleagues watched their boss pace inside his glass-walled office. The reporters couldn't know how desperately he was trying to contact Michelle's parents before he could tell his staff what the hell was going on. And so it was, from Kandahar to Calgary to Monterrey that the pieces of the story came sharply into focus, somehow slowly and suddenly at the same time, before the day was out.

I sit on a couch across from Art and Sandy in their finely furnished living room on a bright August morning. I place my tape recorder on a footstool between them as they recount their memories. All of us are uneasy at first, but the dreadful memories soon begin tumbling out.

Art and Sandy remember that they were on the second floor of the art museum, waiting for Cameron and Sandra to catch up. When Sandra finally arrived by herself, they were puzzled.

"I think you better come down and talk to Cameron," Sandra had told them, an edge to her voice.

"He was crying when we got down there," Sandy says. "He said that Michelle had been killed. I collapsed, literally. I was sick to my stomach, which I feel now."

Sandy's face crumples and her voice cracks, so Art jumps in, telling me that Cameron couldn't talk when they approached. His son simply handed him his phone. Michael Louie was on the other end, as distraught as Cameron.

"He told us she had been killed in an IED explosion along with a number of soldiers," Art explains. "I just said: 'Oh, Mike. Oh, Mike. This is terrible.'"

I imagine every cell in my brother's five-foot-ten frame freezing, while his grown son stood bent beside him. As they made their way to the car, Art put his arm around his wife, holding her up while she retched on the street. Their world was collapsing, darkness closing in from all sides.

Back at the Intercontinental Hotel, Art grabbed his cell phone before he and Sandy headed to the Benavides home. Hours after Michelle's boss, Lorne Motley, had been trying to reach him, Art and he finally connected. It was a short, painful call, confirming that Michelle was gone, that the news wasn't just a horrible mistake. My brother was probably matter-of-fact, perhaps curt, trying against all odds to keep his voice steady. He hung up, soon finding himself en route to a travel agency with Sandra to book an early flight home. Meanwhile, Cameron folded himself up on a bed and wept. For hours. Anger rolled through his six-foot-plus frame. Sandra was there and not there. What could she do? "There was absolutely nothing to say," she recalled during our phone call, the memory of the long days and nights that followed still close enough to touch. As a doctor, she was no stranger to death. Perhaps more than most, she knew the anguish of loved ones left behind.

When Sandy and Art embarked on the passenger jet the next day, they faced a long flight home in separate seats—all they could get in a pinch at a busy time of year. Once on board, they confided in the flight attendant, who instantly turned to the passengers for a volunteer to give up a seat so Sandy and Art could sit together. It was all a blur, but someone did, of course.

"It was wonderful," Sandy tells me through tears. "Because to try and make it through sitting there for six hours when you're in such agony...," She trails off, and I let out a heavy sigh.

It was the longest flight in their well-travelled lives, and they still had miles to go after landing at Sea-Tac airport. Art drove their 2004 Lexus sedan from Seattle across the Canada–US border at the Peace Arch and along Highway 99, all the way over the Oak Street Bridge to 33rd

Avenue in Vancouver. Home as midnight and a new year approached. Grief-stricken. Exhausted. In shock.

It's no wonder they could not travel to Trenton for the military repatriation of Michelle's body three days later. Bereft. Flattened by this tsunami-like wave that swept them all the way from Mexico to their home on British Columbia's west coast, they needed rest and each other.

In the aftermath, they both wrestled with getting through the days.

"To be honest with you, Catherine, I gave up wearing my seat belt. I didn't care if I died," Sandy tells me. "And I was *so* jealous sometimes when I would see mothers and daughters walking together in the stores. It was six very grim months. I guess we went for grief counselling then and it helped a bit."

"One of the hardest things was they were constantly talking about it on the news. I'd be going about my daily business, and then all of a sudden, her name was mentioned, or it was in the paper. It basically went on for two years." She pauses and looks at me. "But it was worse if I turned the radio off or stopped reading newspapers because then I couldn't stop thinking about Michelle at all. At least news about other things took my mind off it for a little while."

"I was just sad all the time. I think of her every single day. I talk to her every single day, but I can't bring her back. You know, I often think how she would have loved to have children. It was just a life wasted," Sandy says softly.

I think to myself that they've had enough of this for today when my brother mentions how busy they were preparing for two memorials, one in Vancouver and one in Calgary, in the early weeks following her death. And I remember the outpouring of support from friends and families near and far that flooded into their home at that time as well. Handwritten letters of condolence from ambassadors and an Associated Press photographer based in New York who wrote that "words are puny and weak in the face of death's terrible and awful finality." A family of anonymous citizens mailed them the Canadian flag that they had held high when Michelle's remains travelled along the Highway of Heroes. Sympathy cards from parents of Michelle's friends and more from friends who grew up and went to school and university with her, who worked beside her in newsrooms. They wrote things like "she was quick to smile" and "I saw her walking with great purpose and abundant enthusiasm." One friend recalled a pajama party when Michelle brought her baby dolls by

Michelle stops to smile at the camera while travelling with her fiancé. Photo courtesy Michael Louie

mistake and her colleagues razzed her all night long. Or a long-ago friend who remembered a play date with Michelle, digging a tunnel to a fantasy world on the other side of the earth.

"When that was all done, as Sandy said, it was a very, very tough time," Art says, his voice cracking. "Because you're in the latter part of January. It's the worst time of year. It's dark and it's miserable."

I resist the urge to rush over and take my big brother in my arms and hold him tight. It might be my style, but it isn't his, or maybe I'm just too timid. I turn off my tape recorder and sigh another heavy sigh. Art retreats for some quiet time, and Sandy and I eat lunch, bundling up our thoughts and feelings, tucking them away once more.

The following morning, I step along the upstairs hallway and peer over the balustrade into the living room below. I have a bird's-eye view of Sandy, sitting with her legs propped up on a footstool, a paperback in her hands, engrossed in whichever Booker award-winning novel she's reading. She isn't aware of my gaze as I contemplate the void in her life all these years later, an oil portrait of Michelle hanging on the wall beside me—a gift from a stranger who painted it after learning of Michelle's death. It's the only painting of Michelle in their home but not the only image of her—framed photos on end tables, on dressers, on a bookcase, wherever my eyes happen to fall. Michelle is everywhere in this house. All the time.

EPILOGUE

When the Taliban took Kabul following the withdrawal of US troops on August 15, 2021, I felt my world shattering all over again. Images of Afghan civilians clinging to massive jets as they lifted off the tarmac, falling to their deaths, and other horrors: arms that lifted babies up to soldiers on the outer airport wall, the pressing crowd standing outside, knee-deep in a sewage canal, the panic-ridden stories of those at risk—anyone who had worked with NATO forces, journalists, human rights workers, lawyers, judges, parliamentarians and women, especially women. Western promises to protect Afghan civilians now as hollow as those made to citizens in Vietnam decades before. It was as if the news that went on for weeks kept reinforcing what I feared all along: that Michelle had died in vain, just one more senseless casualty and an inevitable outcome of war, wringing my insides out.

When Michael Louie called me, I instantly recognized how his world had also caved again: "Everyone has moved on, Auntie," he blurted. "I know," I said. "I feel exactly the same way. It's hard."

I turned to the news to try and understand what went down. I was outraged, though not entirely surprised, by what I learned. An article in *The Atlantic* and one in the *New Yorker* spelled out in agonizing detail the gross negligence, incompetence and self-serving interests of all parties involved—primarily, the Trump and then Biden administrations in the West and the Ghani administration in Afghanistan.

It left me with a deep sense of betrayal—both on the part of government, the media and the public, for Canadians went to war in our times and for those who served and came home, life isn't the same. For the families of those who didn't come home, life will never be the same either.

When the world turned its attention to Putin's invasion of Ukraine some six months after the fall of Kabul, I paced and protested again. The impact of the complete shift in attention felt personal. I grudgingly allowed that Russia presented a much larger threat to our so-called world order than Afghanistan. Or so we think, anyway. As the country sinks further from the public sphere, the Taliban are busy in their madrassas radicalizing new generations of young men.

Our rapid shifts in attention are driven in part by news and media, an irony that doesn't escape me. No doubt compassion fatigue or complacency or perhaps a combination of both are also at play. Since then, the Israel-Hamas war usurped Russia's war with Ukraine in the media for a while, with the horrific images and human cost of war on full display. Reporters cover other conflicts and the humanitarian disasters that accompany them, as well as international negotiations aimed at finding resolutions, but the lead stories are persistently those that threaten our security.

Over time, I learn that not everyone feels as bleak, that some have found another way to look at it. The very fact that Canadian soldiers made the effort, that people of courage and discipline and goodwill joined those fighting to turn the tide against evil, means something in this world, even if only for a time, even if many died in the process. Lives, like Michelle's, that are cut short, yes, but not wasted. Change for the better may take generations, and politics and evil may continue to undermine our efforts, but we persist because we care. To do otherwise is akin to accepting defeat.

Given this, I sometimes wonder how Michelle's time in Afghanistan might have shaped her future as a reporter and writer. Perhaps it's the legacy I chose to inherit from her. My voice reawakened by her untimely, violent death in a country I'll never visit and yet feel inescapably tied to.

Mid-March, 2024. Bruce and I sit among the Silver Cross families at the Afghanistan Memorial in Victoria waiting for speakers to begin yet another afternoon of remembrance. This one is to mark the tenth anniversary of Canada's final withdrawal from Afghanistan on March 12, 2014. Paul Panone, now a retired lieutenant colonel, reminisces about the simplicity of their departure from Kabul, where the last of Canadian troops were training the Afghan National Army.

"There were no bands, no programs, no marching," he says. "The last Canadian commander of our contingent lowered the lone Canadian flag and handed it to Canada's Ambassador to Afghanistan in a small area in front of NATO headquarters."

"Then we donned on our battle rattle, helmets and slung our rifles and boarded the Chinook Helicopters," Paul says, holding up the green backpack with a small Canadian flag that hung at his side that day. He was third to last in a line of soldiers disappearing into the maw of the aircraft, all captured in an iconic photo.

Gerald Pash, another retired veteran, steps forward, remarking that "in the tide of human affairs there is often much debate. That is predominantly true when the outcome of events is different than desired or anticipated. History does what history does."

I scowl inwardly, as if that comment can possibly sum up how life goes on or doesn't in the face of such loss. But the words of retired military chaplain Jim Short coax me away from such bitter thoughts, speaking more to my heart. "There is power in naming," he says. "It summons forth the life of the person named."

Throughout the afternoon, a roster of dignitaries and veterans reads each name engraved on the memorial, each grouping of names followed by the reverberating ring of a bronze bell. I find myself embedded in this simple act of remembrance, a sense of power in this spoken, collective ritual, a way to touch that which will be forever intangible. And it strikes me that remembering is as vital to humanity as clean air is to our breath.

One of the last to speak, retired Cpt. Trevor Greene rolls up to the podium in his wheelchair, his wife and young son flanking him on either side. Unquestionably a man who commands respect, he's wearing a dark navy suit, with reddish-brown hair covering the skull that an Afghan teenager penetrated with an axe during a consultation with Afghan elders.

The spring sun falls on us as he begins, his voice faltering for a millisecond, perhaps not from emotion but from cognitive trauma. The last name he speaks is that of the soldier who replaced him on the battlefield. A split second later, the bell's piercing ring spills into silence. Like a fleeting embrace. Here, in the now.

ACKNOWLEDGEMENTS

I began with only a cursory grasp of how many people would step forward to provide me with the emotional and material support that I'd need to write this memoir.

My family has been at the forefront. Michelle's parents, Art and Sandra Lang, gave me their blessing to remember Michelle in this way. It's hard to find words to express my gratitude for their willingness to relive the anguish of losing their daughter so that she may be remembered. Thanks also to Michelle's brother, Cameron Lang, and Sandra Benavides-Lang, for sharing memories, happy and sad. And to Michael Louie, for hosting me in Calgary and for staying strong. To my sister, Margaret Menzies, where would our family be were it not for your kind and caring ways? Daniel, Vera and Stephen Menzies, Ellen Newman, Sam Martin, you're all part of this story, always in my heart.

Michelle's colleagues and friends—the clutch of women with whom she worked in the news business—provided outstanding help that also made this work possible. Colette Derworiz, Renata D'Aliesio, Kelly Cryderman and Robin Summerfield shared stories of Michelle that made me laugh and cry, eager to go the distance when I came calling. Their abiding love for Michelle was evident in all their efforts. I cherish the time we spent together: tours in Calgary; the road trip to Bellevue in the Crowsnest Pass; our adventure to Lang Bay, Saskatchewan; a front row seat at World Press Freedom Day in Toronto. Robert Remington, another of Michelle's close colleagues at *The Herald*, often stepped up too, freely offering inside stories, contacts, background and advice.

To Lorne Motley and Monica Zurowski at *The Herald*, thank you for permission to reprint many photographs in this book and for helping in other ways, never closing your doors despite how much time passed since Michelle left on her fateful assignment. Thanks also to Chris Varcoe, Steve Jenkinson and Tony Seskus, who pushed deadlines aside to meet with me.

Thanks to Colleen Silverthorn, Michelle's mate at the *Leader-Post*, for the late lunch at your lovely lakeside home and for your courage to revisit the fun as well as difficult memories.

To everyone who shared stories of Michelle during her time in Afghanistan: André Gauthier, Walter Natynczyk, Gary Lunn, Reg Yu, Adam Sweet, Renée Filiatrault, Bushra Saeed-Khan. This story wouldn't be complete without your contributions. And to Colin Perkel for your excellent journalism, for going the extra mile to ensure there is a record of that deadly day.

And to Mellissa Fung, for taking time to meet and stay in touch. You exemplify the best in advocacy journalism.

To the families of the soldiers who perished, thank you for welcoming me into your circle. Robin and Armande McCormack, Anna Miok, Tina Smith, Heather Middleton, you and your families are role models of resilience. To the guys who demonstrated that vulnerability and courage go hand-in-hand: Jimmy Collins, Barrett Fraser, Fedor Volochtchick and Wolfi Brettner.

To Jodie Densmore, friend and confidante. Because of you, I stand taller on Remembrance Day and December 30, remembering not only Michelle but the mates with whom you served.

Yvonne Blomer, I'm ever so grateful for your guidance and expertise during the developmental stages of writing this memoir and beyond. You hung in there over the long haul and helped keep me sane. I simply couldn't have done this without you.

To my Beta readers, Ella Harvey, Amy Reiswig and Bill Johnstone. You're awesome. Thank you for your time and valuable comments.

Special thanks to Vici Johnstone at Caitlin Press for taking a leap of faith in me, and to editor Sarah Corsie whose enthusiasm about my manuscript lifted me up. Thanks also to Malaika Aleba for your steady hand with marketing.

To Phoebe and Rob Fung in Calgary, Elizabeth Kalmakoff in Regina, my "cousins" in Herbert, Saskatchewan, Renata D'Aliesio in Toronto and Kay Dila in Ottawa, many thanks for your gracious hospitality and more. Thanks also to Sarah and Sanjay Vyas for bringing Michelle's high school and university friends together to reminiscence about her fun-loving ways.

To my husband, Bruce Martin, for staying the course through many trials. I'm ever so grateful to have you by my side.

If it takes a whole village to raise a child, it takes an entire community to bring a book to fruition. To all of these folks and more, thank you for supporting my efforts to remember Michelle in this way.

When Canadian Women for Women in Afghanistan published a tribute to Michelle in their January 2010 newsletter, it opened doors I didn't know existed. I'm indebted to many who welcomed me into the fold and demonstrated how critical education is to achieving justice and gender equality. The amazing team of people at the helm and volunteers across Canada who haven't forgotten Afghan women help counter the despair I sometimes feel, as do the brave women of Afghanistan whose indomitable spirits inspire me. When I stand in solidarity with these strong, brilliant and hard-working women, I do so in honour of Michelle. For me, the humanity she brought to her work will always be part of the fight for women's equality, everywhere.

SUGGESTED READING

Books

A Disappearance in Damascus: A Story of Friendship and Survival in the Shadow of War by Deborah Campbell, Vintage Canada, 2017

A Perfectly Beautiful Place by Michael Elcock, Oolichan Books, 2004

A Thousand Splendid Suns by Khaled Hosseini, Penguin Random House Canada, 2008

All We Leave Behind: A Reporter's Journey into the Lives of Others by Carol Off, Penguin Random House Canada, 2017

Ascent of Women: A New Age is Dawning for Every Mother's Daughter by Sally Armstrong, Random House Canada, 2013

Between Good and Evil: The Stolen Girls of Boko Haram by Mellissa Fung, Harper Collins, 2023

Bitter Roots, Tender Shoots: The Uncertain Fate of Afghanistan's Women by Sally Armstrong, Penguin Canada, 2009

Breaking the Silence: Veterans' Untold Stories from the Great War to Afghanistan by Ted Barris, Dundurn Press, 2011

children of air india: un/authorized exhibits and interjections by Renée Sarojini Saklikar, Nightwood Editions, 2013

Dancing in the Mosque: An Afghan Mother's Letter to her Son by Homeira Qaderi, Harper Perennial, 2022

For Your Tomorrow: The Way of an Unlikely Soldier by Melanie Murray, Penguin Random House, 2012

Hand on My Heart: A Canadian Doctor's Awakening in Afghanistan by Maureen Mayhew, Caitlin Press, 2023

Embedded on the Home Front: Where Military and Civilian Lives Converge edited by Joan Dixon and Barb Howard, Heritage House, 2012

I am Malala: The Girl Who Stood Up for Education and was Shot by the Taliban by Malala Yousafzai with Christina Lamb, Back Bay Books, (Little, Brown and Company), 2013

Masham Means Evening by Kanina Dawson, Coteau Books, 2013

News from the Red Desert by Kevin Patterson, Vintage Canada, 2017

On the Edge of Being: An Afghan Woman's Journey by Dr. Sharifa Sharif, Sumach Press, 2011

Outside the Wire: The War in Afghanistan in the Words of Its Participants edited by Kevin Patterson and Jane Warren, Vintage Canada, 2008

Outspoken: My Fight for Freedom and Human Rights in Afghanistan by Sima Samar with Sally Armstrong, Penguin Random House, 2024

The Best Place on Earth: Stories by Ayelet Tsabari, Harper Collins, 2013

The Breadwinner Trilogy by Deborah Ellis, Groundwood Books, 2009

The Dogs are Eating Them Now: Our War in Afghanistan by Graeme Smith, Knopf Canada, 2013

The Kite Runner by Khaled Hosseini, Anchor Canada (division of Random House Canada), 2003

The Places in Between by Rory Stewart, Penguin Canada, 2004

The Naked Don't Fear the Water: An Underground Journey with Afghan Refugees by Matthieu Aikins, Harper Perennial, 2023

The Punishment of Virtue: Inside Afghanistan After the Taliban by Sarah Chayes, Penguin Books, 2006

The Unexpected War: Canada in Kandahar by Janice Gross Stein and Eugene Lang, Viking Canada, 2007

Under an Afghan Sky: A Memoir of Captivity by Mellissa Fung, Harper Collins, 2011

Veiled Threat: The Hidden Power of the Women of Afghanistan by Sally Armstrong, Penguin Random House, 2003

War Is Not Over When It's Over: Women Speak Out from the Ruins of War by Ann Jones, Picador, 2011

We Are Still Here: Afghan Women on Courage, Freedom, and the Fight to be Heard edited by Nahid Shahalimi, Penguin Canada, 2021

Magazines

"Afghanistan Is Your Fault: The American public now has what it wanted" by Tom Nichols, *The Atlantic*, August 16, 2021

"The Fall of the Islamic Republic: The secret history of the US diplomatic failure in Afghanistan" by Steve Coll and Adam Entous, *The New Yorker*, December 10, 2021

"The Other Afghan Women: What villagers in the heartland see in the Taliban" by Anand Gopal, *The New Yorker*, September 6, 2021

ENDNOTES

1. "Postmedia Awards 2024 Michelle Lang Fellowship in Journalism to Ehsanullah Amiri," Postmedia, January 9, 2024, www.postmedia.com/2024/01/09/postmedia-awards-2024-michelle-lang-fellowship-in-journalism-to-ehsanullah-amiri/.

2. Helen Garner, "Helen Garner: 'I may be an old woman, but I'm not done for yet'," *The Guardian*, May 8, 2020, https://www.theguardian.com/books/2020/may/09/helen-garner-i-may-be-an-old-woman-but-im-not-done-for-yet.

3. Colin Perkel, "The full story of one of Canada's deadliest days," *The Globe and Mail*, December 29, 2010, https://www.theglobeandmail.com/news/world/the-full-story-of-one-of-canadas-deadliest-days/article1321639/.

4. Brandy Schillace, editor-in-chief for British Medical Journal's *Medical Humanities Journal*, the author of two books, including *Death's Summer Coat: What the History of Death and Dying Teaches Us About Life and Living*.

5. Her real name was Evelyn Caldwell, and according to Pierre Berton, she could think as fast as she could type. She was a war correspondent for a short time, having worked her way out of the typical women's section of the newspaper.

6. Canadian Women for Women in Afghanistan rebranded to Right to Learn Afghanistan in September 2024.

7. In July 2011, Canada ended its combat commitment in Kandahar but continued training Afghan national security forces in Kabul and Mazar-e-Sharif. In 2014, Canadian forces left Afghanistan, ending Canada's participation in the mission. "Canada and the War in Afghanistan," www.warmuseum.ca/learn/canada-and-the-afghanistan-war/.

8. Janice Gross Stein and Eugene Lang, *The Unexpected War: Canada in Kandahar* (Toronto, ON: Penguin Canada, 2008).

9. Gross Stein and Lang, *The Unexpected War*, 5.

10. "Canadian Forces personnel who died during operations in Afghanistan," *The Globe and Mail*, July 29, 2017, www.theglobeandmail.com/feeds/

canadian-press/national/canadian-forces-personnel-who-died-during-operations-in-afghanistan/article35839129/.

11. Sky Spirit Studio, Ripple, www.calgary.ca/arts-culture/public-art/8-avenue-se-laneway.html.

12. Frank Slide Interpretive Centre, "Learn," frankslide.ca/learn.

13. Robin Summerfield, "On Lang Bay: My journey to remember a friend lost to war," CBC Radio, September 8, 2017, updated May 4, 2018, https://www.cbc.ca/radio/nowornever/finding-motivation-in-loss-1.4643849/on-lang-bay-my-journey-to-remember-a-friend-lost-to-war-1.4646928.

14. Colette Derworiz, "Saskatchewan names lakes after two Calgarians killed in Afghanistan," February 17, 2015, https://calgaryherald.com/news/local-news/saskatchewan-names-lakes-after-two-calgarians-killed-in-afghanistan.

"The journey to honour Michelle Lang, a fallen Canadian reporter," *Macleans*, August 24, 2017.

15. Margaret Renkl, *Late Migrations: a natural history of love and loss* (Milkweed Editions, Minneapolis, 2019).

16. "Trauma and healing after explosion in Afghanistan," *Ottawa Citizen*, January 4, 2021, updated January 14, 2021, https://ottawacitizen.com/sponsored/inside-the-ottawa-hospitals-world-class-care/trauma-and-healing-after-explosion-in-afghanistan.

17. Jolene Banning, "Tikinagan revival: Why Anishinaabe artists are returning to traditional handcrafted wooden baby carriers," *The Globe and Mail*, July 5, 2019.

The strong connection between babies and the spirit world. They are intimately connected with the Creator, so it's important that parents wrap their babies up tightly to let them know they are loved and they belong here.

18. "Canadian soldiers dismantle, ship Kandahar memorial back home," *The Globe and Mail*, November 13, 2011, www.theglobeandmail.com/news/national/canadian-soldiers-dismantle-ship-kandahar-memorial-back-home/article4243217/.

19. "Missing man formation," Wikipedia, en.wikipedia.org/wiki/Missing_man_formation.

20. Kevin Griffin, "Vancouver high school honours journalist Michelle Lang, who was killed in Afghanistan," *Vancouver Sun*, November 8, 2019, vancouversun.com/news/local-news/vancouver-high-school-honours-journalist-michelle-lang-who-was-killed-in-afghanistan.

21. Catherine Lang, "Lang's legacy reminds us of journalism's ability to change things for the better," *Calgary Herald*, December 27, 2019, calgaryherald.com/opinion/columnists/opinion-langs-legacy-reminds-us-of-journalisms-ability-to-change-things-for-the-better.

22. Robert Remington, "Remembering Michelle Lang: 'Worst news' from Afghanistan is confirmed," *Calgary Herald*, December 27, 2019.

Robert Remington, "Remembering Michelle Lang: Part 2: A trip beyond 'the wire'," *Calgary Herald*, December 28, 2019.

Robert Remington, "Remembering Michelle Lang: Part 3: Premonition and survivor's remorse," *Calgary Herald*, December 30, 2019.

23. Colin Perkel, "'It's as fresh as yesterday': Canadian survivors on trauma, healing 10 years after Afghan blast," *The Globe and Mail*, December 19, 2019, https://www.theglobeandmail.com/canada/article-its-as-fresh-as-yesterday-canadian-survivors-on-trauma-healing-1/.

24. Bill Graveland, "Soldier convicted in fatal training accident in Afghanistan wins appeal," *The Globe and Mail*, September 19, 2014, www.theglobeandmail.com/news/national/soldier-convicted-in-fatal-training-accident-in-afghanistan-wins-appeal/article20692226/.

25. Renata D'Aliesio, "Investigation: The Unremembered," *The Globe and Mail*, October 30, 2015, https://www.theglobeandmail.com/news/veterans/article26499878/.

26. "The passengers of UIA Flight 752: What we know about those we lost in the disaster," *The Globe and Mail*, January 8, 2020, updated March 4, 2022, https://www.theglobeandmail.com/canada/article-students-doctors-children-ukrainian-airliner-crash-victims-had/.

27. Anser Daud, "The losses we can't measure from the fall of Ukraine International Flight 752," *The Globe and Mail*, January 17, 2020, www.theglobeandmail.com/opinion/article-the-losses-we-cant-measure-from-the-fall-of-ukraine-international/.

ABOUT THE AUTHOR

Photo by Roy Patt

Catherine Lang worked as a community newspaper reporter and freelance writer at the outset of her writing career in the 1980s. In 1996, she published *O-Bon in Chimunesu: A Community Remembered*, a creative non-fiction work about the former Japanese-Canadian community on Vancouver Island, with Arsenal Pulp Press; *O-Bon* won the Hubert Evans Non-Fiction Prize at the 1997 BC Book Prizes. She later worked as an editor of provincial legislative debates and in treaty negotiations with Indigenous nations in BC. Lang lives in Victoria, BC.